Robin Robertson's

Vegan *without* Borders

For the animals

Other Books by Robin Robertson

Quick-Fix Vegan

More Quick-Fix Vegan

Quick-Fix Vegetarian

1,000 Vegan Recipes

Hot Vegan

Fresh from the Vegan Slow Cooker

Vegan on the Cheap

The Nut Butter Cookbook

One Dish Vegan

Vegan Planet

Party Vegan

The Vegetarian Meat and Potatoes Book

Robin Robertson's

Vegan *without* Borders

Easy Everyday Meals
from Around the World

Robin Robertson

Photography by Sara Remington

**Andrews McMeel
Publishing**

Kansas City • Sydney • London

Contents

Acknowledgments

There are so many hands and hearts I want to acknowledge, beginning with my mother who taught me how to cook intuitively (I never once saw her use a measuring spoon or cup!) and my father who sparked my sense of culinary adventure.

To the many friends, neighbors, home cooks, and restaurant chefs all over the world who, over the years, have shared with me their knowledge, their secret ingredients, and their enthusiasm for cooking—I thank you.

I also must express a special thanks to the most amazing group of recipe testers, who cooked their way around the world to help make this book what it is: Barbara Bryan, Melissa Chapman, Zsu Dever, Lea Jacobson, Lyndsay Orwig, and Jonathan and Nancy Shanes. If there were a Hall of Fame for recipe testers, surely you would all be inducted.

Much gratitude to the fabulous team at Andrews McMeel for believing in this project and for helping to make this book as wonderful and beautiful as it is, with special thanks to my editor, Jean Lucas; publisher, Kirsty Melville; Julie Barnes, Dave Shaw, Carol Coe, and Andrea Shores.

I also want to thank photographer Sara Remington for bringing her talent to this project and making my recipes look good enough to eat right off the page.

An extra special thanks to my husband Jon for sharing my passion for exploring global cuisines and for helping to make the world a more compassionate place. My love for you is without borders.

Many thanks, also, to my agent and friend, Stacey Glick of Dystel & Goderich Literary Agency, for her many years of support for my work and for helping me navigate in the world of publishing.

I want to express my appreciation to all my friends, fans, and supporters for inspiring me to keep on keeping on. And, finally, lots of love and hugs to my wonderful cats (you know who you are) for bringing joy to my life each day.

Introduction

I began my professional cooking career more than thirty years ago, working my way up the ranks from line cook, to sous chef, and finally the chef at several restaurants, including a French restaurant in Charleston, South Carolina. Eventually I realized that I no longer wanted to work in restaurants or eat animal products. On the same day that I left the restaurant business, I started on the road to a vegan lifestyle and decided to devote my time and talents to developing techniques for preparing great-tasting traditional fare with plant-based ingredients.

Soon after going vegan in 1987, I attended a family gathering where my Italian and Eastern European relatives were serving a variety of ethnic foods. Assuming there would be little for me to eat in the midst of two dozen card-carrying meat eaters, I was elated to discover that many of the family specialties were naturally and traditionally vegan. After enjoying my fill of caponata bruschetta, lentil salad, and *halushki*, I began to explore the potential for vegan dishes and vegan-convertible gems in cuisines all over the world.

I spent the next twenty-five years exploring international cuisines in cities throughout the United States and as far away as Italy. No sooner would I try a Gujarati restaurant or a Thai noodle shop than I'd begin researching and learning the cooking style so I could make those heavenly meals at home, using my culinary skills and background to develop the best ways to adapt the dishes.

From samosas to sushi to Stroganoff, I fell in love with scores of international recipes that I just couldn't—and still can't—get enough of. These became the recipes I wanted to share one day in a special cookbook of my all-time favorites. The book would be a pastiche of plant-based delights from all over the world. The phrase "vegan without borders" sat in my idea file for a long time.

More than twenty cookbooks later, the idea is a reality in what has turned out to be my most personal cookbook to date. *Vegan Without Borders* is the culmination of my years of restaurant experience, family recipes, travels, and more than ten years of writing the "Global Vegan" column for *VegNews Magazine*. Some of the recipes in this book are inspired by the insights and recipes shared with me by many talented cooks I've met over the years, from friends and neighbors who showed me how to prepare their family specialties to colleagues and restaurant chefs who shared a secret ingredient or tip along the way.

I call my collection *Vegan Without Borders* because fantastic flavors know no boundaries, and neither do most vegans when it comes to enjoying great-tasting food. Because many global cuisines are free of the meat-and-potato constraints of the typical Standard American Diet (SAD), food-loving vegans are naturally attracted to the dishes of other cultures, from our love affair with all things hummus to chowing down on bean burritos, or savoring fragrant vegetable stir-fries made with tofu "done right."

Many of the recipes, such as Umbrian Lentil Salad (page 9), Manchurian Cauliflower (page 176) and Ethiopian Spicy Lemon Chickpeas (page 136), are authentically interpreted here. Others, however, have been inspired by certain traditions, while not being bound by them. For example, seitan replaces beef in the Vietnamese Noodle Salad (page 244) known as *bun bo xao*, just as the Jackfruit Gyros (page 50), are made without meat, and the Butternut Mac and Cheese (page 90) contains no dairy. In many cases, I substitute ingredients that are close to the original. For example, I list the original ingredient but also suggest a substitute, such as using grated lime zest instead of less accessible kaffir lime leaves. It was important for me to find the best possible substitutes for otherwise hard-to-find ingredients to enable more people to enjoy preparing these recipes at home.

My goal with *Vegan Without Borders* isn't to give you a comprehensive or encyclopedic collection, but to offer my most loved recipes from Europe, Africa, India, Asia, and the Americas, as found in about twenty different cuisines. While the cuisines of many countries feature prominently, there are others that are absent. This is not intended as a slight against any particular cuisine—I just happen to especially adore the food of the regions featured in this book, and I hope you will, too.

Many of the recipes are especially quick to make, low in fat, gluten free, and/or soy free, or have easy options to make them so. Each of these special features is indicated on the recipe pages. An easy-to-use index of the recipes grouped according to category starts on page 260.

The recipes are intentionally not organized by type of meal (entrees, appetizers, soups, etc.), but by global region, such as Asia and Europe. Within those regions, they are arranged by country. This organization allows you to make any recipe you wish as a stand-alone dish. However, if you want to make a complete meal in a particular cuisine, I also provide several types of menus (see page 266) so you can easily find recipes of the same national origin. At the same time, I encourage you to mix and match recipes from various cuisines.

Each section begins with my own take on the particular country's cuisine to give readers a better understanding of the region, particular ingredients, and flavors. Further understanding of various ingredients can be found in the glossary on page 268. I also provide shopping lists of essential ingredients native to the cuisine, which will help you achieve authenticity on your own. Because naturally vegan dishes can be found in many cuisines around the world, vegans tend to have adventuresome palates. But lots of other people, including omnivores, are also looking for healthy, inexpensive, and innovative recipes. The recipes in *Vegan Without Borders* are healthy and accessible without compromising on flavor.

CHAPTER 1

The Global Melting Pot

My many years of exploring the world's cuisines led me to discover that virtually every culture enjoys a variety of traditional vegan dishes. It's true that some cuisines are unquestionably meat-centric, but many others use very little meat, or use it more as a flavoring or side dish rather than the main event of a meal. Numerous other cuisines showcase vegetables, grains, and legumes, as evidenced by the many plant-based dishes of Asia, India, and the Middle East. Perhaps less well known is the fact that a bounty of flavorful vegan dishes also exists in European countries and beyond.

In these days of global cuisines and fusion foods, ethnic lines often dissolve in the already homogeneous culinary American melting pot. While we enjoy savoring the familiar dishes of our roots, we also like discovering new food flavors, textures, and experiences. This book is a collection of my go-to recipes and most cherished cuisines, from the slow-simmered vegetable stews of France to lightning-quick Asian stir-fries, to simple roasted vegetables and pasta dishes of Italy, and flavorful dals of India.

This book features naturally vegan recipes, but also recipes that, while not traditionally vegan, are easily made so simply by swapping in the right plant-based ingredients—I've already done the research for you and have developed recipes that I find simply thrilling when it comes to enjoying the foods of other cultures. Think of it this way: Much as one might swap chickpeas for black beans in a recipe due to personal preference, why not replace chicken or beef with tofu or seitan, or even mushrooms or eggplant.

Within these pages you will find the traditional flavors of Italian, French, Spanish, and Eastern European cooking as well as a tempting selection of recipes from the Middle East, Africa, India, and Asia. Also featured are plant-based delights from Central and South America, and the United States. The recipes include family-style comfort foods, global ethnic favorites, and even some creative new dishes inspired by the classics, all developed to satisfy a variety of mealtime desires. As long as flavor combinations are pleasing, you can plan entire meals based on a particular region, or combine regions for cross-cultural fare.

It's interesting to note that in many countries throughout the world, eating meat is not a daily occurrence. Whether for economic or religious reasons (or both), many cultures have predominantly plant-based diets, where meat is either not eaten at all or eaten more as a condiment or flavoring rather than the main event. In some cultures, you will find rice to be a mainstay of the people, often paired with beans or vegetables. In certain parts of Italy, pasta replaces rice, but beans and vegetables are common as well. Many naturally vegan Italian dishes such as pasta fagiole, polenta, and bread and cabbage soup are known as *povero*—"poor man's" food. They happen to be some of the most delicious dishes on earth.

Flavor Profiles

For virtually every cuisine, naming a few distinct ingredients will tell you instantly from what part of the world the food originates. It's usually not the protein, starch, or even the vegetables that shout out a particular cuisine; more often, it's the seasonings—spices, herbs, and other flavor-packed ingredients that are the real calling card of a region's cuisine. If you begin with a reasonably neutral ingredient, such as chickpeas (which are eaten in many places throughout the world), cook them with garlic, oregano, basil, and olive oil, and you're visiting the Mediterranean. Use ginger, sesame oil, and soy sauce, and you've crossed borders into Asia. Team chickpeas with paprika, sour cream, and onions, and Eastern European cooking comes to mind. Add tahini, lemon juice, and za'taar spices, and you have the flavors of the Middle East.

By using this book, you will become familiar with the flavor profiles of these global regions, and know how to stock your kitchen with the ingredients needed to prepare them. With the pantry list on page xx, the cuisines of the world will be at your fingertips.

GETTING UMAMI "WOW" IN PLANT-BASED COOKING

Thousands of years ago, people throughout Asia recognized the importance of the "five flavors" for making healthful and delicious meals. They structured their dishes to stimulate all the tongue receptors for salt, sour, bitter, sweet, and one more element, too: a mysterious and nameless flavor-maker that added a savory edge to foods. The elusive element was known in ancient China, the Roman Empire, and in nineteenth-century France by Escoffier, though even he didn't know what it was.

Now known as the "fifth flavor," this element didn't have a name until chemist Kikunae Ikeda named it in 1908: umami, the noun form of the Japanese adjective umai, which means delicious, tasty, and savory. The umami taste comes chiefly from the presence of glutamates in the dish, an amino acid that is abundant in meat and cheese, and less so in vegetables. To artificially add the umami element to vegetable dishes, cooks added the artificial monosodium glutamate (MSG). But certain plant-based ingredients do contain glutamates and other umami-producing ingredients, and if they are used correctly in cooking, vegan dishes can be just as exciting and Mmmm as any other.

When you cook vegan, you can add an umami quality to your foods by including such ingredients as nutritional yeast, soy sauce, mushrooms, wine, balsamic vinegar, miso, olives, sauerkraut, sun-dried tomatoes, umeboshi plums, and many others.

Combining certain ingredients to achieve those special "aha" moments make flavors merge to create that transporting umami quality, and I have developed the recipes in this book for maximum umami, health, and deliciousness.

CHAPTER 2

A Global Vegan Kitchen

Vegan kitchens tend to be "without borders" naturally because once people begin to enjoy various plant-based ingredients that may have been previously unknown to them, they find themselves drawn to exploring cuisines from all over the world. They begin to experiment with different spices, colorful vegetables, and a world of beans, whole grains, and sauces.

The recipes in *Vegan Without Borders* are free of animal ingredients. Some are naturally plant-based while others have been made so by a simple ingredient swap, such as using nondairy milk or vegetable broth, or using plant-proteins such as beans, seitan, or tofu instead of meat. Additionally, some traditional recipes call for copious amounts of lard or butter, but you'll find that my recipes use only a modest amount of oil, and many can be made with no oil at all.

People transitioning to plant-based foods from an omnivorous diet need to pay special attention to their nutrition—many of those who don't succeed dropped their meats and dairy, but didn't take the time to learn about the wondrous variety of vegetables and ingredients by which they can make their meals balanced as well as delicious. It's a good idea to read through the following list even if you are a longtime vegan, as a reminder or perhaps to spark some new ideas.

Ingredients

One of my goals while writing this book was to make it easy to explore cooking from a variety of international cuisines, wherever you live. In order to make the recipes most accessible, I tried, as much as possible, to use ingredients that are easily found in well-stocked supermarkets or natural food stores. Still, there remain a few ingredients that can only be found in ethnic markets or online, but if it is an integral ingredient to a cuisine that you love, it will be worth the effort to get it.

I think vegans, in general, tend to be more open to a variety of cuisines because of the fact that many of the world's cuisines feature plant-based recipes, so it was a natural progression to try them. Cooking with a variety of whole grains, beans, or legumes, and fresh vegetables, fruits, and seasonings allows you to explore the world's cuisines while enjoying a healthful vegan diet. While it's the particular herbs, spices, and techniques that go into giving a recipe its cultural identity, there are also several foundational ingredients that form the canvas upon which all the flavorful brushstrokes are lavished. The following is a brief overview of the basic ingredients used throughout this book.

BEANS

Dried beans, also known as legumes, are widely used throughout the world as a major protein source. Beans are inexpensive, easy to prepare, low in fat, and an important part of a well-balanced vegan diet. Popular bean varieties include chickpeas, black-eyed peas, lentils, split peas, black beans, pinto beans, kidney beans, lima beans, fava beans, and white beans (Great Northern, navy, and cannellini). Once called "poor man's meat," beans are high in protein, fiber, carbohydrates, and B vitamins. Keep a variety of dried beans on hand. For convenience, you can cook dried beans in large batches and then portion and freeze them for ease of use. I also suggest keeping a supply of canned beans on hand, such as black beans, chickpeas, kidney beans, pintos, and cannellini beans.

GRAINS

Considered staple foods throughout the world, grains can be an economical source of high-quality nutrition. Among the many grains to choose from are rice, millet, quinoa, barley, and many others. Each type of grain has its own nutritional value, unique flavor, and cooking characteristics. When combined with beans, vegetables, and seasonings, grains provide great taste and texture, in addition to good nutrition. Some grains, such as quinoa and bulgur, cook faster than others. For convenience, longer-cooking grains, such as brown rice, can be prepared in large batches, portioned, and stored in the freezer.

VEGETABLES AND FRUITS

Fresh produce is loaded with nutrients such as vitamin C, potassium, iron, and calcium and eating a wide variety of vegetables and fruit helps ensure optimum nutritional benefits. In many international cuisines, you are more likely to find vegetables featured as an integral part of a meal rather than as a typically American side dish.

Fresh organic, locally grown produce is optimal; however, when it is unavailable or out of season, or simply too expensive for the budget, nonorganic "supermarket" produce will suffice. Some frozen vegetables can also be incorporated into your meals because they are convenient and economical, and, since they are frozen when they are fresh, they actually retain many of their nutrients. Among the frozen vegetables I keep on hand are artichoke hearts, green peas, bell pepper strips, chopped spinach, corn kernels, and edamame. I also keep some canned vegetables in the pantry, notably tomatoes and tomato products, artichoke hearts, solid-pack pumpkin, and, of course, canned beans of all kinds.

OILS

There are those who follow a no-oil, or low-oil diet. To make this book more accessible to them, many of its recipes feature a no-oil option in which you can, instead, "water sauté" ingredients. Recipes that can be prepared without oil are so noted. If you do use oil, however, here's what I recommend.

The best-quality oils are cold-pressed, or unrefined. A little extra-virgin olive oil adds flavor to salads and other dishes, except for high-heat stir-fries, where you want an oil that has a higher smoking point and will not start breaking down before you get it to the right temperature. A good "all-purpose" oil is grapeseed oil. It has a fairly high smoking point and so it can be used for high-temperature cooking, such as stir-frying or sautéing. Because of its light flavor, it also makes a good component in dressings and sauces.

Toasted or dark sesame oil adds an Asian flavor to salads and other recipes, but think of it as a seasoning rather than a cooking oil, because it is unstable at high temperatures. Add it at the last minute for flavor. Flaxseed oil is an excellent source of omega-3 fatty acids, which are so important for good health. Like toasted sesame oil, flaxseed oil is unstable at high temperatures and should not be used for cooking. Unlike toasted sesame oil, it is virtually flavorless, but you can use it on salads to boost your intake of omega-3s. All of these oils are highly perishable, so be sure to store them in the refrigerator.

Coconut oil is another choice you may want to consider. It can withstand high temperatures and is especially useful for frying. Studies show a very low incidence of heart disease among people who consume coconut oil on a regular basis. In addition, coconut oil aids calcium absorption and is rich in antimicrobial properties. Organic, unrefined food-grade coconut oil is available at natural food stores and online.

NUTS AND SEEDS

Nuts and seeds are staple foods in many cultures in addition to being important protein sources for vegans. Nuts are popular in both sweet and savory dishes and are often enjoyed as a snack food. Due to their high oil content, nuts and seeds go rancid quickly once shelled and should be stored in an airtight container in the refrigerator, where they will keep for several months.

Studies have shown that eating just two ounces of almonds, pecans, or other nuts each day as part of a high-fiber vegan diet can dramatically lower "bad" low-density lipoprotein (LDL) cholesterol.

When nuts or seeds are ground into a paste, they are referred to as butters and are used in a variety of cuisines around the world. Nut and seed butters are rich in protein, fiber, and essential fatty acids and can be used to replace butter or margarine on bread or toast. At least half of the fat in nuts is monounsaturated, which can actually be good for blood cholesterol. Nut butters are a boon to vegans as a versatile source of protein and can be used to make sauces, to enrich soups and stews, and as a healthy fat replacement in baking. They are easier to digest than whole nuts and are easy to make at home.

SALT

Even a small amount of salt can make the difference between a well-seasoned dish and one that lacks flavor. The best salt for general use is sea salt, because it is naturally derived, has a good flavor, and contains minerals that are nutritionally beneficial. There are also a number of "fancy" salts available that are fun to use, such as Himalayan pink salt that has a delicate flavor and the *sulfurous* black salt that can make a vegan omelet taste like one made with eggs. Steer clear of refined table salt. It is bitter, devoid of nutrition, and loaded with chemicals that are added to make it flow freely.

SWEETENERS

Instead of using white table sugar, I usually prefer to use a naturally processed granulated sugar, such as Sucanat or Florida Crystals. For Southeast Asian recipes, date or palm sugar is a good choice because of its deep, almost caramelized flavor.

Natural liquid sweeteners that can be used instead of honey are pure maple syrup, agave nectar, and coconut nectar. Sweeteners such as barley malt and brown rice syrup are about half as sweet as honey, so you may need to experiment to achieve the desired results. Soaked and pureed dates and raisins, as well as molasses, are good natural sweeteners, but their dark color and distinctive flavors make them appropriate for only certain recipes.

VEGETABLE BROTH

Homemade vegetable broth is easy and economical to make, but it can also take up a lot of space in the refrigerator or freezer. You can buy prepared vegetable broth in cans and aseptic containers. However it can be expensive, and the strength and flavor of the various brands can vary greatly. More economical choices include vegan bouillon cubes, powdered vegetable base, and vegetable broth paste. These products are easy to use, and can be made into broth with the addition of boiling water.

It's important to note that the saltiness of the different broths can vary widely. Be sure to taste any broth before using it, because the flavor may impact your finished dish. If the flavor of your broth is stronger than you would like, simply dilute it with water. As broth reduces while cooking, the saltiness increases, so you'll need to judge the saltiness as you cook. For these reasons, the recipes often suggest salting "to taste." My personal favorite product to keep on hand for making vegetable broth is Superior Touch Better Than Bouillon vegetable base paste. It has a good flavor and is easy to use. If you prefer to make homemade broth from scratch, here is a basic recipe.

Vegetable Broth

This basic vegetable broth can be cooled and frozen in several storage containers with tight-fitting lids so you can defrost exactly what you need for a recipe. Be sure to scrub and wash all vegetables well before using.

1 tablespoon olive oil or ¼ cup water

1 large yellow onion, coarsely chopped

2 large carrots, coarsely chopped

1 large russet potato, unpeeled and cut into chunks

2 celery ribs, including leaves, coarsely chopped

3 cloves garlic, crushed

3 quarts water

2 tablespoons soy sauce

1 cup coarsely chopped fresh parsley

2 bay leaves

½ teaspoon salt

½ teaspoon whole black peppercorns

Heat the oil in a large stockpot over medium heat. Add the onion, carrots, potato, celery, and garlic. Cover and cook until slightly softened, about 5 minutes. Add the 3 quarts of water and the soy sauce, parsley, bay leaves, salt, and peppercorns. Bring to a boil, then decrease the heat to medium-low and simmer, uncovered, for 1 hour to reduce the liquid by one-third and bring out the flavors of the vegetables.

Strain the liquid through a fine-mesh sieve into another pot, pressing the juices out of the vegetables with the back of a large spoon. Discard the solids. The broth is now ready to use. For a stronger broth, bring the broth back to a boil, and reduce the volume by one-quarter. This broth keeps well in the refrigerator for up to 3 days if kept tightly covered, or portioned and frozen for up to 4 months.

Makes about 2 quarts

PLANT PROTEINS

Beyond beans and legumes, other main sources of plant-based protein are tofu (soybean curd), tempeh (compressed soybeans), and seitan (wheat-meat). Here is some basic information about each.

TOFU

Tofu, a curd made from soybeans, is a rich protein source. In China, tofu is called "meat without the bones." Nutritionally, tofu is very high in protein, calcium, iron, and B-complex vitamins. Its lack of flavor makes tofu a blank canvas for the imaginative cook because it readily absorbs other flavors and seasonings. Before using tofu, drain it well and press out the water to give it a firmer texture and allow it to absorb more flavor as it cooks. Regular tofu is also known as Chinese bean curd, and silken tofu is called Japanese-style tofu. Both are available in soft, firm, and extra-firm varieties. Firm and extra-firm regular tofu are used in stir-fries and other dishes that require a sturdy texture that retains its shape during cooking. Soft regular tofu can be used in recipes where a softer texture is desired. Silken tofu is used in recipes requiring a smooth, creamy texture, such as smoothies, sauces, and puddings. Regular tofu and silken tofu are not used interchangeably in most recipes—when tofu is called for in my recipes, it means regular Chinese tofu, unless "silken" is specified. Regular tofu is also sold baked and marinated in a number of flavors, which can be used without further seasoning.

Regular tofu may be stored unopened in the refrigerator until the expiration date on the package. Once opened, it is best to use it right away, although it can be submerged in fresh water in a covered container (to prevent it from absorbing surrounding flavors) and kept in the refrigerator for several days. Silken tofu is usually sold in aseptic containers that can be kept unrefrigerated until opened. Once opened, however, it should be used within two to three days.

Tofu is generally packaged in water, so it must be drained before using it in recipes. To remove even more moisture, cut the tofu into slabs and place them on a cutting board or baking sheet lined with two or three layers of paper towels. Cover the tofu with paper towels and blot to help enable the tofu to better absorb flavors.

To remove most of the moisture from regular tofu and thereby achieve a firmer texture, place a baking sheet on top of the tofu after blotting. Weight down the sheet with canned goods or a heavy skillet and allow to sit for one hour, then use as desired. Another way to change the texture of regular tofu is to freeze it. (Do not freeze silken tofu.) Once thawed, the tofu will be chewier and more porous, making it ideal for marinating and sautéing. To freeze tofu, cut drained and pressed tofu into thin slices and wrap in plastic or place in an airtight container. When you are ready to use the tofu, defrost it, then squeeze it to remove any excess moisture. Once thawed, it should be used within two to three days. Since frozen tofu will keep for several months, this is a good way to store tofu that is near its expiration date.

TEMPEH

Originating in Indonesia, tempeh is made of fermented, compressed soybeans that are formed into firm cakes. Tempeh has a distinctive flavor and chewy texture and can be cubed, crumbled, or grated to resemble ground meat. It marinates well and turns a crisp, golden brown when fried. High in protein and B vitamins, including vitamin B_{12}, tempeh can be found in the refrigerated section of natural food stores and some supermarkets. Tempeh is sold in 8- or 12-ounce packages, depending on the brand. It can be sliced lengthwise, cut into strips, cubed, or grated. Tempeh must be stored in the refrigerator, where it will keep unopened for several weeks (check the expiration date). Once opened, however, it should be tightly wrapped and used within three to four days. Tempeh also may be stored in the freezer for a month or so.

Steaming Tempeh For best results, I recommend that you steam tempeh before using it to mellow its flavor and also to make it more digestible. When recipes call for "steamed tempeh," it simply means that before using it in a recipe, the tempeh should be steamed in a steamer basket over boiling water for at least 15 minutes. Once it is steamed, tempeh can then be used as desired in recipes.

SEITAN

Called "wheat-meat" because it is made from the protein part of wheat, seitan (pronounced "say-TAN") is a versatile ingredient that can be ground, diced, cubed, or sliced. Made with vital wheat gluten flour and water (and seasonings), seitan can be purchased ready-made in the refrigerated or freezer sections of most natural food stores. However, because it can be expensive to buy and is easy to make at home, I suggest making your own. A recipe for homemade seitan is below. In addition to being a good source of protein, vitamin C, and iron, seitan is also low in fat and calories: One 4-ounce serving contains only 70 calories and 1 gram of fat.

Homemade Seitan

This recipe makes about 2 pounds that can be divided into 8-ounce portions, tightly wrapped, and frozen for later use. You can also keep seitan in the refrigerator for up to five days, either in a covered container in its cooking broth or portioned and tightly wrapped in freezer wrap and placed in freezer bags. Cooking instructions are provided to make seitan either on top of the stove or in a slow cooker. This seitan can be used in any of the recipes in this book that call for seitan.

2 cups vital wheat gluten

¼ cup nutritional yeast

3 tablespoons tapioca flour

1 teaspoon onion powder

1 teaspoon garlic powder

½ teaspoon salt

¼ teaspoon freshly ground black pepper

1½ cups cold water

6 tablespoons soy sauce

2 tablespoons olive oil

4 cups cold vegetable broth

In a food processor or mixing bowl, combine the vital wheat gluten, nutritional yeast, tapioca flour, onion powder, garlic powder, salt, and pepper and pulse or stir to mix. Add the water, 2 tablespoons of the soy sauce, and the oil and process or stir to mix well. Turn out the mixture onto a flat surface and knead for 2 minutes into a soft dough. Set the dough aside to rest for 5 minutes.

Stovetop Method: Divide the dough into four equal pieces and place them in a large pot with enough cold cooking broth to cover. Add the remaining 4 tablespoons of soy sauce and bring almost to a boil, then lower the heat to a simmer and cook for 1 hour.

Slow Cooker Method: Divide the dough into four equal pieces and place them in a slow cooker with enough cooking broth to cover. Add the remaining 4 tablespoons of soy sauce, cover with the lid, and cook on low heat for 6 to 8 hours.

After cooking (either method): Transfer the cooked seitan to a baking sheet to cool. Once cool, tightly wrap the portions of seitan, placing some of it in the freezer for later use, and the remainder in the refrigerator (whatever you plan to use within a few days). The seitan can now be cut or sliced to use in recipes.

Makes about 2 pounds seitan

Note: Seitan will keep in the refrigerator for 4 to 5 days and in the freezer for several weeks. The cooking liquid may be strained and used as a broth in sauces, soups, and other recipes or frozen in a tightly covered container and used to make the next batch of seitan.

OTHER PLANT-BASED PROTEINS

Textured vegetable protein (TVP) is a handy ingredient to keep in your pantry. Sold as dehydrated granules that double in size when reconstituted with a hot liquid, TVP is one of the most economical meat alternatives you could buy. Look for TVP in natural food stores and well-stocked supermarkets, where it is often sold in bulk. To rehydrate, place the desired amount in a heatproof bowl and cover with boiling water.

A popular TVP-like product is called Butler Soy Curls, which are made from textured non-GMO, whole soybeans. They are easy-to-use strips with a great texture and can be used in most recipes calling for seitan, tempeh, or extra-firm tofu.

DAIRY AND EGG ALTERNATIVES

There are a variety of ways to replace dairy products and eggs in recipes, including nondairy milk, vegan mayonnaise, and vegan cheeses.

Nondairy milk, including those made from soy, almonds, rice, oats, and coconut, can be used in recipes in the same way dairy milk is used. For savory recipes, it's important to use plain "unsweetened" varieties, however, as some brands of nondairy milk contain added sugar, even those labeled simply "plain." I generally use plain unsweetened almond milk for both savory and sweet recipes. Coconut milk is sold in a variety of ways: in refrigerated cartons next to the soy and almond milk, or the canned variety that has a richer texture and distinctive flavor making it most suitable for Thai or Indian recipes or in certain desserts. Other products, such as vegan versions of mayonnaise, cream cheese, sour cream, yogurt, and various types of cheese, are available to use instead of dairy products.

In addition to nondairy milks, you can buy (or make your own) vegan mayonnaise, sour cream, cream cheese, and a variety of cheeses made from nuts, soy, and rice. When buying such products, read the label to be sure the product does not contain casein or other dairy by-products that are sometimes added to make the cheese melt better. When you need a solid butter alternative, look for a nonhydrogenated vegan buttery spread, such as Earth Balance.

There are a number of egg substitutes. Depending on the recipe and the function eggs serve in it, alternatives include ground flaxseeds blended with water; silken tofu;

applesauce or other pureed fruit, vegetable, or bean; and egg replacement powder made from vegetable starch and leaveners.

Kitchen Equipment

A few good basic kitchen tools and equipment can go a long way to making your cooking life easier. You don't have to buy the most expensive equipment available. Just get the best quality you can afford, and buy only what you need. For example, there's no reason to get a huge set of pots and pans (or other equipment) when just a few basics will do.

MUST HAVES

BASIC TOOLS

Every kitchen needs cutting boards, a colander, spatulas, vegetable peeler, vegetable brush, box grater, wooden spoons, and a potato masher.

Knives: Every kitchen needs three basic knives: a paring knife for peeling and trimming; a long serrated knife for slicing bread, tomatoes, and other fragile foods; and a good (8- or 10-inch) chef's knife for virtually everything else. Buy the best quality knives you can afford and keep them sharp. You can chop more quickly and safely with sharp knives than with dull ones.

Pots and Pans: Every kitchen needs at least one pot big enough to boil pasta and make several quarts of vegetable stock. You also need a couple of smaller saucepans, including one with a steamer insert for steaming vegetables. Two or three heavy-bottomed skillets, ranging in size from 8 to 16 inches in diameter, are a must. At least one skillet should have a nonstick surface. One cast-iron skillet is also a good investment. All pots and skillets should have lids that fit well.

Baking Pans: At least two sheet pans are a must (9 by 13-inch is a good size); muffin tins, 9 by 5-inch loaf pan, 8 by 8-inch square baking pan, and a 9 by 13-inch baking dish or lasagna pan; a pie plate, springform pan (you'll thank me), and two 9-inch round cake pans.

Mix It Up: Stock your kitchen with a few mixing bowls, measuring cups and spoons, and a glass measuring pitcher for liquids.

Food Processor: A food processor is essential for making pesto, pureeing vegetables, chopping nuts, and making bread crumbs. It is also great for making pie dough, chopping vegetables, and numerous other mixing and chopping tasks. The trick is knowing when it will be faster to cut, whisk, or chop by hand, and that can usually be determined by the quantity of food involved. In addition to a large-capacity processor, some people also have a smaller model that they use for smaller tasks.

Blenders, Great and Small: Specifically, (a) a high-speed blender, such as a Vitamix, is ideal for making smooth creamy sauces, soups, and desserts; and (b) an immersion blender, handy for pureeing soups right in the pot. Also called a stick blender, it's easier to clean than a regular blender and it saves the time of pouring your recipe into a blender container.

Salad Spinner: The easiest and quickest way to dry your salad greens after washing them. It gets every drop of water off your lettuce, leaving it crisp and ready for your salad.

NICE-TO-HAVES

SMALL BUT MIGHTY

Small hand tools that come in handy include a citrus zester, Microplane grater, and an olive/cherry pitter.

Mandoline: A great tool when you need very thin slices very fast. It allows you to cut uniform slices, from thick to paper thin, with ease and swiftness—just watch your fingers because the blades are super sharp. Note: The plastic Benriner slicer is a smaller, less expensive, version of the stainless-steel mandoline, making it a good choice if you're on a budget.

Spice Grinder: Not a "must-have" but an electric spice grinder (or coffee grinder) can be very handy especially if you like to make your own spice blends from whole spices.

Steamer: This can be a dedicated saucepan with a fitted perforated steamer pan and lid, or a small collapsible perforated steamer insert to use in your existing saucepans; or a bamboo or similar steamer. It will be put to use for steaming items such as vegetables, dumplings, tempeh, to name a few.

Kitchen Tips

In addition to keeping a well-stocked pantry, here are a few other tips to help make your cooking time more enjoyable.

Organize your workspace. Before you start cooking, assemble all of the ingredients and the equipment you'll need to make a recipe. That includes measuring out the ingredients in advance. This is called *mise en place.* If you do this before you begin to cook, it will save you time, reduce stress, and may even improve your cooking skills by helping you avoid kitchen mishaps, such as missing ingredients or burning the onions while you search for a spatula.

Read the entire recipe—twice. It's much easier to prepare a recipe when you are familiar with it. Be sure to read through a recipe to avoid any midrecipe surprises.

Plan ahead. Keep essential ingredients on hand to prevent time-wasting extra shopping trips for one or two ingredients: for example, stock, cooked beans, and vegetable broth in the freezer; or buy canned vegetable broth and beans to stash in the pantry.

Be flexible. Even when we try to plan ahead and have everything we need on hand to make a recipe, sometimes we run out of an ingredient at the last minute. When that happens, don't panic. Just figure out whether you have something on hand to substitute for the missing ingredient. To avoid running out of the ingredients you use most frequently, keep a grocery list handy in the kitchen so you can write down items the minute you run out or that are getting low.

Swap it. If you don't like a particular ingredient in a recipe, or perhaps you don't have it on hand, chances are you can still make the recipe. It's often a simple matter of substituting one ingredient for another, such as using white beans instead of chickpeas, or basil instead of cilantro.

Season to taste. With the help of my dedicated recipe testers, I have done my best to use seasonings in these recipes that should please most palates. However, you should still use your own judgment regarding the use of various herbs and spices, depending on your personal tastes as well as to adjust for variables such as the strength (and saltiness) of your vegetable broth, or the heat of your chiles.

CHAPTER 3

A Pantry Without Borders

The first step toward enjoying international cooking at home is to develop a well-stocked pantry filled with a variety of ingredients, including sauces and spices. If you like to cook recipes from around the world, then a well-stocked pantry can be a valuable asset. When your larder is full of the ingredients used in these recipes, you'll be all set to transport your taste buds anywhere on the planet.

A well-stocked kitchen should also include fresh staples, such as onions, carrots, and celery, fresh lettuce and other salad ingredients, and a wide selection of vegetables and fruits, including fresh herbs whenever possible. Include a range of dried or canned beans, such as chickpeas, cannellini beans, lentils, kidney beans, and pintos. Stock your pantry with a variety of pasta, rice, and other grains, extra-virgin olive oil, and canned tomato products, including paste, puree, and diced and whole tomatoes. Keep on hand a supply of dried herbs, spices, sea salt, and other basic seasonings, as well as standard baking items, such as flours, baking soda, baking powder, and extracts. By keeping a variety of basic ingredients on hand, you'll always be ready to create fabulous international meals whenever you want them.

For Mediterranean flavors, for example, line your shelves with olives, capers, sun-dried tomatoes, artichoke hearts, dried mushrooms, and roasted red peppers. For those times when you want to cook with an Asian flair, be sure to keep on hand tamari, toasted sesame oil, chili paste, sriracha sauce, fresh ginger, rice vinegar, hoisin sauce, and other flavor enhancers. With a variety of ingredients at your fingertips, you can prepare interesting, healthful meals in a snap.

Some pantry ingredients, such as nuts, seeds, certain oils, and whole-grain flours, can go rancid quickly and should be kept in the refrigerator, especially if not using right away. In addition, some nonperishable pantry items should be stored in the refrigerator once the package or container is opened. In the freezer you should stock cooked and portioned beans, grains, as well as international flavor-makers such as small portions of tomato paste, chipotle chiles in adobo, and pesto.

The following lists of pantry items are especially important in an international vegan kitchen. For your convenience, I've divided the pantry list into two sections: The first section is a Basic Pantry List that includes such cross-cultural staples as canned and dried beans, grains, pasta and noodles, vegetable broth paste, nut butters, and tomato products. It features items that you will need for virtually any type of cooking you may want to do. The second section, a Global Pantry List, features particular ingredients needed to cook in various cuisines. You may notice some crossover ingredients, which is indicative as to how different cuisines use many of the same ingredients. This list is organized according to a general geographical region, since many cuisines in close proximity use similar sauces, herbs, spices, and other ingredients. Since herbs and spices are the cornerstone of any cuisine, I've listed several of the ones used in each cuisine.

Not included in the list are the general items found in most kitchens such as sea salt, black peppercorns, and baking needs such as all-purpose flour, baking soda, baking powder, cornstarch, and extracts. Also not listed are general perishable staples common to a variety of cuisines, such as fresh vegetables and fruits, including cooking basics such as onions and garlic, lemons and limes, or tofu and tempeh.

Basic Pantry List

The items in this list are useful to have on hand in any vegan kitchen. They can be used to prepare recipes from most of the countries and regions highlighted in this book, with some ingredients being used to a greater or lesser degree.

Beans and legumes, dried and canned (chickpeas, kidney beans, cannellini beans, black beans, lentils, and so on)

Dried fruit: cranberries, raisins, figs, apricots, peaches, and so on

Dried mushrooms

Flours: Vital wheat gluten flour, chickpea flour, all-purpose flour, white whole wheat flour, cornmeal, and so on

Grains: rice (brown, basmati, jasmine, risotto, wild, etc.), quinoa, barley, bulgur, oats (rolled and/or steel-cut)

Instant coffee or espresso powder (for baking)

Nondairy milk: almond, soy, rice, coconut, and so on

Noodle varieties (rice sticks, cellophane noodles, udon, soba, and so on)

Nut butters (peanut, almond, tahini, and so on)

Nutritional yeast

Nuts: almonds, walnuts, pecans, cashews, peanuts, pine nuts, and so on

Oils: olive, flaxseed, sesame, grapeseed, walnut, coconut (unrefined)

Pasta varieties (linguine, penne, rigatoni, and so on)

Seeds: sesame, sunflower, flax

Sweeteners: sugar (raw natural, confectioners', etc.), agave nectar, maple syrup, molasses

Tomato products, canned (diced, whole, puree, paste)

Vegetable broth or soup base (aseptic containers, canned, paste, powder, or cube—preferably low sodium)

Vinegars: balsamic, rice, sherry, cider

Global Pantry List

In addition to the basic ingredients listed here, these ingredients (including herbs and spices) are of relevance to the specific world cuisines.

EUROPE
artichoke hearts, canned, frozen, or marinated

capers

grape leaves

herbs and spices: basil, bay leaves, caraway seeds, cilantro, dill, fennel seed, herbes de Provence, marjoram, mint, oregano, paprika (hot, sweet, and smoked), parsley, poppy seeds, red pepper flakes, rosemary, savory, thyme

olives

polenta (ground cornmeal)

roasted red peppers

sun-dried tomatoes (dehydrated or oil-packed)

THE AMERICAS
chiles, dried and fresh

chipotles in adobo sauce

coconut milk

corn and wheat tortillas

cornmeal/masa harina

herbs and spices: annatto, allspice, bay leaf, cilantro, cinnamon, coriander, cumin, oregano, parsley, thyme, liquid smoke

quinoa

tomato salsa

MIDDLE EAST AND AFRICA

bulgur

chickpea flour, chickpeas

chiles, dried and fresh

couscous

dates

dried apricots

harissa sauce

herbs and spices: cayenne, cinnamon, coriander, cumin, paprika, turmeric, *za'taar* spice blend, berbere spice blend, baharat spice blend

phyllo dough

pistachios

pita bread

pomegranate molasses

tahini

teff flour

INDIA

basmati rice

cashews

chickpeas

chickpea flour

chiles, dried and fresh

chutney

ginger

herbs and spices: cilantro, curry leaves, cardamom, mustard seeds, coriander, cumin, mango powder, turmeric, curry paste or powder, garam masala

lentils

pistachios

rosewater

tamarind paste

ASIA

chili pastes/sauces: sambal oelek, sriracha, sweet chili sauce

chiles, dried and fresh

coconut milk, unsweetened (canned)

ginger

herbs and spices: cilantro, coriander, cumin, star anise, Szechuan peppercorns, Thai basil

hoisin sauce

jasmine rice

sushi rice

kaffir lime leaves

lemongrass

miso paste

rice flour

rice paper wrappers

rice vinegar

sea vegetables: nori (for sushi), agar (thickener), kelp or kombu (to make dashi stock)

soy sauce: tamari, mushroom (vegan oyster sauce), black (sweet)

tamarind paste

toasted sesame oil

toasted sesame seeds

unsweetened jackfruit (canned or frozen)

wasabi paste

About the Recipes

The way anyone likes their food seasoned, as well as the size of their portions, are among the things that make us individuals. To that end, most of the recipes in this book yield four average servings. However, if you know that your family tends to eat smaller portions, or if you plan to serve a few other dishes or courses with a particular recipe, then you may be able to stretch six or more portions out of a recipe designed to feed four hearty appetites as a one-dish meal. In terms of seasonings, certain cuisines are known for their spiciness so I tried to strike a balance in these recipes to keep heat levels reasonably authentic without alienating the average palate that might not have a high tolerance for heat. No one knows their heat and spice preferences as well as you do, so please use your own discretion when adding spices to recipes. All of these recipes were tested by a number of people with varying taste preferences. If you prefer your food milder or hotter, please feel free to adjust the seasonings accordingly.

Here are some specific points about the ingredients used in the recipes:

When olive oil is listed in a recipe, it refers to extra-virgin olive oil.

When salt is listed, sea salt is preferred.

For sugar, I recommend an organic natural sugar, such as Sucanat.

When chopped scallions (aka green onions) are listed, it refers to both the white and green parts.

When specific can or jar sizes are called for, these sizes are based on what is available in my local store. If your store carries 15-ounce canned beans and the recipe calls for a 16-ounce can, go with the size found in your store. Such a small size differentiation won't affect the recipe results.

When vegan butter is called for, I recommend Earth Balance buttery spread.

For soy sauce, I suggest using wheat-free tamari for best flavor and quality.

Categories

To make it easy to spot recipes that use little or no oil, as well as those who require recipes that are gluten free or soy free, each recipe features information indicating these categories. Most of the recipes are naturally low-fat and many call for no oil or very little oil. For example, in many cases, a choice is given to sauté ingredients in either water or a small amount of oil. Many of the recipes are also either gluten free, soy free, or both. Wherever possible, easy substitutions are noted to make a recipe either gluten or soy free. For example, substitute gluten-free pasta for regular pasta or use coconut aminos instead of soy sauce. In addition, many of the recipes are especially quick and easy to make, requiring 30 minutes or less active time.

LOW OIL OR NO OIL

The recipe uses 1 tablespoon of oil or less.

QUICK AND EASY

The recipe can be completed in less than 30 minutes of active time. (This doesn't include time spent soaking nuts, a final chilling, or other inactive time.)

GLUTEN FREE

The recipe contains no wheat, rye, or barley. You'll need to make sure certain ingredients you may use (such as soy sauce, oats, etc.) are gluten free.

SOY FREE

The recipe contains no tofu, tempeh, edamame, soy sauce, or miso. You'll need to use a soy-free vegan buttery spread (Earth Balance makes one) when vegan butter is called for.

For your convenience, beginning on page 260 are lists of the recipes in this book organized according to category.

Note: The categories listed with the recipes refer to the primary ingredients listed within each recipe, not when made with optional ingredients or variations.

CHAPTER 4

Europe

I could fill an entire book with my favorite recipes from almost any country in Europe, so for this book of my personal favorites from around the world, I had to choose carefully. From a culinary point of view, the food of Europe can be divided into two major groups: Mediterranean Europe, featuring the cuisines of the sun-drenched countries of France, Italy, Spain, and Greece, and the northern regions, which include, among others, the United Kingdom and Eastern Europe.

Some of the most familiar and popular plant-based dishes hail from the countries that surround the Mediterranean Sea and so that is where we begin. Mediterranean Europe is home to many of the world's most delicious naturally vegan recipes, such as the farinata of Liguria, or the ratatouille of southern France, using distinctive ingredients of the region, including olives and olive oil, garlic, tomatoes, eggplant, peppers and chiles, fragrant herbs, such as basil, oregano, thyme, and rosemary, and nuts, such as almonds, hazelnuts, and walnuts.

Although northern European countries aren't especially known for their vegetables, a number of tasty, naturally vegan recipes hail from the countries of Eastern Europe as well as the British Isles. While meat, seafood, and dairy products dominate these regions, there are also a number of wholesome dishes, notably the crisp potato pancakes and earthy mushroom soups, that showcase vegetables, beans, and grains, including hearty fare featuring potatoes, barley, noodles, cabbage, and white beans. Seasonings often include horseradish, mustard, and paprika, as well as dill and other herbs.

Italy

Included here are recipes drawn from several regions of Italy, as well as Sardinia and Sicily. The reason is simple: I'm half Italian, so these wonderful flavors are coded in my DNA. I especially love Northern Italian cooking for its well-known emphasis on vegetables, grains, and beans. Consider also the seductive richness of many pasta, risotto, polenta, and gnocchi dishes, or the grilled vegetables, salads, and bean and vegetable soups, such as minestrone and pasta fagiole.

But I also love the pastas and tomato sauces of the South—these were the dishes I grew up on. People are surprised to learn that Italy's most famous ingredients actually come from other regions of the world. Tomatoes were brought to Italy from South America, and pasta was introduced from China by Marco Polo. The Italians brought them together for one of the most popular dishes in the world. The abundant use of fresh produce, herbs, and spices, along with pasta dishes such as Trofie alla Pesto with Green Beans and Potatoes (page 11), rice dishes known as risotto often made with local mushrooms or artichokes, and cornmeal dishes (polenta) such as Polenta Rustica with Kale and Bean Ragout on page 14, make Italy a vegan's culinary dream come true. In Italy (as well as other countries) meat is often used as a side, or merely to flavor soups and sauces.

The foods of Sicily and Sardinia are unique unto themselves, but each with remarkable plant-based culinary treasures. Sardinia is Italy's leading producer of organic produce and tomatoes are grown in abundance, as are artichokes, chickpeas, fava beans, zucchini, and eggplant. Native dishes are redolent of herbs, including wild fennel, mint, basil, and myrtle. Sicilians are known for preparing vegetables such as zucchini, eggplant, or cipollini onions in a sweet and sour sauce. In addition to Sicily's beloved tomatoes and eggplant, fava beans, artichokes, and other vegetables are prepared with garlic, olive oil, hot chiles, olives, pine nuts, or capers, and lots of fragrant basil or parsley, as well as dried fruit such as raisins or figs, as in Sicilian-Style Cauliflower on page 15.

Farinata with Sun-Dried Tomatoes and Olives

Made with chickpea flour, *farinata* is actually more of a savory pancake than a bread. It's easy to make this Ligurian specialty that can be served as an appetizer or as part of the main meal. *Farinata* is often prepared without embellishment, but I sometimes add a fresh herb such as rosemary or sage, or chopped olives and sun-dried tomatoes, as in this recipe.

1 cup water

1 cup chickpea flour

2 tablespoons plus 1 teaspoon olive oil

½ teaspoon salt

Freshly ground black pepper

3 tablespoons minced kalamata olives

3 tablespoons minced sun-dried tomatoes

In a mixing bowl, whisk together the water and chickpea flour until smooth. Add the oil, salt, a few grinds of pepper, olives, and tomatoes, and mix until well blended. Cover and set aside at room temperature for 1 hour.

Preheat the oven to 425°F. Oil a 12-inch pizza pan and heat in the oven until hot. Carefully remove the pan from the oven and add the batter, spreading evenly. Bake until the top is firm and the edges are golden brown, about 15 minutes. Cut into thin wedges and serve immediately.

Variation: Omit the olives and tomatoes from the batter and spread the baked farinata with a thin layer of pesto.

Serves 6

GLUTEN-FREE
SOY-FREE

Artichoke Crostini with Chickpeas and Arugula

To acknowledge the thin crisp flatbread of Sardinia known as *carasau*, the bread for this crostini is sliced very thin. The luscious topping is a fragrant blend of typical Sardinian ingredients, including chickpeas, artichokes, and fennel. To make this gluten-free, use a gluten-free bread instead of the ciabatta loaf.

1 loaf Italian ciabatta bread, thinly sliced

2 tablespoons olive oil, plus more for brushing bread

1 clove garlic, crushed

1 (15-ounce) can chickpeas, drained and rinsed

1 cup cooked artichoke hearts (frozen, canned, or marinated), well drained

3 tablespoons freshly squeezed lemon juice

2 tablespoons water

Salt and freshly ground black pepper

2 cups chopped arugula or baby spinach

¼ cup oil-packed sun-dried tomatoes, drained and chopped

¼ cup coarsely chopped basil

Fennel Gremolata (optional; recipe follows)

Preheat the oven to 425°F. Arrange the bread in a single layer on a baking sheet and brush with oil. Bake until golden, about 5 minutes. Set aside.

In a food processor, mince the garlic, then add the chickpeas, artichoke hearts, lemon juice, remaining 2 tablespoons of oil, 2 tablespoons of water, and salt and pepper to taste. Process until almost smooth, then add the arugula, tomatoes, and basil and pulse to combine. Spread the mixture onto each crostini. Sprinkle each crostini with the fennel gremolata, if using. Serve immediately.

Serves 4

GLUTEN-FREE OPTION
SOY-FREE
QUICK AND EASY

Fennel Gremolata

This gremolata adds a bold and fragrant note to a variety of dishes such as soups, stews, and pastas. It's made with popular Sardinian ingredients, fennel and citrus, making it an ideal complement to the artichoke crostini.

Combine the fennel fronds, pine nuts, zest, garlic, fennel seed, and salt in a small bowl. Mix well and use immediately or cover and refrigerate until needed.

Serves 4 to 6

GLUTEN-FREE
SOY-FREE
QUICK AND EASY
NO OIL

3 tablespoons minced fennel fronds

1½ tablespoons finely chopped toasted pine nuts

1½ tablespoons finely grated lemon or orange zest

1 clove garlic, minced

½ teaspoon ground fennel seed

Pinch of salt

Tuscan White Bean Soup

One prominent feature in central Italy is the wide use of beans, especially chickpeas, favas, and cannellini beans. Beans are used so often in Tuscan cooking, Tuscans are sometimes called "bean eaters." Creamy white cannellini beans are featured in this Tuscan-inspired soup made with a tomatoey broth and the addition of a small soup pasta such as ditalini. For gluten free, use a gluten-free pasta.

1 tablespoon olive oil or ¼ cup water

1 medium yellow onion, minced

3 cloves garlic, minced

1 (14-ounce) can crushed tomatoes

1 teaspoon dried oregano

1 teaspoon dried basil

½ teaspoon red pepper flakes

6 cups vegetable broth

1 bay leaf

Salt and freshly ground black pepper

1 cup small soup pasta, such as ditalini

1 medium zucchini, chopped

3 cups cooked cannellini beans, or 2 (15.5-ounce) cans, drained and rinsed

2 tablespoons minced fresh Italian parsley

Heat the oil or water in a large pot over medium heat. Add the onion and cook for 5 minutes to soften. Add the garlic and cook, stirring, for 1 minute. Blend in the tomatoes, oregano, basil, and red pepper flakes. Stir in the broth. Add the bay leaf and salt and pepper to taste and bring to a boil. Lower the heat to medium and simmer for about 20 minutes. Return to a boil and stir in the pasta, zucchini, and beans. Decrease the heat to a simmer and cook until the pasta and zucchini are just tender, about 10 minutes. Add a little more broth, if needed. Remove the bay leaf, then taste and adjust the seasonings if needed. Stir in the parsley and serve hot.

Serves 4 to 6

GLUTEN-FREE OPTION
SOY-FREE
LOW OIL

Umbrian Lentil Salad

This hearty salad is inspired by a similar dish that I enjoyed for lunch at a small café in Assisi in the Umbrian region of Italy where lentils are quite popular. The salad was served to me at room temperature with warm crusty Italian bread, and I encourage you to do the same.

Cook the lentils in a pot of boiling salted water until tender but firm, 30 to 40 minutes. Drain well and rinse under cold water, then drain again.

While the lentils are cooking, combine the oil, vinegar, maple syrup, mustard, coriander, red pepper flakes, and salt and pepper to taste in a small bowl. Stir to combine well. Set aside.

In a large bowl, combine the cooked, drained lentils with the arugula, onion, walnuts, raisins, capers, and parsley. Pour on the dressing and toss to mix well. Serve at room temperature or cover and refrigerate and serve chilled.

Serves 4

GLUTEN-FREE
SOY-FREE

2 cups brown lentils

2 tablespoons olive oil

3 tablespoons cider vinegar

2 teaspoons maple syrup
or agave nectar

2 teaspoons spicy brown mustard

½ teaspoon ground coriander

¼ teaspoon red pepper flakes

Salt and freshly ground black pepper

2 to 3 cups chopped arugula

¼ cup minced red onion

½ cup toasted walnut pieces

½ cup raisins

3 tablespoons capers

2 tablespoons chopped parsley or basil

Trofie alla Pesto with Green Beans and Potatoes

This classic Ligurian dish combines pasta and pesto with green beans and potatoes for a hearty and delicious meal. Trofie pasta is a specialty of the region where it is rolled by hand and commonly served with Pesto Genovese. For gluten-free, substitute a gluten-free pasta.

If making homemade trofie, make the pasta first and set aside.

In a food processor, combine the garlic, pine nuts, and salt and process to a paste. Add the basil, drizzle in the oil, and process until smooth. Transfer to a bowl, cover with plastic wrap, and place directly on the surface of the pesto. Set aside. Steam the potatoes over a pot of simmering water until tender, about 10 minutes. Set the potatoes aside, then steam the green beans over simmering water until tender, about 6 minutes. Set aside.

Cook the pasta in a large pot of boiling salted water until it is al dente. Drain the pasta and return to the pot. Gently stir in the steamed potatoes and green beans, reserved pesto, and 2 to 3 tablespoons of the hot pasta water. Cook for a few minutes, until heated through and combined. Season with salt and pepper. Serve immediately.

Serves 4

GLUTEN-FREE OPTION
SOY-FREE

1 pound trofie pasta (recipe follows) or purchased trofie, gemelli, or cut fusilli

3 cloves garlic, crushed and chopped

2 tablespoons pine nuts

Salt

2 cups tightly packed fresh basil leaves

⅓ cup olive oil

8 ounces small new potatoes, quartered or sliced

8 ounces green beans, trimmed and cut into 2-inch pieces

Freshly ground black pepper

Trofie Pasta

The Ligurian pasta known as trofie is made with flour, water, and a little salt. No eggs are used to make it—and it doesn't even require a pasta-making machine, as its unique twisted shape with tapered ends is rolled by hand. This classic Genovese pasta is traditionally served with a pesto sauce.

3 cups all-purpose flour, plus more for dusting

1 teaspoon salt

1 cup cold water, or more if needed

Combine the flour and salt in a large bowl. Slowly add the water, mixing it into the flour with a fork.

When combined, flour your hands and knead the dough with your hands. If the dough is too dry, add a tablespoon of water (or more as needed). If the dough is sticky, sprinkle in a little more flour. Transfer the dough to a lightly floured board and knead well for 5 minutes, or until the dough is smooth. Cover the dough with a kitchen towel or plastic wrap and set aside for 30 minutes.

Lightly flour a work surface and a baking sheet. Cut off a piece of the dough and roll it into a long rope about ⅓ inch thick. Cut the rope into small pieces, about ½ inch long. Roll the piece of dough away from you with the palm of your hand to form a cylinder. Turn your hand up at a 45-degree angle, then gently roll the cylinder back toward you to form a twisted spiral with tapered ends. Repeat until all the dough is used. Transfer the trofie to a lightly floured, parchment-lined baking sheet.

Makes 1 pound trofie

SOY-FREE
NO OIL

Fregola with Roasted Zucchini and Tomatoes

Fregola is a tiny, rustic Sardinian pasta that resembles Israeli couscous. In the summer months, I especially enjoy its nutty flavor tossed with roasted diced zucchini and tomatoes. For a one-dish meal, I add in some chickpeas or cannellini beans. It is good served hot, warm, or cold. Toasted pine nuts are a good addition as well. If fregola is unavailable, substitute your favorite small pasta shape.

Preheat the oven to 425°F. Spread the zucchini, shallots, and tomatoes in a single layer on a well-oiled rimmed baking sheet. Drizzle with a small amount of olive oil and season with salt and pepper. Roast the vegetables until tender and slightly caramelized, 20 to 30 minutes, turning once about halfway through. Remove from the oven, set aside, and keep warm.

While the vegetables are cooking, cook the fregola in a pot of boiling salted water until just tender, about 20 minutes, or according to the package directions. Drain and return to the pot.

Combine the fregola with the roasted vegetables and toss gently to combine. Taste and adjust the seasonings, adding more salt and pepper, if needed. Serve hot or warm, garnished with pine nuts and fresh basil leaves.

Serves 4 to 6

SOY-FREE
LOW OIL

3 zucchini (12 ounces), cut into ¼-inch dice

3 shallots, finely chopped

2 cups cherry tomatoes, halved lengthwise

Olive oil

Salt and freshly ground black pepper

1 (16-ounce) package fregola sarda

2 tablespoons toasted pine nuts or chopped walnuts

2 tablespoons fresh basil leaves, (torn, if large)

Polenta Rustica with Kale and Bean Ragout

In the past, Italian meals were frequently meatless because the people could not afford meat. In fact, many of the so-called upscale dishes found in contemporary restaurants developed from what was considered Italian "peasant food," a general category called *povero* (poor). Polenta is a delicious example of the *povero* cuisine of Tuscany. The kale and bean ragout make this a satisfying one-dish meal.

Ragout

1 tablespoon olive oil or ¼ cup water

1 medium yellow onion, chopped

1 red or yellow bell pepper, seeded and chopped

3 cloves garlic, run through a garlic press

3 tablespoons tomato paste

1 teaspoon dried oregano

1 teaspoon salt

½ teaspoon freshly ground black pepper

½ cup dry white wine (optional)

1 (14.5-ounce) can diced fire-roasted tomatoes, undrained

1½ cups vegetable broth

1 bay leaf

1 (15.5-ounce) can cannellini beans, drained and rinsed

4 cups chopped Tuscan kale or spinach

½ cup chopped fresh basil leaves

Polenta

5 cups water

½ teaspoon salt

1½ cups cornmeal polenta

To make the ragout, heat the oil or water over medium-high heat in a large pot. Add the onion, bell pepper, and garlic. Cover and cook until the vegetables are softened, stirring occasionally, about 5 minutes. Stir in the tomato paste, oregano, salt, and pepper. Stir in the wine, if using. Add the tomatoes and their juices, broth, and bay leaf and bring to a boil. Lower the heat to medium, stir in the cannellini beans and simmer, uncovered, for 15 minutes. Remove the bay leaf and discard. Stir in the kale and basil and cook for 5 minutes longer to wilt the kale. Taste and adjust the seasonings, if needed. Keep warm.

To make the polenta, bring the water to a boil in a large pot. Add the salt and slowly stream in the polenta, whisking constantly. Decrease the heat to medium-low and stir continuously until the polenta pulls away from the sides of the pot, about 20 minutes.

To serve, spoon the polenta into shallow bowls and top each serving with a large spoonful of the ragout. Serve hot.

Serves 4

GLUTEN-FREE
SOY-FREE
LOW OIL

Sicilian-Style Cauliflower

Sicilian cooking often incorporates dried fruit, such as figs or raisins with vegetables or pasta. If figs are unavailable, substitute raisins. Garlic and olive oil add depth and pine nuts provide a bit of crunch.

Preheat the oven to 425°F. Lightly oil 1 or two baking sheets. Cut the cauliflower into ½-inch-thick slices (some of the slices will come apart where the core has been removed—that's okay). Arrange the slices (and pieces) of cauliflower on the prepared baking sheets. Drizzle or brush lightly with olive oil and season with salt and pepper. Roast until tender on the inside and lightly browned on the outside, turning once, about 15 minutes total. Keep warm.

While the cauliflower is roasting, heat 1 tablespoon of olive oil in a small skillet over medium heat. Add the garlic and cook until fragrant, about 30 seconds. Add the figs and pine nuts and cook until the pine nuts are lightly toasted, about 1 minute. Stir in the red pepper flakes to taste. To serve, transfer the cauliflower to a shallow bowl and top with the garlic and fig mixture. Serve hot, sprinkled with parsley.

Serves 4

GLUTEN-FREE
SOY-FREE
LOW OIL

1 head cauliflower, ends trimmed, and cored

Olive oil

Salt and freshly ground black pepper

3 cloves garlic, finely minced

½ cup dried figs, coarsely chopped

¼ cup pine nuts

¼ to ½ teaspoon hot red pepper flakes

2 tablespoons chopped Italian parsley

Tiramisu Pie

The traditional Italian "pick-me-up" dessert is usually made with ladyfingers or cake and mascarpone cheese. This version uses shortbread cookie crumbs to make a crumb crust for a tiramisu pie and a filling made with cashews and vegan cream cheese.

Crust

2 cups vegan shortbread cookies, purchased or homemade (recipe follows)

3 tablespoons vegan butter, melted

Filling

⅓ cup sugar

2 tablespoons cornstarch

⅓ cup almond milk

1 cup raw cashews, soaked for 3 hours or overnight, then drained

2 tablespoons strong brewed coffee

2 tablespoons Kahlúa or 2 teaspoons brandy or rum extract

1 teaspoon pure vanilla extract

8 ounces vegan cream cheese, softened

Unsweetened cocoa powder, for garnish

To make the crust, preheat the oven to 350°F. Lightly oil a 9-inch pie plate or spray it with cooking spray. In a small bowl, combine the cookie crumbs and butter and mix well to moisten the crumbs. Transfer the crumb mixture to the pie plate and press the crumbs firmly into the bottom and sides of the pan to make a crust. Bake for 10 minutes, then remove from the oven and set aside to cool.

To make the filling, combine the sugar, cornstarch, and almond milk in a small saucepan, stirring until well blended. Heat, stirring, just to a boil, then decrease the heat to a simmer and cook, stirring until thickened. Set aside to cool.

In a high-speed blender or food processor, combine the soaked and drained cashews with the coffee, Kahlúa, and vanilla and blend until completely smooth and creamy. Add the vegan cream cheese and process until well blended and smooth and creamy. Add the reserved almond milk mixture and process until well blended. Scrape the batter into the prepared crust. Refrigerate for at least 2 hours or up to 10 hours.

To assemble, when ready to serve, dust the top of the pie with cocoa powder.

Serves 8

Shortbread Cookies

These cookies are delicious on their own, but they can also be used to make a flavorful crumb crust for the Tiramisu Pie (page 16).

Preheat the oven to 375°F. Line two baking sheets with parchment paper and set aside.

In a food processor, combine the sugar, butter, and cream cheese, and process until smooth and well blended. Add the flour and baking powder and pulse until well combined. Do not overmix.

Transfer the cookie dough to a flat work surface between two sheets of parchment paper or plastic wrap. Roll out the dough to ½ inch thick.

Using a pastry cutter, small drinking glass, or cookie cutter, cut the cookies into the desired shape and arrange them on the prepared baking sheets. Bake until golden, about 15 minutes. Let cool for several minutes before using.

Makes about 2 dozen cookies

1 cup natural sugar

½ cup vegan butter, at room temperature

½ cup vegan cream cheese, softened

2 cups white, whole wheat, or all-purpose flour

1 teaspoon baking powder

France

I'll always have a soft spot for French cooking since my training as a chef began with this classic cuisine and I eventually worked my way up the ranks to chef in a French restaurant.

French cuisine is often synonymous with meat, cheese, and cream, so it is not especially known as vegan-friendly. However, many French dishes are easily transformed into vegan fare by a simple ingredient swap: For example, I use vegetable broth and vegan cheese to make the Brandy-Laced Onion Soup on page 20. Similarly, mushrooms are used instead of chicken livers to make a pâté called Pâté au Champignon (page 21). In the same way, you can simply omit the tuna from a salade niçoise or a pan bagnat, and you will have a delectable vegetable salad and sandwich, respectively.

Additionally, the Provençal region in southern France is known for its vegetable and bean-centric dishes. Typical Provençal cuisine is a celebration of fresh vegetables, such as ratatouille, the famous stew of eggplant, zucchini, and tomatoes in perfect harmony. By roasting the vegetables, I give the dish more depth of flavor in my recipe for Roasted Ratatouille with Basil Pistou (page 28).

In Provence, olive oil is typically favored over butter and mayonnaise used elsewhere in France. Provençal cooking is similar to northern Italian, with its pistou, a basil pesto (made without cheese) that is used to season the ratatouille mentioned above, as well as the classic French minestrone soup known as soupe au pistou. Similarly, olive oil is used in the making of socca, a Niçoise version of the Italian farinata, a pancake made with chickpea flour and pissaladière, a French version of pizza.

Brandy-Laced Onion Soup

Nearly thirty years ago, in a restaurant kitchen far far away, I spilled several gallons of scalding hot onion soup on myself. But that hasn't stopped me from adoring this classic French soup. The key to its great flavor is caramelizing the onions before adding the broth. French onion soup is usually made with beef broth, so if you can find vegan "beef" broth, such as "No-Beef Broth" it will add an extra flavor dimension. For gluten free, use a gluten-free bread; for soy-free, use coconut aminos instead of Worcestershire or soy sauce.

1 tablespoon olive oil, plus more for brushing bread

4 large sweet yellow onions, thinly sliced (12 to 14 cups)

Salt and freshly ground black pepper

1 teaspoon dried thyme

⅓ cup brandy

½ teaspoon smoked paprika

5 cups vegetable broth

1 teaspoon vegan Worcestershire sauce or soy sauce

4 to 6 slices French or Italian bread, cut to fit your soup bowls, if necessary

⅓ cup shredded vegan mozzarella cheese (optional)

Heat the oil in a large pot over medium heat. Add the onions and season with salt and pepper. Cook, stirring, to coat the onions with the oil. Cover and cook until the onions are softened, about 10 minutes, then uncover and continue to cook, stirring, until the onions begin to caramelize, about 20 minutes longer. Stir in the thyme, brandy, and smoked paprika, then add the broth and Worcestershire sauce. Taste and adjust the seasonings, adding more salt and pepper if needed. Simmer for another 30 to 45 minutes to blend the flavors.

Preheat the oven to 400°F. Brush the bread slices with olive oil and arrange on a baking sheet. Sprinkle with salt and pepper, and a little smoked paprika and thyme, if desired. Bake until toasted, turning occasionally, about 15 minutes total. If using vegan cheese, sprinkle it on the bread during the last 5 minutes of baking.

To serve, ladle the soup into bowls and top each serving with a slice of the toasted bread. Serve immediately.

Serves 4 to 6

GLUTEN-FREE OPTION
SOY-FREE

Pâté au Champignon

This rich, nicely seasoned mushroom pâté is a great way to begin a French dinner. Plan on making it the day before needed, if possible, so the flavors can meld. Serve with crackers or thin slices of toasted baguette. Leftovers make a great sandwich filling.

Preheat the oven to 350°F. Lightly oil an 8- or 9-inch loaf pan and set aside.

Heat the oil in a large skillet over medium heat. Add the onion and garlic, and cook, stirring, until softened, 5 minutes. Add the mushrooms and continue cooking until the mushrooms are softened, about 5 minutes longer. Stir in the paprika, thyme, sage, salt, pepper, allspice, and cayenne, mixing well. Continue cooking until any remaining liquid is absorbed. Set aside.

In a food processor, combine the lentils, walnuts, and tofu and process until smooth and well blended. Add the oats, nutritional yeast, wheat gluten, brandy, soy sauce, and lemon juice. Process until smooth and well combined. Add the reserved mushroom mixture and pulse to combine well, leaving some texture. Taste and adjust the seasonings, if needed.

Spoon the pâté mixture into the prepared loaf pan, packing well. Smooth the top and cover with aluminum foil. Place the pan inside a 9 by 13-inch baking dish. Pour 1 inch of water into the bottom of the pan. Carefully place in the oven and bake for 1 hour. Uncover and bake 5 minutes longer.

Remove the pan from the oven and set aside to cool. Refrigerate for at least 3 hours or overnight before serving.

To serve, run a knife around the edge of the pan to loosen, then transfer the pâté to a serving plate. Garnish with a sprinkling of paprika and a sprig of thyme, or as desired. Serve cool or at room temperature.

Serves 8

LOW OIL

1 tablespoon olive oil

1 small yellow onion, chopped

3 cloves garlic, chopped

12 ounces mushrooms (any kind), chopped

1 teaspoon smoked paprika

1 teaspoon dried thyme

½ teaspoon ground dried sage

½ teaspoon salt

½ teaspoon freshly ground black pepper

⅛ teaspoon ground allspice

⅛ teaspoon cayenne pepper

1½ cups cooked brown lentils, well drained

1 cup toasted walnut pieces

1 cup extra-firm tofu, well drained and crumbled

⅓ cup old-fashioned rolled oats

¼ cup nutritional yeast

¼ cup vital wheat gluten

2 tablespoons brandy

2 tablespoons soy sauce

1 tablespoon freshly squeezed lemon juice

Thyme sprig, for garnish

Pissaladière

This savory caramelized onion tart hails from Nice in the Provence region of France. Known for its thick dough and lusty topping of flavorful onion confit and luscious Caillette or Niçoise olives, this sophisticated pizza can be enjoyed as an appetizer or main dish. To save time, you can use ready-made pizza dough for the crust instead of making your own. You can also divide the dough into quarters and make four individual sizes instead. Use a gluten-free pizza dough to make this gluten free.

Dough

1 (.25 ounce) package active dry yeast (2¼ teaspoons)

1 teaspoon sugar

¾ to 1 cup warm water (105 to 115°F)

2½ to 3 cups all-purpose flour

1 teaspoon salt

1 tablespoon olive oil

Topping

2 tablespoons olive oil

3 large sweet yellow onions, halved and thinly sliced (about 2 pounds)

½ teaspoon salt

¼ teaspoon freshly ground black pepper

1 teaspoon herbes de Provence or dried thyme

⅓ cup pitted and halved kalamata olives (or niçoise or caillette olives)

In a small bowl, combine the yeast, sugar, and ¾ cup of the warm water, stirring to mix. Set aside for 5 minutes. In a large bowl, combine 2½ cups of the flour and the salt. Add the yeast mixture and the oil, stirring to make a smooth dough. Add up to ¼ cup additional water, if needed.

On a lightly floured work surface, knead the dough for about 5 minutes, working in as much of the remaining ½ cup of flour as needed if the dough is sticky. Transfer the dough to a lightly oiled bowl, turning the dough to coat with the oil. Cover the bowl with plastic wrap and let rise in a warm place until doubled, about 45 minutes.

While the dough is rising, make the topping. Heat the oil in a large skillet over medium heat. Add the onions, salt, and pepper. Cook, stirring frequently, until the onions soften and turn golden brown, about 10 minutes. Decrease the heat to medium-low and stir in the herbes de Provence. Cover and cook 20 minutes longer, or until the onions are soft and caramelized. Taste and adjust the seasonings, if needed. Set aside to cool. Preheat the oven to 425°F. Lightly oil an 11 by 17-inch baking pan and set aside.

Punch the dough down and transfer to a lightly floured surface. Let it rest for about 3 minutes, then stretch the dough to fit the baking pan. It should be about ¼- inch thick. Arrange the dough on the prepared pan. Spread the onion mixture evenly onto the dough, leaving a ½-inch border of exposed dough around the edge. Arrange the olives on top of the onions, spacing them evenly. Bake for 16 to 20 minutes, or until the crust is nicely browned.

Serves 4

GLUTEN-FREE OPTION
SOY-FREE

Portobellos with Béarnaise Sauce

Béarnaise, with its shallot-tarragon wine reduction, is the classier cousin to the already haute hollandaise sauce, only this version is even better than the classic because it omits the butter and eggs while keeping the flavor. A dream over these pan-seared portobellos, the sauce is also fabulous over grilled or roasted asparagus, cauliflower, and other vegetables, and it makes a lovely topping for a vegan eggs Benedict.

¼ cup dry white wine

2 tablespoons minced shallots

2 tablespoons chopped fresh tarragon

⅔ cup raw cashews, soaked for 3 hours or overnight, then drained

⅓ cup water or vegetable broth, plus more as needed

1 tablespoon freshly squeezed lemon juice

½ teaspoon Dijon mustard

¼ teaspoon sea salt

2 tablespoons olive oil

4 large portobello mushrooms, stems removed and gills scraped out

In a small saucepan, combine the wine, shallots, and tarragon and simmer over medium heat until the liquid is mostly absorbed—watch carefully so it doesn't burn. Remove from the heat and set aside.

In a high-speed blender, combine the soaked and drained cashews with the water and lemon juice and blend until completely smooth and creamy. Add the mustard, salt, and reserved shallot mixture and blend again. Keep warm.

Heat the olive oil in a large skillet over medium heat. Add the mushrooms and cook for about 5 minutes, or until the mushrooms are tender and nicely browned on both sides. Season with salt and pepper to taste. Serve hot topped with the sauce.

Serves 4

SOY-FREE
GLUTEN-FREE
QUICK AND EASY

Potato Gratin Dauphinois

This comfort food recipe is traditionally double-cooked in seasoned cream and then baked with Gruyère cheese. My healthier version is made without dairy and skips the traditional "cook in a saucepan of cream" step, but the results are still rich tasting and delicious. A mandoline works great for slicing the potatoes—just be careful of your fingers! For a little crunch, you can sprinkle the top with 2 to 3 tablespoons of panko crumbs about halfway through the baking time, if desired—but if you do, it will no longer be gluten-free.

Preheat the oven to 375°F. Generously oil a large gratin dish or shallow baking dish. Set aside.

In a high-speed blender, combine the soaked and drained cashews and vegetable broth. Process until smooth and creamy. Add the garlic, vegan cream cheese, vegan sour cream, thyme, nutmeg, and salt and pepper to taste. Add a little almond milk if the sauce is too thick. Set aside.

Layer the potato slices in the prepared baking dish, slightly overlapping each other. Season each layer of potatoes with salt and pepper, and top each layer with some of the reserved sauce. Bake for 1 hour or longer, until the potatoes are soft, and the top is golden brown. Serve hot sprinkled with the chives.

Serves 6

GLUTEN-FREE
NO OIL

1 cup raw cashews, soaked for 3 to 4 hours, then drained

1 cup vegetable broth

2 cloves garlic, crushed

1 cup vegan cream cheese

1 cup vegan sour cream

1 teaspoon minced fresh thyme, or ½ teaspoon dried

Pinch of ground nutmeg

Salt and freshly ground black pepper

Plain unsweetened almond milk, as needed

1½ to 2 pounds baking potatoes, peeled and cut crosswise into ⅛-inch slices

2 tablespoons chopped chives or scallions

Green Beans Provençal

This simple side dish holds a special place in my heart as it was one of the original recipes I made in my first French cooking class. It's so simple, yet so flavorful, especially when you use fresh local green beans, tomatoes, and basil.

1½ pounds fresh green beans or haricots verts, ends trimmed

1 tablespoon olive oil

1 shallot, minced

3 cloves garlic, minced

1½ cups cherry or grape tomatoes, halved or quartered

1 tablespoon capers

Salt and freshly ground black pepper

2 tablespoons chopped fresh basil leaves

Steam the green beans in a steamer basket over boiling water until just tender, 4 to 7 minutes, depending on their size.

While the green beans are steaming, heat the olive oil in a medium skillet over medium heat. Add the shallot and garlic and cook for 2 minutes to soften. Stir in the tomatoes and capers and season with salt and pepper.

When the green beans are cooked, add them to the skillet with the tomato mixture. Add the basil and toss gently to combine. Serve hot.

Serves 4

SOY-FREE
GLUTEN-FREE
LOW OIL
QUICK AND EASY

Vegetable Pan Bagnat

Pan bagnat is the "bathed bread" sandwich from the south of France. Typically it contains tuna, but you won't miss the fish with all the great flavors going on in this vegan version. Since this sandwich must be prepared in advance in order for the bread to become flavored with the other ingredients, it makes a great choice for a picnic.

Cut the mushroom caps into very thin slices. Heat 1 tablespoon of the oil in a large skillet over medium-high heat. Working in batches, add the mushroom slices and sear on both sides. Season with salt and pepper to taste. Transfer the cooked mushrooms to a plate and cook the remaining mushroom slices. When all the mushrooms are cooked, combine them all in the skillet and set aside.

In a small bowl, combine the vinegar, soy sauce, and mustard, stirring to blend. Pour the mixture over the mushrooms, turning to coat. Set aside to cool.

In a food processor, combine the white beans and garlic and process to a paste. Add the tahini, sun-dried tomatoes, lemon juice, water, and salt and pepper to taste. Process until smooth. Set aside.

Use a serrated knife to cut the bread in half horizontally. Use your hands to pinch out the soft center of the bread from inside both halves of the loaf to make room for the filling.

Spread the white bean mixture inside both halves of the loaf. Remove the mushrooms from the marinade and layer them over the white bean mixture, alternating with layers of the roasted peppers, artichoke hearts, spinach, tomato, and olives. Drizzle with the remaining marinade and season with salt and pepper to taste. Replace the top half of the loaf and wrap the entire loaf tightly in plastic. Place the sandwich on a large plate and top with another plate, lid, or pan. Weigh the top down with canned goods. Refrigerate for at least 4 hours or up to 12 hours. When ready to serve, unwrap the sandwich and cut it with a serrated knife into four to six wedges.

Serves 4 to 6

2 large portobello mushroom caps, gills scraped out

2 tablespoons olive oil

Salt and freshly ground black pepper

2 tablespoons sherry vinegar

1 tablespoon tamari soy sauce

½ teaspoon Dijon mustard

1½ cups cooked white beans, or 1 (15-ounce) can, drained and rinsed

3 cloves garlic, crushed

¼ cup tahini (sesame paste)

2 tablespoons minced reconstituted or oil-packed sun-dried tomatoes

3 tablespoons freshly squeezed lemon juice

2 tablespoons water

1 large round crusty bread loaf

2 roasted red bell peppers (home-roasted or jarred), cut into strips

1 (6-ounce) jar marinated artichoke hearts, drained and sliced

1 cup packed baby spinach or kale leaves

1 large ripe tomato, thinly sliced

⅓ cup pitted and chopped kalamata olives

Roasted Ratatouille with Basil Pistou

Roasting the vegetables in this classic French mélange deliciously intensifies the flavor of the dish which is further enhanced by the addition of basil pistou. You'll want to serve this with a warm crusty baguette.

1 large yellow onion, chopped

1 eggplant, peeled and
cut into ½-inch dice

2 zucchini, halved lengthwise
and cut into ¼-inch slices

1 red bell pepper, seeded and chopped

2 cups cherry or grape tomatoes,
halved lengthwise

3 cloves garlic, chopped

1 teaspoon dried thyme

1 teaspoon dried marjoram

½ teaspoon dried oregano

Salt and freshly ground black pepper

2 tablespoons olive oil

3 tablespoons Basil Pistou
(recipe follows)

2 tablespoons chopped
fresh Italian parsley

Preheat the oven to 425°F. Lightly oil a large baking dish or roasting pan.

In a large bowl, combine the onion, eggplant, zucchini, bell pepper, tomatoes, and garlic. Sprinkle on the thyme, marjoram, and oregano and season generously with salt and pepper to taste. Drizzle on the oil and toss to combine. Spread the vegetable mixture into a large baking dish. Roast until the vegetables are tender, about 45 minutes, turning once or twice to cook evenly. To serve, transfer to a serving bowl, add the pistou and parsley and toss to combine. Serve hot.

Serves 4 to 6

GLUTEN-FREE
SOY-FREE

Basil Pistou

Pistou is the French version of basil pesto. Made without cheese or pine nuts, pistou can be used in the same ways as pesto: as a pasta sauce, in salad dressings or soups, or to flavor vegetable dishes, as it does in Roasted Ratatouille (page 28). Best of all, it freezes well, so portion it into 1- to 2-tablespoon amounts and freeze for later use.

2 cups packed fresh basil leaves

4 cloves garlic, chopped

¼ cup olive oil

½ teaspoon salt

A few grinds of freshly ground black pepper

In a food processor, combine the basil leaves, garlic, olive oil, salt, and pepper. Process until thoroughly blended, scraping down the sides as needed. Transfer to a container with a tight-fitting lid. Use immediately or cover and refrigerate until needed.

Makes about ⅔ cup pistou

GLUTEN-FREE
SOY-FREE
QUICK AND EASY

Mousse au Chocolat

Rich, chocolatey, and delicious, this creamy chocolate mousse, made without the traditional eggs, butter, or cream, is the perfect ending to a fancy French dinner—or any dinner, for that matter! I especially like the added flavor dimension provided by the Frangelico (or brandy), but you can leave it out if you prefer.

Melt the chocolate in the top of a double boiler over gently simmering water, stirring frequently. Set aside.

In a high-speed blender, combine the cashews, maple syrup, Frangelico, and vanilla and blend until smooth. Add the tofu and blend until smooth. Add the reserved melted chocolate and blend until smooth and creamy.

Transfer to individual dessert dishes, cover, and refrigerate until well chilled.

When ready to serve, sprinkle the top of each dessert with the hazelnuts or chocolate curls.

Serves 4

GLUTEN-FREE
QUICK AND EASY
NO OIL

1 cup vegan semisweet chocolate chips

½ cup raw cashews, soaked for 3 hours, then drained

¼ cup maple syrup or agave nectar

2 tablespoons Frangelico or brandy

1 teaspoon vanilla extract

6 ounces extra-firm silken tofu, drained and blotted dry

2 tablespoons toasted chopped hazelnuts or chocolate curls, for garnish

Spain and Portugal

It wasn't until I left the restaurant business that I began to explore the foods of Spain and Portugal. People sometimes erroneously compare Spanish cooking to Mexican, when in fact it is much closer to Italian. While Spaniards use the Mediterranean ingredients of tomatoes, garlic, chiles, and olive oil, their cooking was also influenced by the Moors, as evidenced by their use of cumin, almonds, rice, and saffron, as illustrated with the delectable Saffron-Almond Rice Pudding on page 42. Although meat and fish are eaten liberally throughout Spain, the region is also known for well-seasoned dishes that use fresh produce, beans, and grains. Similarly, while seafood is prominent in the cuisine of Portugal, many flavorful plant-based dishes are part of the Portuguese culinary tradition, including the delicious Portuguese Kale Soup (page 34).

Like everybody else back in the nineties, I fell in love with tapas, the bite-size snacks that delight the palate but don't fill you up, such as Patatas Bravas (page 36) and Pan-Seared Mushrooms with Garlic and Sherry (page 35). These "small plates" are an important social custom in Spain and are also enjoyed in Portugal, where they are known as *pestiscos*; they are eaten as appetizers in anticipation of a traditional late-evening supper. Tapas menus include small dishes with a wide range of complex flavors and varied textures. Tapas can be as simple as marinated olives or roasted almonds or more elaborate dishes, such as savory pastries and toasted bread with spreads, or marinated or fried vegetables.

Portuguese Kale Soup

This restorative soup, made with white beans, kale, potatoes, and lots of garlic, is especially delicious because of the addition of dry sherry that brings all the flavors together. I like to add a small amount of red pepper flakes for a little heat, but you can omit it (or add more) if you like. For an even heartier soup, add some vegan chorizo before serving.

1 tablespoon olive oil or ¼ cup water

1 large yellow onion, chopped

4 large cloves garlic, minced

1 large Yukon Gold potato, peeled and chopped

3 cups cooked cannellini or other white beans or 2 (15.5-ounce) cans, drained and rinsed

6 cups vegetable broth

3 tablespoons dry sherry

¼ teaspoon red pepper flakes

Salt and freshly ground black pepper

8 ounces kale, stemmed and coarsely chopped (about 6 cups)

Heat the oil or water in a large pot over medium-high heat. Add the onion, cover, and cook until softened, about 5 minutes. Add the garlic and cook for 1 minute. Add the potato, beans, broth, sherry, red pepper flakes, and salt and black pepper. The amount of salt needed will depend on the saltiness of your broth. Cook for 1 hour. Stir in the kale and cook 30 minutes longer, or until the vegetables are tender and the flavors are well blended. Taste and adjust the seasonings, if needed. Serve hot.

Serves 4 to 6

GLUTEN-FREE
SOY-FREE
LOW OIL

Pan-Seared Mushrooms with Garlic and Sherry

Redolent of garlic and Spanish sherry, these mushrooms are great served with warm, crusty bread. Adjust the amount of red pepper flakes used according to your own heat tolerance. Although traditionally served as tapas on small plates, you can also serve these flavorful mushrooms over rice or noodles or as a topping for sautéed seitan.

In a large skillet, heat the oil over medium-high heat. Add the mushrooms and cook, stirring, until seared, 2 to 3 minutes. Decrease the heat to medium and add the garlic, sherry, lemon juice, red pepper flakes, paprika, and salt and pepper to taste. Cook, stirring, until the garlic and mushrooms are softened, about 5 minutes. Remove from the heat, sprinkle with minced parsley, and serve hot on small plates.

Serves 4

GLUTEN-FREE
SOY-FREE
LOW OIL
QUICK AND EASY

1 tablespoon olive oil

3 cups white mushrooms, halved if small, quartered if large

4 cloves garlic, finely minced

3 tablespoons dry sherry

1½ tablespoons freshly squeezed lemon juice

¼ to ½ teaspoon hot red pepper flakes

¼ teaspoon Spanish paprika

Salt and freshly ground black pepper

2 tablespoons minced fresh parsley

Patatas Bravas

These boldly seasoned potatoes doused with a spicy sauce can be found as a "small plate" in virtually any tapas bar. When you make them at home, the challenge will be limiting yourself to just a small plate of them!

1½ pounds russet potatoes, peeled and cut into ½-inch dice

2 tablespoons olive oil

2 teaspoons Spanish sweet paprika or smoked paprika

Salt and freshly ground black pepper

¼ cup minced yellow onion

3 cloves garlic, minced

3 tablespoons tomato paste

1½ tablespoons sherry vinegar

½ teaspoon sugar

¼ teaspoon cayenne

¼ cup vegan mayonnaise

½ teaspoon hot sauce

2 tablespoons minced fresh parsley

Preheat the oven to 425°F. Lightly oil a rimmed baking sheet and set aside. In a bowl, combine the potatoes with 1 tablespoon of the oil, ½ teaspoon of the paprika and salt and pepper to taste, tossing to coat. Spread the potatoes in a single layer on the prepared pan and roast them until tender and nicely browned, turning once, 20 to 30 minutes.

While the potatoes are roasting, make the sauce. In a saucepan, heat the remaining 1 tablespoon of oil over medium heat. Add the onion, cover, and cook until tender, 3 minutes. Stir in the garlic and cook until fragrant, about 30 seconds. Stir in the tomato paste, vinegar, sugar, cayenne, and the remaining paprika.

Remove from the heat, and stir in the mayonnaise and hot sauce, and season with salt and pepper to taste. Mix well and set aside.

Combine the potatoes with the reserved sauce and sprinkle with the parsley. Serve warm on small plates.

Serves 6

GLUTEN-FREE
QUICK AND EASY

Roasted Romesco Vegetable Stacks

Who knew vegetables could look so fancy? These delicious vegetable stacks are worthy of the center of your plate thanks to the luscious romesco sauce made with roasted bell peppers, tomatoes, and almond butter. If you have any leftover romesco sauce, try it as a topping over baked potatoes, or as a dipping sauce for roasted cauliflower or fried tofu.

To make the vegetables, preheat the oven to 425°F. Lightly oil two rimmed baking pans. Arrange the vegetable slices in a single layer on the pans. Drizzle with a little olive oil and season with salt and pepper to taste. Roast until slightly browned on the edges and just tender, turning once about halfway through, about 30 minutes.

While the vegetables are roasting, make the sauce. Heat the oil in a skillet over medium heat. Add the onion, garlic, and chile and cook until softened, about 5 minutes. Stir in the tomatoes and roasted red bell pepper. Cook for 10 minutes, then stir in the vinegar, almond butter, and salt and pepper to taste. Cook another 5 minutes or until the vegetables are soft. Transfer the mixture to a food processor or high-speed blender. Process until smooth and creamy. Taste and adjust the seasonings, if needed. Keep warm.

When ready to serve, spread a spoonful of sauce on each of four dinner plates. Stack the vegetables on top of the sauce. Spoon more of the sauce on top of each stack. Sprinkle each stack with parsley. Serve hot.

Serves 4

GLUTEN-FREE
SOY-FREE

Vegetables

1 large red onion, cut into ¼-inch slices

1 medium eggplant, cut into ½-inch slices

1 large yellow bell pepper, seeded and cut vertically into 4 rectangular pieces

4 portobello mushroom caps, gills scraped out

1 large ripe tomato, cut into ½-inch slices

Olive oil

Salt and freshly ground black pepper

Sauce

1 tablespoon olive oil

¼ cup chopped yellow onion

2 cloves garlic, chopped

1 small hot red chile, seeded and chopped

1 (14.5-ounce) can diced fire-roasted tomatoes, well drained

1 roasted red bell pepper (home-roasted or jarred), coarsely chopped

2 tablespoons red wine vinegar

¼ cup almond butter

Salt and freshly ground black pepper

2 tablespoons chopped fresh parsley

Vegetable Paella

Saffron is traditional in this voluptuous Spanish stew, but if you don't have any you can leave it out and you'll still have a delicious dish. If you're not a fan of eggplant, substitute diced mushrooms. For a heartier dish, add 8 ounces of diced seitan, vegan sausage, or steamed tempeh.

Heat the oil in a large saucepan or Dutch oven over medium heat. Add the onion and cook for 5 minutes to soften. Add the garlic, eggplant, and bell pepper and cook 3 minutes longer. Stir in the rice, 1 cup of the broth, and the saffron, paprika, bay leaf, oregano, red pepper flakes, and diced tomatoes and their juice. Bring to a boil, then lower the heat to medium. Season with salt and pepper to taste, cover, and simmer for 20 minutes. Stir in the chickpeas, artichoke hearts, peas, and olives. If the mixture seems dry, add the remaining ½ cup of broth. Stir in the parsley and lemon zest and cook until the rice and vegetables are tender, about 10 minutes longer. Remove and discard the bay leaf. Taste and adjust the seasonings, if needed. Serve hot.

Note: You can use brown rice instead of white if you prefer, but it will take longer to cook, so allow more time.

Serves 4

GLUTEN-FREE
SOY-FREE
LOW OIL

1 tablespoon olive oil

1 large yellow onion, chopped

2 cloves garlic, minced

1 medium eggplant, peeled and cut into ½-inch dice

1 red bell pepper, seeded and coarsely chopped

1 cup uncooked short-grain white rice

1½ cups vegetable broth

1 pinch of saffron threads

1 teaspoon smoked paprika

1 bay leaf

1 teaspoon dried oregano

½ teaspoon red pepper flakes

1 (28-ounce) can diced fire-roasted tomatoes, undrained

Salt and freshly ground black pepper

1½ cups cooked chickpeas, or 1 (15.5-ounce) can, drained and rinsed

1 (6-ounce) jar marinated artichoke hearts, drained and chopped

1 cup frozen green peas

½ cup sliced pimiento-stuffed green olives

2 tablespoons chopped fresh Italian parsley

1 teaspoon finely minced lemon zest

Spicy Pinto Empanadas

The term empanada comes from the Spanish word empanar, which means to wrap in bread (or pastry). This recipe makes four main-dish–size empanadas, or you could divide the dough into smaller pieces and roll out for mini empanadas. I like to make both the pastry and filling in advance, so they have time to cool before assembly. Use soy-free vegan butter to make this soy free.

Pastry

2 cups all-purpose flour

3 tablespoons vegan butter

3 tablespoons olive oil

½ teaspoon salt

Cold water, as needed (about 7 tablespoons)

Filling

1 tablespoon olive oil

1 small red onion, chopped

2 cloves garlic, minced

½ teaspoon dried oregano

½ teaspoon ground cumin

½ teaspoon salt

¼ teaspoon freshly ground black pepper

½ teaspoon cayenne

1 cup cooked or canned pinto beans, coarsely mashed

¾ cup cooked mashed sweet or white potatoes

1 chipotle in adobo, minced

¼ cup fresh or thawed frozen corn kernels

2 tablespoons sliced pimiento-stuffed green olives

2 tablespoons raisins

To make the pastry, combine the flour, butter, oil, and salt in a food processor and pulse until crumbly. With the machine running, slowly drizzle in just enough water to make a smooth dough (about 7 tablespoons). Shape the dough into a ball and wrap it in plastic wrap. Refrigerate for at least an hour or overnight.

To make the filling, heat the oil in a skillet over medium-high heat. Add the onion and cook for 5 minutes to soften. Stir in the garlic and cook 1 minute longer, then stir in the oregano, cumin, salt, pepper, and cayenne. Add the beans, potatoes, chipotle, corn, olives, and raisins. Mix well, mashing the filling until it is incorporated but still with some texture. Add more salt to taste, if needed. Set aside to cool. Preheat the oven to 400°F.

To assemble, first divide the pastry into four equal pieces and roll them out into 5- to 6-inch circles on a lightly floured work surface. Spoon one-quarter of the filling mixture onto each dough round, then fold one end of the dough over the filling to meet the opposite end of the dough. Use your fingers to seal and pinch the edges to enclose the filling, then press down on the edges with the tines of a fork.

Place the empanadas on an ungreased baking sheet. Pierce the top of the pastry with a fork and brush the tops with a little olive oil or nondairy milk. Bake for about 25 minutes or until golden brown.

Serves 4

SOY-FREE

Eggplant Piri-piri

Piri-piri sauce is a classic Portuguese sauce made with hot chiles. It is simple to make and can be used whenever you want a really hot condiment. I especially like it with eggplant, but it's also delicious paired with seitan and mushrooms. The sauce can be refrigerated in an airtight container for up to a week or frozen for up to 6 months.

To make the eggplant, preheat the oven to 425°F. Lightly oil a baking pan. Arrange the eggplant and bell pepper in a single layer on the prepared baking pan. Drizzle lightly with olive oil and season with salt and pepper to taste. Roast until tender and browned on the outside, turning once, about 20 minutes total.

While the eggplant is roasting, make the sauce. Heat the oil in a saucepan over medium heat. Add the onion, garlic, and ginger; cook for 5 minutes, stirring to coat evenly. Stir in the chiles, tomato paste, and ketchup and cook 2 minutes longer. Transfer the mixture to a high-speed blender and add the paprika, salt, vinegar, and Worcestershire sauce, if using. Process until smooth. Taste and adjust the seasonings, if needed.

To serve, toss the eggplant with as much as the sauce as desired. Sprinkle with basil. Serve any remaining sauce on the side. Serve hot.

Note: For soy free, omit the optional Worcestershire sauce.

Serves 4

GLUTEN-FREE
SOY-FREE

Eggplant

1 large or 2 medium eggplants (2½ to 3 pounds total), cut into ½-inch dice

1 green or yellow bell pepper, seeded and cut into 1-inch dice

Olive oil

Salt and freshly ground black pepper

Sauce

1 tablespoon olive oil

1 medium yellow or red onion, finely chopped

3 cloves garlic, minced

2 teaspoons grated fresh ginger

1 to 2 tablespoons crushed dried piri-piri or bird's-eye chiles or hot red pepper flakes

2 tablespoons tomato paste

2 tablespoons ketchup

1 tablespoon smoked paprika

1 teaspoon salt

3 tablespoons cider vinegar or freshly squeezed lemon juice

1 tablespoon vegan Worcestershire sauce (optional)

Basil leaves, for garnish

Saffron-Almond Rice Pudding

I prefer to make rice pudding using leftover cooked rice rather than starting from scratch with raw rice because it's quicker and it's a great way to use leftover rice. My favorite rice for rice pudding is brown basmati rice, but if you like a creamier texture, try sushi rice, arborio rice, or jasmine rice.

1 tablespoon pure maple syrup or agave nectar

1 tablespoon almond butter

2 teaspoons natural sugar

½ teaspoon ground cinnamon

Few pinches of saffron

⅛ teaspoon salt

1 cup almond milk

2 cups cooked basmati rice (or your favorite rice)

½ cup toasted slivered almonds

In a small saucepan, combine the maple syrup, almond butter, sugar, cinnamon, saffron, and salt over medium heat. Slowly add the almond milk, stirring to blend. Add the cooked rice and cook, stirring until the rice is heated through and the mixture begins to thicken. Decrease the heat to medium-low, stirring occasionally, until the desired consistency is reached. For a thinner pudding, add a little more almond milk. For a creamier texture, use an immersion blender to blend a portion of the rice pudding right in the saucepan. To serve, spoon the pudding into bowls and sprinkle with toasted almonds.

Serves 4

GLUTEN-FREE
SOY-FREE

Greece

Greek cuisine is a showcase for olives, eggplant, oregano, peppers, tomatoes, and zucchini. Although Greek cooking incorporates its own unique blending of herbs and spices, I find it similar in many ways to that of Italy and Spain. However, Greek cooking also shares striking similarities to Middle Eastern cuisines, with its popular enjoyment of stuffed grape leaves, phyllo dough, and pita bread, as well as the use of lemons, artichokes, mint, cinnamon, and rice.

Greek food is often humble fare, but it is always full-flavored and prepared with seasonal ingredients such as Greek Tomato Bruschetta (page 47), best made with only the ripest tomatoes.

Economic conditions and religious observances contributed to an abundance of plant-based dishes such as dolmades (stuffed grape leaves), fakes salata (lentil salad), briam (roasted vegetables), and fassolada (white bean soup). Pasta and rice dishes are common, as are beans, legumes, and spinach and other leafy greens known as horta, as well as olives, olive oil, and garlic. Recipes for Greek Rice and Spinach (page 56) and Spanakopita Tart (page 51) combine many of these ingredients to delicious effect, and lemons dominate the flavor profile, as do such herbs and spices as oregano, dill, and cinnamon.

Orzo and Chickpea Salad

This refreshing salad is loaded with a variety of textures and flavors from juicy tomatoes and briny olives to crisp cucumbers and celery. It makes a satisfying lunch served alone or on a bed of torn Romaine lettuce. For added flavor and protein, top this salad with some Vegan Feta (page 49). To make this recipe gluten-free, use your favorite type of gluten-free pasta to replace the orzo.

1¼ cups orzo

1½ cups cooked chickpeas, or 1 (15.5-ounce) can, drained and rinsed

5 scallions, minced

1 cup grape or cherry tomatoes, halved or quartered

½ English cucumber, peeled and chopped

½ cup kalamata olives, pitted and halved

⅓ cup thinly sliced celery

2 tablespoons minced fresh parsley

2 cloves garlic, minced

2 tablespoons freshly squeezed lemon juice

½ teaspoon natural sugar

1 teaspoon minced fresh oregano, or ½ teaspoon dried

½ teaspoon salt

¼ teaspoon freshly ground black pepper

3 tablespoons olive oil

2 tablespoons toasted pine nuts

Cook the orzo in a saucepan of boiling salted water until just tender. Drain and run cold water over the orzo in the colander, then drain again. Transfer the orzo to a large bowl. Add the chickpeas, scallions, tomatoes, cucumber, olives, celery, and parsley. Set aside.

In a small bowl, whisk together the garlic, lemon juice, sugar, oregano, basil, salt, and pepper. Whisk in the oil in a slow, steady stream until emulsified and smooth. Pour the dressing onto the salad and toss well to combine. Taste and adjust the seasonings, if needed. Serve immediately or cover and refrigerate until needed. Sprinkle with pine nuts before serving.

Serves 4 to 6

GLUTEN-FREE OPTION
SOY-FREE
QUICK AND EASY

Greek Tomato Bruschetta

Sometimes referred to as "Greek bruschetta," dakos is a popular meze, or small plate, on Crete. The easy and delicious tomato topping is best made when fresh ripe tomatoes are at their peak. Dakos are traditionally made with barley rusks, but I use grilled or toasted crusty bread instead.

Place the chopped tomatoes in a bowl. Add the olive oil, oregano, salt, and pepper. Toss to combine. Drain off any liquid.

Spoon the tomato mixture onto the toasted bread and top with the vegan feta. Sprinkle with additional oregano and black pepper, if desired.

Serves 4

QUICK AND EASY

2 large ripe tomatoes, chopped

1 tablespoon olive oil

1 teaspoon minced fresh oregano

¼ teaspoon salt

¼ teaspoon freshly ground black pepper

8 (½-inch) slices crusty Italian bread, grilled or toasted

½ cup Vegan Feta (recipe follows)

Vegan Feta

This vegan alternative to feta adds flavor to the bruschetta on page 47 and Greek Rice and Spinach on page 56. It also delivers protein, flavor, and an authentic appearance to a Greek salad.

In a shallow bowl, combine the olive oil, lemon juice, vinegar, miso, salt, and oregano stirring to mix well. Crumble the tofu and add to the marinade, turning gently to coat well. Cover and marinate at room temperature for 1 hour. If not using right away, refrigerate until needed. Properly stored, it will keep for up to a week in the refrigerator.

Note: Mellow white miso, also known as "sweet" miso or "Shiro" miso, has a milder, more delicate flavor than darker miso varieties. White miso is also lower in salt and fermented for a shorter time.

Makes about 1½ cups feta

GLUTEN-FREE
QUICK AND EASY

¼ cup olive oil

2 tablespoons freshly squeezed lemon juice

2 tablespoons white wine vinegar

1½ teaspoons mellow white miso (see Note)

1 teaspoon salt

½ teaspoon dried oregano

8 ounces extra-firm tofu, drained, pressed, and blotted dry

Jackfruit Gyros

The meaty texture of jackfruit, and its ability to absorb surrounding flavors, makes it an ideal choice for these gyros. Look for frozen or canned water- or brine-packed jackfruit in Asian markets or well-stocked supermarkets (do not get the kind packed in syrup). You can shred the jackfruit in a food processor if you don't want to use your hands. If jackfruit is unavailable, substitute your choice of seitan, steamed tempeh, mushrooms, or reconstituted Soy Curls.

1 (20-ounce) can jackfruit in water or brine, rinsed, drained, and pulled apart into shreds

1 tablespoon olive oil

1 medium yellow onion, halved lengthwise and thinly sliced

2 cloves garlic, minced

2 teaspoons dried oregano

½ teaspoon ground coriander

¼ teaspoon ground cumin

1 tablespoon soy sauce

¾ cup vegetable broth

Salt and freshly ground black pepper

3 tablespoons freshly squeezed lemon juice

4 pita loaves, warmed

Shredded lettuce

Sliced tomato

Tzatziki Sauce (page 54)

Use your fingers to shred the jackfruit or shred it in a food processor using the shredding disk. Set aside. Heat the oil in a large skillet over medium-high heat. Add the onion and cook until softened, about 5 minutes. Lower the heat to medium and stir in the garlic, then add the jackfruit, stirring to combine. Cook for 20 minutes, stirring occasionally, until browned and caramelized. Stir in the oregano, coriander, cumin, soy sauce, and broth. Season to taste with salt and pepper. Decrease the heat to a simmer and cook for 10 minutes, then stir in the lemon juice and continue cooking until most of the liquid has evaporated. Spoon the jackfruit mixture into warm pitas along with shredded lettuce, sliced tomato, and tzatziki sauce.

Serves 4

LOW OIL

Spanakopita Tart

This quicker version of spanakopita, the famous spinach pie, takes a shortcut by using phyllo on the bottom only. In lieu of a top crust, the trimmings from the phyllo are used as a topping. Olive oil is used instead of butter to brush the layers of flaky pastry.

Steam the spinach in a perforated metal steamer basket over a saucepan of boiling water until tender, about 3 minutes. Drain well, squeezing out any excess moisture. Finely mince the spinach and set aside.

Heat the olive oil in a large skillet over medium heat. Add the onion, cover, and cook until softened, about 5 minutes. Add the garlic and cook, stirring, until softened, about 1 minute. Add the spinach, dill, oregano, salt, pepper, and nutmeg. Cook, stirring, until all the liquid is absorbed.

Pulse the tofu in a food processor. Add the spinach mixture and the lemon juice and process until well mixed. Taste and adjust the seasonings, adding more salt if needed. Set aside.

Preheat the oven to 375°F. Unwrap the phyllo pastry and remove five sheets. Cover with plastic wrap, then a damp towel. Tightly seal the remaining sheets and reserve for another use. Place one sheet in a lightly oiled, 10-inch tart pan, pressing it gently into the bottom and sides of the dish. Using a pastry brush, lightly brush a small amount of olive oil on the pastry. Top with another sheet of pastry and brush with a little more oil. Repeat this layering procedure with 4 more sheets and oil. Spread the filling on the pastry and smooth the top. Trim the excess pastry to within 1 inch of the tart pan. Roll the trimmed edges inward and tuck into the rim of the dish to make a neat edge. Brush the rolled edge with oil. Sprinkle the pastry trimmings on top of the tart.

Bake until golden brown, about 30 minutes. Let rest for 15 minutes, then cut into squares. Serve warm or at room temperature.

Serves 6

1 pound fresh spinach, stemmed and well washed

1 tablespoon olive oil, plus more for brushing

1 large yellow onion, minced

4 cloves garlic, minced

2 teaspoons fresh minced dill or 1 teaspoon dried dill

1 teaspoon fresh minced oregano or ½ teaspoon dried

1 teaspoon salt

¼ teaspoon freshly ground black pepper

Pinch of freshly grated nutmeg

1 (16-ounce) package firm tofu, drained and crumbled

2 tablespoons freshly squeezed lemon juice

1 (16-ounce) package phyllo pastry, thawed overnight in the refrigerator

Baked Eggplant Fries

Crunchy and delicious, these "fries" are a surefire way to make an eggplant lover out of just about anyone. And because they're baked, not fried, they're good for you too! Serve them as a side dish with Jackfruit Gyros (page 50) for a hearty lunch or casual supper. Dipping them in tzatziki sauce is a must!

1 large eggplant, peeled and sliced vertically into ½-inch slices

½ cup flour of choice (all-purpose, rice, or chickpea are good choices)

½ teaspoon salt

¼ teaspoon freshly ground black pepper

⅛ teaspoon cayenne

1 cup plain unsweetened almond milk or other nondairy milk

2 tablespoons ground flaxseed, blended with ¼ cup water in a blender until thick

1 tablespoon freshly squeezed lemon juice

1 cup dry bread crumbs

3 tablespoons nutritional yeast

2 teaspoons dried oregano

1 teaspoon dried basil

1 teaspoon smoked paprika

Tzatziki Sauce (page 54), for serving

Cut the eggplant slices lengthwise into ½-inch strips. If the strips are too long, cut them in half. Set aside. Preheat the oven to 425°F. Lightly oil a baking sheet and set aside.

In a shallow bowl, combine the flour, salt, pepper, and cayenne and mix well. In a second shallow bowl, combine the almond milk, flaxseed mixture, and lemon juice, stirring to blend. In a third shallow bowl, combine the bread crumbs, nutritional yeast, oregano, basil, and paprika.

Dredge the eggplant strips in the flour mixture, then dip them in the milk mixture, and then roll them in the bread crumb mixture. Arrange the strips in a single layer on the prepared baking sheet. Bake for 15 minutes, then flip over and bake for about 10 minutes longer, or until golden brown and crispy. Sprinkle the hot fries with salt. Serve hot with a bowl of the sauce.

Serves 4

NO OIL

Tzatziki Sauce

The refreshing and flavorful sauce made with yogurt, cucumber, and seasonings is extremely versatile. Try it on Jackfruit Gyros (page 50) or Baked Eggplant Fries (page 52). It's also good as a dip for warm pita bread or crunchy pita chips.

3 cloves garlic, crushed

½ small cucumber, peeled, seeded, and quartered

¼ cup vegan yogurt

¼ cup vegan sour cream

1 tablespoon freshly squeezed lemon juice

2 tablespoons chopped fresh dill, mint, or parsley

Salt and freshly ground black pepper

In a food processor, combine the garlic and cucumber and process until finely minced. Add the yogurt, sour cream, lemon juice, dill, and salt and pepper to taste. Process until well blended, then transfer to a bowl. Taste to adjust the seasonings if needed. Cover and refrigerate until needed.

Makes about 1 cup sauce

GLUTEN-FREE
QUICK AND EASY
NO OIL

Stifado

The predominant feature of this Greek stew is lots of onions. Typically small pearl onions are used, but I prefer shallots or cippollini onions. Of course, this hearty stew, made with seitan, mushrooms, and tomatoes, can be made with chopped regular onions as well. Reconstituted Soy Curls, diced tempeh, or extra-firm tofu, or large butter beans can be substituted for the seitan.

Heat the oil in a large, deep skillet or saucepan over medium heat. Add the seitan and cook until browned all over, about 7 minutes. Remove from the pan, and set aside. To the same pan, add the shallots and cook until lightly browned and softened, about 10 minutes. Add the mushrooms and cook 5 minutes longer, then stir in the garlic and cook for 1 minute longer. Add the tomato paste and wine and cook another minute or two, stirring to blend. Stir in the tomatoes and their juices, the broth, cinnamon stick, bay leaves, oregano, and salt and pepper to taste. Bring to a boil, then decrease the heat to a simmer. Add the reserved seitan and cook for 10 to 15 minutes longer to blend flavors and reduce the sauce by about one-third. For a thicker sauce, stir in the cornstarch mixture, constantly stirring until thickened. Taste and adjust the seasonings, if necessary. Remove the cinnamon stick and bay leaves. Serve hot.

Serves 4

SOY-FREE
LOW OIL

1 tablespoon olive oil

1 pound seitan, cut into 1-inch dice

1 pound small shallots or cippollini onions, peeled and quartered

8 ounces mushrooms (any kind), chopped

4 cloves garlic, minced

2 tablespoons tomato paste

½ cup dry red wine

1 (14.5-ounce) can diced tomatoes, undrained

1½ cups vegetable broth

1 cinnamon stick

2 bay leaves

1 teaspoon dried oregano

Salt and freshly ground black pepper

2 tablespoons cornstarch dissolved in ¼ cup water

Greek Rice and Spinach

When you keep cooked rice on hand, this "spinach rice," or spanakorizo, can be ready in minutes. Top with Vegan Feta (page 49) for extra flavor. Add some cooked white beans to make it a hearty meal.

1 tablespoon olive oil or ¼ cup water

1 medium yellow onion, finely chopped

3 cloves garlic, minced

9 ounces fresh spinach, washed, trimmed, and coarsely chopped

3 cups cooked rice

2 teaspoons minced fresh oregano, or 1 teaspoon dried

½ cup kalamata olives, pitted and chopped

⅓ cup minced reconstituted or oil-packed sun-dried tomatoes

Salt and freshly ground black pepper

2 to 3 tablespoons freshly squeezed lemon juice

Heat the oil or water in a large pot or skillet over medium heat. Add the onion and cook until softened, about 5 minutes. Add the garlic and cook, stirring, 1 minute longer. Add the spinach and cook, stirring until wilted, about 1 minute. Stir in the rice, oregano, olives, tomatoes, and salt and pepper to taste. Cook, stirring, until the rice is hot and the flavors are well blended. Just before serving, sprinkle with the lemon juice. Taste and adjust the seasonings, if needed. Serve hot.

Serves 4

GLUTEN-FREE
SOY-FREE
LOW OIL
QUICK AND EASY

Baklava Bites

These addictively tasty bites give you the flavor of baklava without the fuss—or the pastry or honey! Just a few ingredients combined in the food processor, roll 'em up, and pop 'em in your mouth.

   If your dates are not moist, you may want to soak them in hot water for 20 minutes to soften. But then be sure to drain them well and blot them so they don't add too much moisture to the mixture.

In a food processor, pulse the walnuts until coarsely ground. Add the dates, almond meal, agave, vanilla, and cinnamon. Pulse until crumbly and well mixed. If the mixture is too dry, add a little water until the mixture sticks together. If the mixture is too wet, add more walnuts or almond meal.

Pinch off a small piece of the mixture and roll it firmly in your hands to make a ball, then set it on a plate. Repeat with the remaining mixture until it is used up. Refrigerate for about 30 minutes before eating.

Note: You can make your own almond meal by finely grinding blanched almonds.

Makes about 24 bites

GLUTEN-FREE
SOY-FREE
QUICK AND EASY
NO OIL

2 cups walnut pieces

½ cup pitted dates

⅓ cup almond meal (see Note)

¼ cup agave nectar

1 teaspoon vanilla extract

¼ teaspoon ground cinnamon

Eastern Europe

I mentioned that I'm half Italian, but my other half is Hungarian, so I also have an affinity with the dishes of Eastern Europe. The harsh winters and prominence of animal agriculture makes Eastern Europe less than a vegan wonderland. I knew a vegan student who actually spent two weeks in Poland subsisting on bread and beer. The fact is that while meat and dairy are on the daily menu in most Eastern European countries, the region is not without its plant-based fare. You just may have to look a little harder to find it.

From Budapest to Bucharest, there are more than a few wholesome dishes that showcase hearty vegetables, such as cabbage, potatoes, and beets, as well as beans and grains, found in such recipes as Potato Pancakes (page 61) and Serbian Potato Salad (page 68). These include robust stews and soups featuring barley, mushrooms, white beans, and noodles, often seasoned with paprika, dill, or black pepper, such as my Triple Mushroom Soup with Sour Cream and Dill (page 60). Mustard, horseradish, and pickled vegetables are typical condiments.

Despite how the boundary lines have been redrawn, through it all, the foods of countries such as Hungary, Poland, and Romania maintain many similarities. In some instances, you will find the same basic dishes under slightly different names. Take the ultimate Eastern European comfort food, and my personal favorite: the savory dough pillows filled with potato and other ingredients can be called pierogi, pyrohy, or piroghi, among other variants. Similar comparisons can be made for stuffed cabbage rolls, bean and barley soup, cabbage and noodles, potato pancakes, and other dishes.

Many of the regional meat recipes bearing names such as goulash, paprikash, and Stroganoff are ideal vehicles for tempeh or seitan. Merely swap out the meat, add a dollop of vegan sour cream, and you've got some great comfort food.

Triple Mushroom Soup with Sour Cream and Dill

This soup is inspired by the two soups (mushroom and white bean) served at my sister's house on Christmas Eve in keeping with her husband's Slovak traditions. Three kinds of mushrooms are used to contribute to this soup's rich flavor. Porcini powder is easy to make yourself: Just put a few pieces of dried porcini mushrooms in an electric spice grinder (or coffee grinder) and grind to a powder.

1 tablespoon olive oil or ¼ cup water

1 large yellow onion, chopped

1 carrot, peeled and minced

1 celery rib, minced

2 cloves garlic, minced

8 ounces white mushrooms, thinly sliced

4 ounces cremini mushrooms, finely chopped

3 tablespoons dry white wine

1 tablespoon soy sauce

½ teaspoon porcini powder

5 cups mushroom or vegetable broth

Salt and freshly ground black pepper

1½ cups cooked white beans, or 1 (15.5-ounce) can, drained and rinsed

2 tablespoons minced fresh dill, or 1 tablespoon dried

½ cup vegan sour cream

Heat the oil or water in a large pot over medium heat. Add the onion, carrot, and celery and cook, stirring occasionally, until softened, about 5 minutes. Add the garlic and both kinds of mushrooms and cook for 5 minutes longer to soften. Stir in the wine, soy sauce, and porcini powder, then add the broth, and salt and pepper to taste. Bring to a boil, then decrease the heat to a simmer and cook for 15 minutes.

Stir in the dill. Taste and adjust the seasonings, if needed. To serve, ladle the soup into bowls and add a spoonful of sour cream to each serving.

Serves 4

GLUTEN-FREE
QUICK AND EASY
LOW OIL

Potato Pancakes

A favorite throughout Eastern Europe where they are traditionally served as a side dish or snack, potato cakes are especially delicious served hot with vegan sour cream or cinnamon-laced applesauce. For convenience, I like to make them ahead of time and then reheat them in the oven when ready to serve. Use a gluten-free flour to make this gluten-free.

Peel and coarsely grate the potatoes, using a box grater with large holes. Place them in a colander and set it over a large bowl. Use your hands to squeeze the liquid from the potatoes. Pour off the liquid from the potatoes and place the potatoes in the bowl. Using a box grater with large holes, grate the onion and add to the potatoes along with the flour, parsley, baking powder, salt, and pepper. Mix well.

Preheat the oven to 275°F. Heat a thin layer of oil in a large skillet over medium heat. Scoop a heaping spoonful of the potato mixture and press it flat with your hand, then gently place it in the hot oil. Repeat this process to make three or four more potato pancakes and add them to the pan. Do not crowd. Fry until golden brown on both sides, turning once, about 8 minutes total.

Repeat with the remaining potato mixture, adding more oil to the skillet as needed. Remove the cooked potato pancakes to paper towels to drain excess oil, then transfer to an ovenproof platter and keep them warm in the oven until all the pancakes are cooked.

Serves 4

GLUTEN-FREE OPTION
SOY-FREE

1½ pounds russet potatoes

1 small yellow onion

¼ cup unbleached all-purpose flour

1 tablespoon minced fresh parsley

½ teaspoon baking powder

1 teaspoon sea salt

¼ teaspoon freshly ground
black pepper

Grapeseed or other neutral oil,
for frying

Seitan Jagerschnitzel

Thinly sliced seitan absorbs the flavor of the rich mushroom sauce in these German "hunter's cutlets." You can use any kind of mushrooms you like, but I prefer using a variety of different kinds to add interest and flavor dimension to the dish.

Heat 1 tablespoon of the oil in a large skillet over medium heat. Add the seitan and season to taste with salt and pepper. Cook until browned on both sides, about 5 minutes. Remove the seitan from the skillet and set aside on a plate. (Cover with aluminum foil to keep warm.)

Return the skillet to the heat and add the remaining tablespoon of oil. Add the onion and sauté until softened, about 5 minutes. Add the tomato paste, mushrooms, wine, soy sauce, caraway seeds, paprika, and thyme, if using. Cook, stirring frequently, for about 3 minutes.

Stir in the broth and bring to a boil, stir in the cornstarch mixture, decrease the heat to a low simmer and cook, stirring constantly, until the sauce has thickened and the mushrooms are tender, 2 to 3 minutes. Stir in the browning sauce, if using, and then stir in the sour cream. Taste and adjust the seasonings, if needed. Return the seitan to the skillet and continue to cook until the seitan is heated through.

Serves 4

QUICK AND EASY

2 tablespoons olive oil

4 seitan cutlets or 8 ounces seitan, thinly sliced

Salt and freshly ground black pepper

1 small yellow onion or 2 shallots, minced

1 teaspoon tomato paste

8 ounces fresh mushrooms (single variety or assorted), thinly sliced

⅓ cup dry white wine

1 tablespoon soy sauce

½ to 1 teaspoon caraway seeds, crushed or whole

1 teaspoon sweet Hungarian paprika

½ teaspoon dried thyme (optional)

1½ cups vegetable broth

1 tablespoon cornstarch, dissolved in 2 tablespoons water

1 teaspoon browning sauce (optional) (Kitchen Bouquet or Gravy Master are vegan)

½ cup vegan sour cream

Halushki

Halushki is a mild-tasting comfort food made with cabbage and noodles that was a family favorite when I was growing up. It is simple peasant fare that needs no embellishment. However, if you like, you can sprinkle on about ½ teaspoon of liquid smoke a few minutes before serving. Chopped vegan bacon also makes a tasty addition. The vegan butter is optional but recommended to add richness to this dish—for soy free, use a soy-free vegan butter. To make this gluten free, use gluten-free noodles.

2 tablespoons olive oil

1 large sweet yellow onion, chopped

1 medium head cabbage,
cored and chopped

Salt and freshly ground black pepper

2 cloves garlic, minced

8 to 12 ounces egg-free noodles

1 tablespoon vegan butter (optional)

2 tablespoons minced
fresh dill or parsley

Heat the oil in a large pot over medium heat. Add the onion and cabbage. Season lightly with salt and cook, stirring occasionally, until softened. Add the garlic and continue to cook, stirring occasionally, until the onion and cabbage are soft, about 15 minutes. Season with salt and pepper to taste.

Cook the noodles in a large pot of boiling salted water until just tender. Drain well, then stir into the cabbage mixture. For a richer flavor, stir in the vegan butter. Add the dill and cook for a few minutes longer until the flavors are well blended. Taste and adjust the seasonings, adding more salt and pepper if needed.

Serves 4 to 6

GLUTEN-FREE OPTION
SOY-FREE
QUICK AND EASY

White Bean Goulash

Mushrooms and sauerkraut team up with white beans in this new twist on Hungarian goulash based on my mother's recipe. Serve over freshly cooked noodles.

Rinse the sauerkraut under cold running water and drain well. Transfer to a bowl and set aside.

Heat the oil or water in a large saucepan or Dutch oven over medium-high heat. Add the onion and cook, stirring occasionally, until softened, about 5 minutes. Stir in the garlic and paprika and cook for 1 minute longer. Stir in the mushrooms and caraway seeds and cook for a few minutes, stirring occasionally, to lightly brown the mushrooms. Add the wine, then stir in the reserved sauerkraut, the beans, and 1 cup of the broth.

In a small bowl, blend the tomato paste with the remaining ½ cup of the broth, then add it to the goulash. Bring it to a boil, then decrease the heat to low and simmer uncovered, stirring occasionally, until the liquid reduces by about one-third and the flavors are blended, about 20 minutes.

Pour about ½ cup of the simmering liquid into a small bowl and whisk in the vegan sour cream. Stir the sour cream mixture back into the goulash, season with salt and pepper to taste, and simmer over low heat to blend the flavors, about 5 minutes. Serve hot.

Serves 4

GLUTEN-FREE
LOW OIL

1 (16-ounce) can sauerkraut, drained

1 tablespoon olive oil or ¼ cup water

1 large yellow onion, chopped

2 cloves garlic, minced

2 tablespoons sweet Hungarian paprika

8 ounces mushrooms, any kind, chopped, sliced, or quartered

1 teaspoon caraway seeds

½ cup dry white wine

3 cups cooked white beans, or 2 (15-ounce) cans, drained and rinsed

1½ cups vegetable broth

2 tablespoons tomato paste

½ cup vegan sour cream

Salt and freshly ground black pepper

Roasted Brussels Sprouts and Walnuts

If you think you don't like Brussels sprouts, it may be because you've never had them prepared this way. Roasting transforms these tiny orbs into delicious flavor bombs, seasoned with nothing more than salt and pepper and a little olive oil and lemon juice. The walnuts add a delightful crunch.

1½ pounds Brussels sprouts, ends trimmed

2 tablespoons olive oil

½ teaspoon sea salt

¼ teaspoon freshly ground black pepper

½ cup walnut pieces

Squeeze of fresh lemon juice, for serving

Preheat the oven to 400°F. Lightly oil a baking sheet and set aside. If the Brussels sprouts are small, leave them whole. If they are on the large side, cut them in half lengthwise. Place the Brussels sprouts in a bowl. Add the oil, salt, and pepper and toss to combine. Transfer them to the prepared baking sheet and roast for 15 minutes, then remove from the oven, stir the sprouts so they brown evenly, then sprinkle the walnut pieces among the sprouts. Return the pan to the oven and continue to roast, until the sprouts are crisp and browned on the outside and tender inside, about 15 minutes longer. Transfer to a bowl and serve hot sprinkled with a little lemon juice.

Serves 4

GLUTEN-FREE
SOY-FREE

Serbian Potato Salad

The first time I had Serbian potato salad it was because it was the only available vegan option in the restaurant I was in. It was served as a wrap sandwich, with no sides (not even a pickle!) at the cost of ten dollars. Despite that experience, the great flavor of the potato salad stayed with me, so I've re-created it—now I can enjoy it any time I like . . . and I don't have to pay ten dollars for it.

5 large Yukon Gold potatoes, peeled and diced

1 small yellow onion, minced

3 scallions, minced

⅓ cup chopped roasted red pepper (optional)

2 to 3 tablespoons white vinegar

1 clove garlic, minced

3 tablespoons olive oil

½ teaspoon sugar

1 teaspoon salt

½ teaspoon freshly ground black pepper

Cook the potatoes in a pot of boiling salted water until just tender. Drain the potatoes, then peel and dice them and transfer to a large bowl. Add the onion, scallions, and roasted bell pepper, if using. Set aside.

In a small bowl, combine the vinegar, garlic, oil, sugar, salt, and pepper. Mix well to blend. Add the dressing to the potatoes and toss to combine. Cover and refrigerate for several hours or overnight to meld the flavors before serving. Taste and adjust the seasonings, if needed. For the best flavor, serve at room temperature.

Serves 4

GLUTEN-FREE
SOY-FREE
QUICK AND EASY

Easy Apple Strudel

This delicious dessert will look like it took all day to prepare, but it actually goes together quickly thanks to the already prepared puff pastry. I recommend Pepperidge Farm brand because it is vegan and easy to find in most supermarkets.

Preheat the oven to 375°F. Combine the sugar, flour, and cinnamon in a medium bowl. Add the apples, pecans, and cranberries and toss to coat. Set aside.

Unfold the pastry sheet onto a lightly floured work surface. Roll the pastry into a 16 by 12-inch rectangle. With the short side facing you, spoon the apple mixture onto the bottom half of the pastry sheet to within 1 inch of the edge. Roll up like a jelly roll. Transfer the strudel to a baking sheet, seam side down. Tuck the ends under to seal and cut several slits in the top of the pastry. Brush the top lightly with oil, if desired, to help brown the top. Bake for 35 minutes or until golden brown. Remove from the oven and set aside to cool for 20 minutes. To serve, cut into slices, using a serrated knife, and sprinkle with the confectioners' sugar, if using.

Serves 8

SOY-FREE

2 tablespoons natural sugar

1 tablespoon all-purpose flour

1 teaspoon ground cinnamon

2 large Granny Smith apples, peeled, cored and chopped

½ cup ground toasted pecans

2 tablespoons sweetened dried cranberries

1 (10 by 15-inch) sheet vegan puff pastry, thawed

Confectioners' sugar (optional)

British Isles

It seems somewhat ironic that the term vegan originated in a part of the world that has a scarcity of traditional vegan food. From sausages and meat pies to roasts and rarebit, meat and dairy clearly dominate the traditional foods of the British Isles. Further, the climate and growing season produce mainly cold-tolerant vegetables, such as potatoes, cabbages, turnips, and carrots.

However, even though British vegetable dishes may not be varied or plentiful, they certainly have imaginative names such as punchnep (Welsh potatoes and turnips), rumbledethumps (Scottish potatoes and cabbage), stump (English root vegetable puree), and bashed neeps (Scottish rutabaga). Irish food is generally associated with meaty pub fare, such as corned beef and cabbage, Irish stew, and meat pies. While meat dominates the Irish menu, there are still a number of ways for vegan eyes to smile on Irish cuisine. Most notable is the prolific use of two comfort food favorites: potatoes and cabbage. (Case in point, Cauliflower Colcannon on page 78.) Most traditional "meat and potato" recipes of the British Isles, such as Cottage Pie (page 74) or Portobello Pasties (page 79) only needed a little tinkering to transform many of them into vegan versions.

English Garden Salad

Little gem lettuce has spoiled me for other types of lettuce—it's everything we love about butter and romaine lettuce, all in one compact little head. If you can't find Little Gem lettuce, substitute another type of lettuce, such as Boston or Bibb.

4 ounces thin asparagus or young green beans, trimmed and cut into 1-inch pieces

1 cup green peas, fresh or frozen

2 to 3 heads Little Gem lettuce or other tender lettuce, coarsely chopped (about 5 cups total)

8 cherry or grape tomatoes, halved lengthwise

½ English cucumber, thinly sliced

4 red radishes, trimmed and thinly sliced

1 tablespoon chopped fresh tarragon leaves

1 tablespoon snipped fresh chives

1 tablespoon torn small fresh mint leaves

3 tablespoons olive oil

2 tablespoons freshly squeezed lemon juice or white wine vinegar

¼ teaspoon salt

⅛ teaspoon freshly ground black pepper

Pinch of sugar

Steam the asparagus and peas over boiling water, using a steamer pot with a perforated insert until crisp-tender, 2 to 3 minutes. Run cold water over the vegetables to stop the cooking process, then drain and pat dry.

Transfer the cooled vegetables to a large bowl. Add the lettuce, tomatoes, cucumber, radishes, and fresh herbs.

In a small bowl, combine the oil, lemon juice, salt, pepper, and sugar. Drizzle over the salad and toss gently to combine. Serve immediately.

Serves 4

GLUTEN-FREE
SOY-FREE
QUICK AND EASY

Cottage Pie

Also known as shepherd's pie, this animal-friendly version of the classic potato-topped meat and vegetable pie is made with cooked French lentils. It can also be made with cooked chopped tempeh or seitan, if you prefer. Use coconut aminos instead of soy sauce to make this soy free. For gluten free, use a gluten-free flour.

Gravy

1 tablespoon olive oil

2 tablespoons all-purpose flour

1¼ cups vegetable broth

2 tablespoons soy sauce

1 teaspoon minced fresh thyme, or ½ teaspoon dried

1 teaspoon minced fresh marjoram, or ½ teaspoon dried

Salt and freshly ground black pepper

¼ cup plain unsweetened almond milk

Filling

1 tablespoon olive oil

1 large onion, chopped

1 large carrot, peeled and chopped

2 cups cooked French lentils

1 cup fresh or frozen corn kernels, thawed

½ cup frozen peas, thawed

1 tablespoon soy sauce

1 teaspoon minced fresh thyme, or ½ teaspoon dried

Salt and freshly ground black pepper

Potato Topping

2 pounds Yukon Gold or russet potatoes, peeled and diced

⅓ cup plain unsweetened almond milk

1 tablespoon vegan butter (optional)

To make the gravy, heat the oil in a saucepan over medium heat. Add the flour and cook, stirring for 30 seconds. Stir in the broth, soy sauce, thyme, marjoram, and salt and pepper to taste. Continue to cook, stirring, until the sauce thickens, about 5 minutes. Stir in the milk, then taste to adjust the seasonings, if needed. Set aside.

To make the filling, heat the oil in a large skillet over medium heat. Add the onion and carrot. Cover and cook until soft, about 7 minutes. Stir in the cooked lentils, corn, peas, soy sauce, thyme, and salt and pepper to taste. Stir in the prepared gravy. Remove from the heat and set aside. Preheat the oven to 350°F. Lightly oil a 2-quart baking dish (any shape) and set aside.

To make the potato topping, first cook the potatoes in a pot of boiling salted water until soft, about 15 minutes. Drain the potatoes well and return them to the pot. Add the almond milk and butter, if using, and season with salt to taste.

To assemble, spoon the filling mixture into the prepared baking dish. Spread a layer of the potatoes on top. Bake until the filling is hot and the top is golden, about 30 minutes.

Serves 4

GLUTEN-FREE OPTION
SOY-FREE OPTION

Soda Bread Scones

Classic Irish soda bread gets transformed into tasty scones. These are especially good served warm and best if eaten on the same day they are made. These scones are delicious on their own with a little dab of vegan butter or as an accompaniment to a hearty soup or stew.

1¼ cups plain unsweetened almond milk

1 tablespoon white vinegar

1 tablespoon grapeseed or other neutral oil

3 cups white or whole wheat flour

1 teaspoon baking soda

½ teaspoon baking powder

½ teaspoon salt

½ cup raisins

Preheat the oven to 375°F. Combine the milk, vinegar, and oil in a bowl and set aside.

In a large bowl, combine the flour, baking soda, baking powder, and salt. Mix until blended. Stir in the raisins. Add enough of the milk mixture to make a stiff dough. Shape the dough into a ball, then flatten on a lightly floured work surface to make a large round disk about 1 inch thick. Use a floured knife to cut the dough into 8 wedges. Carefully transfer the wedges to a lightly oiled baking sheet. Bake until golden brown, 16 to 20 minutes, or when a toothpick inserted in the center comes out clean. Cool the loaf on a wire rack.

Makes 8 scones

SOY-FREE
LOW OIL

Winter Vegetables with Horseradish Sauce

Roasting winter vegetables adds a rich depth of flavor to them and brings out their natural sweetness. If you're not a fan of a particular vegetable (or can't find it), leave it out and add more of your favorites. The horseradish sauce adds a bold accent.

To make the sauce, combine the sour cream, mayonnaise, horseradish, vinegar, mustard, salt, and pepper in a medium bowl and stir together until smooth and creamy. Cover and refrigerate for 2 to 3 hours or overnight to allow flavors to meld.

To prepare the vegetables, preheat the oven to 425°F. Lightly oil a large shallow baking pan or line it with parchment paper or spray it with cooking spray. Combine the cut vegetables in a large bowl. Add the garlic, thyme, olive oil, and season with salt and pepper. Toss to combine and coat the vegetables. Spread the vegetables in a single layer in the prepared pan. Roast the vegetables for 45 to 50 minutes, stirring once halfway through, or until the vegetables are tender and beginning to turn golden brown.

Serve the vegetables hot with the sauce on the side.

Serves 4

GLUTEN-FREE

Horseradish Sauce

⅔ cup vegan sour cream

2 tablespoons vegan mayonnaise

2 to 3 tablespoons grated fresh horseradish or prepared horseradish (be sure it is vegan)

1½ teaspoons cider vinegar

1 teaspoon Dijon mustard

½ teaspoon salt

¼ teaspoon freshly ground black pepper

Vegetables

1 large red onion, cut into ½-inch dice

2 large carrots, cut into ½-inch slices

1 large parsnip, cut into ½-inch slices

1 turnip, small rutabaga, or celery root, peeled and cut into ½-inch dice

3 golden beets, trimmed and scrubbed or 1 large sweet potato, peeled and cut into 1-inch dice

1 small butternut squash, peeled, seeded, and cut into 1-inch dice

4 whole cloves garlic, crushed

2 tablespoons chopped fresh thyme

2 tablespoons olive oil

Salt and freshly ground black pepper

Cauliflower Colcannon

Colcannon is typically a pairing of creamy mashed potatoes and soft-cooked cabbage with leeks. Some versions use kale instead of the traditional cabbage. This version uses both—with the added feature of cauliflower replacing some of the potatoes. A few slices of crisp, chopped tempeh bacon make a good addition. Since leeks and kale can be sandy, be sure to wash them well before using and remove the tough stems from the kale. A soy-free vegan butter will make this a soy-free recipe.

1 pound Yukon Gold potatoes, peeled and diced

Salt

1 pound cauliflower florets

1 tablespoon olive oil

1 medium yellow onion, chopped

1 leek (white part only), rinsed and chopped

2 cloves garlic, minced

3 cups finely shredded kale

3 cups finely shredded green cabbage

¼ cup hot plain unsweetened almond milk

2 tablespoons vegan butter

Freshly ground black pepper

Place the potatoes in a saucepan with enough cold water to cover. Bring to a boil over high heat. Decrease the heat to a simmer, salt the water, cover, and cook for 5 minutes. Add the cauliflower and continue to simmer until tender, about 15 minutes longer.

While the potatoes and cauliflower are cooking, heat the oil in a large saucepan over medium heat. Add the onion, leek, and garlic and cook until softened, about 5 minutes. Add the kale and cabbage, season with salt and pepper, cover, and cook until tender, about 10 minutes.

When the potatoes and cauliflower are cooked, drain them and return to the pot. Add the almond milk, butter, and salt and pepper to taste. Mash well, then stir in the kale and cabbage mixture and serve hot.

Serves 6

GLUTEN-FREE
SOY-FREE OPTION

Portobello Pasties

The national dish of Cornwall, England, the traditional Cornish pasty is a baked pastry filled with beef, diced potato, turnip, and onion, seasoned with salt and pepper. These savory pockets are the epitome of comfort food, with a delectable homey filling enclosed in pastry. This recipe makes four large pasties, a satisfying meal when served with a crisp green salad.

To make the pastry, combine the flour and salt in a mixing bowl. Cut in the shortening. Add enough water to moisten the dry ingredients. Shape into a ball, then cover and set aside.

To make the filling, heat the oil in a large skillet over medium heat. Add the onion and cook until softened, 5 minutes. Add the carrot, potato, and garlic and cook, stirring for 4 minutes. Add the mushrooms, soy sauce, thyme, salt, and pepper, and cook 5 minutes to soften. Stir in the peas. Cook, stirring until the vegetables are tender and any liquid has evaporated, about 5 minutes. Remove from the heat and set aside to cool. Taste and adjust the seasonings, if needed.

To assemble, preheat the oven to 400°F. Lightly oil a baking sheet and set it aside.

Divide the dough into four pieces. Roll out each piece of the dough into a 5-inch circle on a lightly floured surface. Spoon the filling mixture onto the center of each dough circle. Fold the dough over the filling, sealing the edges tightly with the tines of a fork. Cut slits in the top of the pasties and arrange them on the prepared baking sheet. Bake until golden brown, 35 to 45 minutes.

Serves 4

Pastry

1½ cups all-purpose flour

¼ teaspoon salt

½ cup vegan shortening

¼ cup cold water

Filling

1 tablespoon olive oil

1 yellow onion, minced

1 carrot, shredded

1 russet potato, shredded

3 cloves garlic, minced

3 portobello mushrooms, trimmed and finely chopped

1 tablespoon soy sauce

½ teaspoon dried thyme

½ teaspoon salt

¼ teaspoon freshly ground black pepper

½ cup thawed frozen peas

Lemon Posset

In Britain, posset used to refer to a drink, but now it is a term for a dessert pudding. This version is made creamy with cashews and tofu or vegan cream cheese. It's the perfect ending to a hearty meal.

1 cup raw cashews, soaked for 3 hours, then drained and blotted dry

1 cup firm silken tofu or vegan cream cheese, blotted dry

⅔ cup superfine sugar

⅓ cup freshly squeezed lemon juice (preferably from Meyer lemons)

2 teaspoons finely grated lemon zest

1 teaspoon vanilla extract

Mint sprigs, for garnish

Lemon zest, for garnish

Place the cashews in a dry food processor or high-speed blender and process until finely ground. Loosen the cashews from the processor or blender. Add the tofu, sugar, lemon juice, zest, and vanilla. Process for several minutes until completely smooth, scraping down the sides of the machine as needed. Transfer the pudding into dessert glasses, cover each with plastic wrap, and refrigerate for at least 1 hour to chill. Just before serving, garnish each posset with a sprig of mint and lemon zest.

Serves 4

GLUTEN-FREE
QUICK AND EASY
NO OIL

CHAPTER 5

The Americas

As much as I love the international dishes I share in this
book, some of my favorites can be found right here at home.
The United States is home to a number of specialty cooking
traditions, including the Tex-Mex of the Southwest, Cajun and
Creole cooking native to Louisiana, Low-Country cooking of
the Carolinas, and New England, where the cold winters are
warmed by stews, squashes, and berries introduced to the early
settlers by Native Americans. Some days I crave the vibrant
flavors of our neighbors to the south, from the bold spiciness of
Mexico and South America to the refreshing tropical cuisine of
the Caribbean islands, with such tasty bites as Spicy Plantain
Fritters with Mango-Papaya Relish (page 112).

Having lived in different parts of the country and traveled to the
others, I've come to think of many of the dishes from all of these
areas simply as home cooking.

The United States

Within the various regions of the United States, we find distinct cuisines that reflect the traditions of the original settlers. As in all countries, indigenous produce informs the varied cuisines of the United States.

In the Southwest, the cooking has a strong Mexican influence, with its use of chiles, cumin, cilantro, and lime. Louisiana's Cajun cooking is said to be the only cuisine actually invented in America. In addition to French influences, the Cajuns learned about filé (ground sassafras leaves) from the Indians and okra from the freed African slaves. Many traditional Cajun and Creole recipes are easily adapted to the vegan kitchen such as vegetable jambalaya and gumbo, for those who want a taste of New Orleans cuisine, minus the crawfish and andouille sausage.

New England boasts satisfying comfort foods, including my takes on two of them: Easy Boston Baked Beans (page 93) and Brown Bread with Walnuts and Raisins (page 97). New England ingredients, such as cranberries, maple syrup, squash, pumpkins, apples, hazelnuts, and molasses, as well as other ingredients have long been a part of Native American culture. Corn was one of the most widely used crops prepared by Native Americans who also cooked with root vegetables, squashes, wild peas, watercress, mulberries, nuts, leeks, and onions.

When I was a chef in Charleston, South Carolina, I learned to cook in the regional "low country" style where rice, beans, and greens grace dinner tables in homes and restaurants alike. I came away from there with a number of favorite dishes. The South is also home to several flavorful stews, from the jambalaya of New Orleans, to the burgoo of Kentucky, the Lowcountry's Frogmore stew and my personal favorite, Brunswick Stew (page 88). While none of these stews are traditionally vegan, they contain enough vegetables and seasonings to adapt to satisfying plant-based versions.

Chickpea Nuggets with Buffalo Barbecue Ranch Sauce

Make a batch of these all-American (but animal-friendly) nuggets and then cool and refrigerate some to use right away. For extra decadence, you can batter-dip and fry them. Instead of shaping into nuggets, you can flatten the mixture into patties or cutlets to use in a variety of recipes for sautés and stir-fries. The nuggets can also be wrapped tightly and frozen for later use. The broth can be frozen and used to make your next batch of nuggets or as a base for soups, sauces, or gravies.

Cooking Broth

6 cups water

2 tablespoons vegetable broth base (paste or powder)

2 tablespoons soy sauce

1 medium yellow onion, quartered

2 cloves garlic, crushed

Nuggets

½ cup cooked chickpeas

1 cup cold vegetable broth

2 tablespoons soy sauce

1 cup vital wheat gluten, plus more as needed

⅓ cup chickpea flour

⅓ cup nutritional yeast

1 teaspoon garlic powder

½ teaspoon onion powder

Olive oil, for cooking

Buffalo Barbecue Ranch Sauce (recipe follows), for serving

To make the broth, combine the water, vegetable broth base, soy sauce, onion, and garlic in a large pot. Set aside.

For the nuggets, place the chickpeas in a food processor and process until smooth. Add the broth and soy sauce and process until blended. Add the vital wheat gluten, chickpea flour, nutritional yeast, garlic powder, and onion powder. Process until well blended. If the dough is too soft, add a couple more tablespoons of vital wheat gluten.

Turn the dough out onto a floured surface and knead for 3 to 5 minutes. Stretch the dough into a log shape about 1 inch thick. Cut the log at 1-inch intervals.

Add the nuggets to the reserved broth and bring just to a simmer. Cover and simmer for 45 minutes, turning about halfway through. Do not allow the broth to boil.

Remove from the heat and allow the nuggets to cool for 30 minutes in the broth, then use a slotted spoon to remove them from the broth. Use at once or cover and refrigerate until needed.

To serve, sauté the nuggets in a skillet in a small amount of oil until golden brown, about 4 minutes per side. Serve with Buffalo Barbecue Ranch Sauce or your favorite dipping sauce.

Serves 4

LOW OIL

Buffalo Barbecue Ranch Sauce

As an homage to the decadent overload that defines much of America's fast food, I developed this sauce that has the heat of Buffalo wing hot sauce, the sweet tang of barbecue sauce, and the creaminess of ranch dressing. This makes an ideal dipping sauce for the chickpea nuggets (page 86).

Combine the mayonnaise, hot sauce, and barbecue sauce in a bowl. Stir until well blended. Taste and adjust the flavor if needed, adding a little more hot sauce for a spicier sauce, or a little extra barbecue sauce to make it a bit sweeter.

Makes about ¾ cup sauce

GLUTEN-FREE
QUICK AND EASY
NO OIL

⅓ cup vegan mayonnaise

3 tablespoons hot sauce
(Texas Pete's is a good choice)

3 tablespoons barbecue sauce

Brunswick Stew

The origin of this classic Southern stew is in contention with Virginia, Georgia, and North Carolina all laying claim to different versions. Since the main difference in the various regions has to do with the type of meat used, I say, let them duke it out while we enjoy this vegan version of the tomato-based stew, thick with lima beans, corn, and potatoes. Like most stews, this tastes even better the day after it's made. A small amount of liquid smoke added near the end of the cooking time adds a pleasant smoked nuance.

1 tablespoon olive oil

8 ounces seitan, steamed tempeh, or reconstituted Soy Curls, cut into ½-inch pieces

1 large sweet yellow onion, finely chopped

1 large carrot, peeled and chopped

2 cloves garlic, minced

3 cups vegetable broth

2 large Yukon Gold potatoes, diced

1 (15-ounce) can fire-roasted diced tomatoes, undrained

8 ounces fresh or frozen baby lima beans or butter beans

1½ cups fresh or frozen corn kernels

1½ teaspoons grated fresh ginger

2 tablespoons tamari

2 teaspoons prepared mustard

1 teaspoon natural sugar

½ teaspoon ground allspice

½ teaspoon Tabasco

Salt and freshly ground black pepper

½ teaspoon liquid smoke

Heat the oil in a large saucepan or Dutch oven over medium heat. Add the seitan and cook until browned, about 5 minutes, stirring occasionally. Remove from the pot and set aside. Reheat the saucepan and add the onion, carrot, and garlic. Add ¼ cup of the broth, cover, and cook until softened, about 5 minutes, stirring occasionally. Uncover, and stir in the potatoes, tomatoes, lima beans, corn, ginger, tamari, mustard, sugar, allspice, Tabasco, and salt and pepper to taste. Bring to a boil. Decrease the heat to low and simmer, uncovered, until the vegetables are tender, 40 to 45 minutes, stirring occasionally. During the last 5 minutes of cooking time, add the reserved seitan and the liquid smoke.

Note: For extra bulk, you can add some sliced and sautéed vegan sausage links just before serving, if desired.

Serves 4 to 6

LOW OIL

Three-Corn Cornbread

Cornbread is a favorite accompaniment to comfort foods such as chili, stew, and greens and beans. If you have a cast-iron skillet, you'll want to use it for this recipe. Otherwise, it can be baked in a glass or metal baking pan. For a spicy version, add one or two minced canned chipotle chiles.

Preheat the oven to 400°F. Oil a 9-inch cast-iron skillet or an 8-inch square baking pan and place in the oven to heat while you make the batter.

In a medium bowl, combine the nondairy milk and lemon juice and set aside.

In a large bowl, combine the cornmeal, flour, baking powder, baking soda, and salt and set aside. Add the corn kernels, creamed corn, maple syrup, and the reserved milk mixture. Stir to combine the ingredients.

Remove the hot skillet from the oven and scrape the batter into it. Bake for about 30 minutes or golden brown and a toothpick inserted in the center comes out clean. Let cool on a cooling rack for 10 minutes before removing from the pan. Serve hot or warm.

Serves 6 to 8

SOY-FREE
NO OIL

½ cup plain unsweetened nondairy milk

1 teaspoon freshly squeezed lemon juice

1¾ cups yellow cornmeal

½ cup all-purpose flour

2 teaspoons baking powder

½ teaspoon baking soda

½ teaspoon salt

1 cup cooked fresh or frozen corn kernels, thawed

1 (16-ounce) can creamed corn

1 tablespoon maple syrup

Butternut Mac and Cheese

Few dishes are more classically American than mac and cheese and this version is one of my favorites. Butternut squash is the secret ingredient in the creamy rich sauce made with cashews and an arsenal of spices. For a variation, add some cooked green vegetables, such as broccoli or peas. To make this gluten free, use gluten-free pasta and bread crumbs.

1 cup diced butternut squash

8 ounces elbow macaroni or other bite-size pasta

½ cup raw cashews, soaked overnight and drained

2½ cups plain unsweetened almond milk

2 tablespoons freshly squeezed lemon juice

1 teaspoon Dijon mustard

½ cup nutritional yeast

2 tablespoons cornstarch

1 teaspoon salt

1 teaspoon onion powder

½ teaspoon garlic powder

½ teaspoon smoked paprika

¼ teaspoon freshly ground black pepper

¼ cup panko bread crumbs

Steam the butternut squash in a steamer pot with a perforated basket over boiling water until tender, about 8 minutes. Set aside. Cook the macaroni in a pot of boiling salted water until it is al dente. Drain and return to the pot. Preheat the oven to 375°F. Lightly oil a 9-inch baking dish.

In a high-speed blender, combine the drained cashews and ½ cup of the almond milk and process until smooth. Add the cooked squash, lemon juice, mustard, nutritional yeast, cornstarch, salt, onion powder, garlic powder, paprika, and pepper, along with the remaining almond milk and blend until completely smooth and creamy.

Add the sauce mixture to the drained macaroni and stir to combine. Taste and adjust the seasonings, if needed. Transfer the mixture to the prepared baking dish and sprinkle with the panko. Bake for 20 to 30 minutes, or until bubbly.

Serves 4

GLUTEN-FREE OPTION
SOY-FREE
NO OIL

Garlicky Greens and Beans

Leafy greens and protein-rich beans are a nutritional match made in heaven that can be found all over the world. I decided to feature it in the United States section, not just as an homage to the melting pot of America in general, but to one of my favorite combos from the American South: collards and black-eyed peas. Feel free to change up the greens and beans in this recipe as desired, although if you use more delicate greens, such as chard or spinach, the cooking time will be greatly reduced. You can vary this recipe by using a different combination of greens or beans.

1 pound collard greens
(or mustard greens), well washed

1 tablespoon olive oil

3 cloves garlic, minced

1 cup vegetable broth

1 tablespoon cider vinegar

1 teaspoon natural sugar

¼ teaspoon red pepper flakes

Salt and freshly ground black pepper

1½ cups or 1 (15-ounce) can red beans
or black-eyed peas, drained and rinsed

Remove the thick stems from the greens. Coarsely chop the greens and add them to a pot of boiling salted water, stirring until wilted. Lower the heat to a simmer and cook until almost tender, about 15 minutes. Drain the greens and set aside.

In the same pot, heat the oil over medium heat. Add the garlic and cook until softened and fragrant, about 30 seconds. Add the greens, then stir in the vegetable broth, vinegar, sugar, red pepper flakes, and salt and pepper to taste. Bring to a boil, then decrease the heat to low, stir in the beans, and cover partially. Cook, stirring occasionally, until the greens are tender, about 10 minutes longer. Serve hot.

Serves 4

GLUTEN-FREE
SOY-FREE
LOW OIL
QUICK AND EASY

Easy Boston Baked Beans

Boston baked beans have long been a traditional New England favorite. You can begin this recipe with dried beans, if you like, but to save time, I start with canned beans that have been drained and rinsed thoroughly. The addition of liquid smoke adds a smoky flavor to the beans, but they taste great without it, too.

Preheat the oven to 350°F. Heat the oil in a skillet over medium heat. Add the onion, cover, and cook until soft, about 10 minutes. Remove from the heat and set aside.

In a large baking dish, combine the tomatoes, molasses, water, sugar, mustard, and salt, stirring to blend. Add the beans, the reserved onion, and the liquid smoke, if using. Stir to mix well. Cover and bake for 30 minutes, then uncover and bake 15 minutes longer.

Serves 4 to 6

GLUTEN-FREE
SOY-FREE
LOW OIL

1 tablespoon olive oil

1 medium yellow onion, chopped

½ cup canned crushed tomatoes

⅓ cup molasses

¼ cup water

1 tablespoon natural sugar

2 tablespoons Dijon mustard

½ teaspoon salt

3 cups cooked or 2 (15-ounce) cans navy beans, drained and rinsed

½ teaspoon liquid smoke (optional)

Blue Ribbon Chocolate Layer Cake

This rich and chocolaty cake is my go-to chocolate cake. It's so delicious it could easily win a blue ribbon at a state fair—or at your own dinner table. Best of all: It contains no eggs or dairy.

To prepare the cake, preheat the oven to 350°F. Lightly oil two 9-inch cake pans or spray with cooking spray. Set aside.

In a medium bowl, combine the ground flaxseed with ½ cup of the almond milk; set aside to hydrate while you measure out the other ingredients.

In a large bowl, combine the flour, sugar, cocoa powder, baking soda, and salt. Mix well, using a whisk to thoroughly combine and "lighten" the dry ingredients. Set aside.

Once the flaxseed meal is hydrated (it will be thickened), add the remaining almond milk, coffee, maple syrup, oil, and vinegar.

Add the wet ingredients to the dry ingredients and use the whisk to mix them together so that a smooth batter forms (don't mix too much—just enough so that everything is wet). The batter will be runny.

Quickly pour the batter into the prepared pans and bake for 30 to 35 minutes, until a toothpick inserted in the middle comes out clean. Do not overbake.

Let the cakes cool in the pans for 10 minutes, then run a knife around the cake between the cake and pan, then turn out onto the cooling racks. Let cool completely before frosting.

CONTINUED ON NEXT PAGE

Cake

2 tablespoons ground flaxseed

1 cup almond milk

2½ cups unbleached all-purpose flour

1¼ cups natural sugar

⅔ cup unsweetened cocoa powder

2 teaspoons baking soda

½ teaspoon salt

1 cup strong coffee (or 1 cup water plus 2 teaspoons instant coffee or espresso powder)

½ cup maple syrup

3 tablespoons grapeseed oil or other neutral oil

2 teaspoons cider vinegar

Frosting

1¼ cups nondairy semisweet chocolate chips

⅔ cup raw cashews, soaked 4 hours, then drained and blotted dry

¼ cup water

¼ cup maple syrup

6 ounces extra-firm silken tofu, blotted dry

1 teaspoon vanilla extract

To make the frosting, melt the chocolate chips in a microwave or on the stovetop over simmering water. Keep warm.

Grind the drained and blotted cashews in a high-speed blender. Add the water and maple syrup and blend until smooth. Add the tofu and vanilla and blend until completely smooth and creamy. Add the melted chocolate and process until smooth and well blended. Transfer to a bowl, cover, and refrigerate until well chilled, 2 to 4 hours.

To assemble, place one layer of the completely cooled cake on a plate. Spread it with about ¾ cup of the chilled frosting. Top with the second layer and spread the top and sides of the cake with the remaining frosting. If not serving right away, refrigerate until needed. Serve chilled or at room temperature.

Serves 8 to 10

Brown Bread with Walnuts and Raisins

This wholesome loaf is inspired by the traditional Boston brown bread made by pouring the batter into a coffee can and steaming it in a few inches of water on top of the stove. Breaking with tradition, this version adds walnuts and raisins to the batter and bakes in the oven.

Grease a 9 by 5-inch loaf pan. Preheat the oven to 325°F.

In a large bowl, combine the cornmeal, wheat flour, all-purpose flour, baking soda, and salt.

In a separate bowl, combine the almond milk, molasses, maple syrup, and vinegar. Stir the wet ingredients into the dry ingredients until just moistened. Fold in the walnuts and raisins. Scrape the batter into the prepared pan, spreading evenly.

Bake for 1 hour or until a wooden pick inserted in the center comes out clean. Carefully remove the bread from the pan. Cool on a rack at least 30 minutes before slicing.

Makes 1 loaf

SOY-FREE
NO OIL

1 cup yellow cornmeal

1 cup whole wheat pastry flour

½ cup all-purpose flour

1 teaspoon baking soda

¾ teaspoon salt

1½ cups plain unsweetened almond milk

½ cup molasses

¼ cup maple syrup

1 tablespoon white vinegar

½ cup walnut pieces

½ cup raisins

Mexico

Anyone who has enjoyed authentic Mexican food knows that there is far more to this flavorful cuisine than the ubiquitous tacos and burritos that have become fast food favorites in the United States. Mexico boasts many regional specialties, where the sauces and ingredients vary greatly from each other, such as mole poblano, the world-famous sauce from Puebla State, which combines chocolate and chiles, and the tangy borracha sauce, which blends chiles with tequila and fruit juices.

Mexican cuisine is a blend of ancient Mexican Indian cooking with Spanish and other European influences. Mexican Indians had long made use of the native corn, tomatoes, beans, and squash, which inspired the Black Bean and Butternut Tortilla Bake on page 102, while the Spanish brought wheat, olives, rice, and introduced citrus fruits as a way to season food, as in the Cilantro-Jicama Slaw with Lime-Orange Dressing on page 105.

Mexican cooking also features produce such as avocados, jicama, and several varieties of chiles, as well as seasonings such as cumin, cilantro, and oregano. The abundance of beans, grains, and fresh vegetables in Mexican cooking make it a natural for vegan recipes.

Avocado and Tomato Salsa Verrines

Verrine is the name given to a sweet or savory dish layered in clear glasses or bowls, usually served as an appetizer or dessert. This one is a savory version, with layers of avocado, black beans, and tomato salsa. You can also serve this family style, by layering the ingredients in a larger clear glass bowl.

3 large ripe tomatoes, peeled, seeded, and chopped

1 hot red chile, seeded and minced

4 scallions, minced

1 large clove garlic, finely minced

2 tablespoons freshly squeezed lime juice

Salt and freshly ground black pepper

2 teaspoons olive oil

¼ teaspoon chili powder

2 ripe Hass avocados

1 cup cooked black beans

½ cup chopped fresh cilantro leaves

In a bowl, combine the tomatoes, chile, three of the scallions, and the garlic. Add 1 tablespoon of the lime juice and salt and pepper to taste. Stir gently to combine. Cover and let stand at room temperature for 30 minutes.

In a separate bowl, combine the remaining tablespoon of lime juice, oil, and chili powder. Add the avocados, season with salt and pepper, and toss gently to coat.

Divide the black beans evenly among four clear glasses, such as large wine or martini glasses, or in a large glass bowl, if serving family style. Top the beans with an equal amount of the avocado mixture. Top the avocado with an equal amount of the tomato salsa. Sprinkle the cilantro on top of each serving and serve immediately.

Serves 4

GLUTEN-FREE
SOY-FREE
QUICK AND EASY
LOW OIL

Black Bean and Butternut Tortilla Bake

Loaded with flavor, this comfort food casserole combines butternut squash with black beans and tomatoes, layered with tortillas. Assemble ahead of time for an easy weeknight meal. To make this gluten-free, use gluten-free tortillas.

1 butternut squash, halved lengthwise, and seeded (about 2½ pounds)

1 tablespoon olive oil

1 medium red onion, chopped

2 cloves garlic, minced

1½ cups cooked black beans or 1 (15.5-ounce) can, drained and rinsed

1 (14.5-ounce) can fire-roasted diced tomatoes, drained

1½ tablespoons chili powder (or to taste)

Salt and freshly ground black pepper

1 cup tomato salsa

2 tablespoons freshly squeezed lime juice

8 (7-inch) flour tortillas

Preheat the oven to 400°F. Place the butternut squash halves, cut side down, in a baking pan large enough to hold the squash. Add ½ inch of water and cover tightly and bake until tender, about 30 minutes. Remove the squash from the pan and set aside to cool. Decrease the oven temperature to 375°F.

Heat the oil in a large skillet over medium heat. Add the onion and garlic and cook until softened, about 5 minutes. Stir in the beans, tomatoes, chili powder, and salt and pepper to taste and simmer for 5 to 10 minutes. Remove from the heat.

Scoop the cooled squash into a food processor. Add the salsa, lime juice, and ½ cup of the bean mixture. Process until well blended. Lightly oil a 9 by 13-inch baking dish.

Spread a thin layer of the squash mixture into the bottom of the prepared baking dish. Arrange 4 of the tortillas on top, overlapping as needed. Spread the remaining bean mixture over the tortillas and cover with another layer of tortillas. Top with the remaining squash mixture, spreading evenly. Bake until hot and bubbly and lightly browned on top, about 30 minutes.

Serves 4 to 6

GLUTEN-FREE OPTION
SOY-FREE
LOW OIL

Garden Fideos

Fideos, a thin noodle used in Mexican and Spanish cooking, are available in Latino markets and well-stocked supermarkets. If fideos noodles are unavailable, substitute capellini or vermicelli pasta. You can use a gluten-free pasta to make this gluten free.

Heat the oil in a large pot over medium-high heat. Add the noodles and cook, stirring constantly, until the noodles begin to brown, about 1 minute. Add the onion, bell pepper, and garlic and cook for 3 minutes to soften. Be careful not to burn. Stir in the broth, then add the tomatoes, scallions, chipotle, oregano, and salt and pepper to taste. Bring to a boil, then decrease the heat to a simmer and cook until most of the liquid is absorbed, about 10 minutes. Transfer to a serving dish and sprinkle with the cilantro and avocado.

Serves 4

GLUTEN-FREE OPTION
SOY-FREE
QUICK AND EASY

2 tablespoons olive oil

8 ounces fideos noodles or vermicelli, broken into 2-inch pieces

1 small yellow onion, finely chopped

1 small red or green bell pepper, seeded and chopped

3 cloves garlic, minced

4 cups vegetable broth

2 ripe tomatoes, chopped

3 scallions, minced

1 chipotle chile in adobo sauce, finely chopped

1 teaspoon dried oregano

Salt and freshly ground black pepper

½ cup chopped fresh cilantro or parsley leaves

1 ripe Hass avocado, peeled, pitted, and diced

Cilantro-Jicama Slaw with Lime-Orange Dressing

A relative of the sweet potato, jicamas taste similarly to water chestnuts and can be eaten raw or cooked. They are especially good in this sprightly slaw. To save time, you can use a julienne peeler to cut the jicama, or even shred it, if you prefer.

In a small bowl, combine the lime juice, marmalade, lime zest, agave, and salt. Mix well, then whisk in the oil and set aside.

In a large bowl, combine the cabbage, jicama, carrot, and cilantro. Pour on the dressing and toss gently to combine. Taste and adjust the seasonings, if needed.

Serves 4

GLUTEN-FREE
SOY-FREE
QUICK AND EASY

¼ cup freshly squeezed lime juice

1 tablespoon orange marmalade

1 teaspoon finely grated lime zest

1 teaspoon agave nectar

½ teaspoon salt

2 tablespoons olive oil

4 cups shredded cabbage

1 large jicama, peeled and cut into thin matchsticks

1 large carrot, shredded

½ cup chopped fresh cilantro

Migas Burritos

I love vegan migas, made with perfectly seasoned tofu and tasty bits of tortilla. I didn't think it could get much better. That is, until I made these burritos filled with migas, avocado, salsa, and vegan sour cream. Instead of tofu, you can substitute mashed beans or potatoes (or some of each).

12 to 16 ounces soft tofu, drained

2 tablespoons nutritional yeast

½ teaspoon salt

1 tablespoon olive oil

1 small yellow onion, minced

2 cloves garlic, minced

1 fresh jalapeño, seeded and minced

2 scallions, minced

2 (6-inch) corn tortillas, torn into bite-size pieces

1 medium tomato, chopped

1 tablespoon minced fresh cilantro

4 large (10-inch) tortillas, warmed

1 ripe avocado, peeled, pitted, and chopped

1 cup tomato salsa

½ cup vegan sour cream

In a medium bowl, combine the tofu, nutritional yeast, and salt and mash well. Mix until well combined. Set aside.

Heat the oil in a large skillet over medium heat. Add the onion and cook until softened, 5 minutes. Add the garlic, jalapeño, scallions, and corn tortilla pieces and cook for 2 minutes. Stir in the tomato and the reserved tofu mixture and cook, stirring, until hot and well combined. Stir in the cilantro, then taste and adjust the seasonings, if needed. Divide the mixture among the four warmed tortillas and top each with avocado, salsa, and sour cream. Roll up the burritos, tucking in the sides as you roll. Serve immediately.

Serves 4

QUICK AND EASY
LOW OIL

Black Bean Caldillo

This hearty stew, made with potatoes, green chiles, and tomatoes, traditionally contains beef. I especially enjoy it made with black beans, although you can substitute diced seitan or Soy Curls for all or part of the beans, if you like.

Heat the oil or water in a large pot over medium-high heat. Add the onion, garlic, and potatoes. Cover and cook, stirring occasionally, for 5 to 7 minutes, to soften the vegetables. Stir in the cumin, then add the tomatoes, chiles, and broth. Bring to a boil, then lower the heat to a simmer and add the black beans, salt, and pepper. Cook, uncovered, until the vegetables are tender, about 30 minutes. Stir in the cilantro and serve hot.

Serves 4 to 6

GLUTEN-FREE
SOY-FREE
LOW OIL
QUICK AND EASY

1 tablespoon olive oil or ¼ cup water

1 large red onion, chopped

3 cloves garlic, minced

1½ pounds Yukon Gold potatoes, chopped

1½ teaspoons ground cumin

1 (14.5-ounce) can diced fire-roasted tomatoes, undrained

1 (14.5-ounce) can crushed tomatoes

1 (8-ounce) jar roasted mild green chiles, drained and chopped

3 cups vegetable broth

3 cups cooked black beans or 2 (15-ounce) cans black beans, drained and rinsed

½ teaspoon salt

¼ teaspoon freshly ground black pepper

½ cup chopped fresh cilantro

Chipotle Corn-Stuffed Peppers

Use the largest bell peppers you can find to hold the delicious stuffing made with pinto beans, rice, corn, and chipotle chiles. I like to use red peppers, but any color will do (or mix them up). For convenience you can assemble them up to 24 hours in advance, cover, and refrigerate, and then they're ready to pop in the oven when you need them.

4 large red bell peppers

1 tablespoon olive oil or ¼ cup water

1 small yellow onion, chopped

2 scallions, minced

1 ripe tomato, finely chopped

2 chipotle chiles in adobo sauce, minced

2 cups cooked fresh or frozen corn kernels

1 cup cooked or canned pinto beans, drained and rinsed

1 cup cooked rice or quinoa

2 tablespoons minced fresh cilantro or parsley

Salt and freshly ground black pepper

½ cup water

Preheat the oven to 350°F. Slice off the tops of the peppers; reserve and set aside. Remove the seeds and membranes of the peppers. Steam the peppers in a perforated steamer pan over a saucepan of boiling water and cook until softened, about 5 minutes. Remove from the steamer and set aside, cut side down. Chop only the pepper tops and set aside.

Heat the oil or water in a large skillet over medium heat. Add the onion and reserved chopped pepper tops and cook until softened, about 5 minutes. Stir in the scallions, tomato, and chipotles and cook for 2 minutes, then add the corn, beans, rice, cilantro, and salt and pepper to taste. Mix well.

Fill the pepper cavities evenly with the stuffing mixture, packing tightly. Arrange the peppers upright in a baking dish large enough to hold them. Add the water to the baking dish, cover tightly, and bake until the peppers are tender and the stuffing is hot, about 30 minutes.

Serves 4

GLUTEN-FREE
SOY-FREE
LOW OIL

Watermelon Paletas

These watermelon Popsicles make a refreshing end to a spicy meal or a cooling snack on a hot day. For best results, use a set of plastic ice-pop molds. The paletas will keep well in the freezer for up to one week.

Cut or scoop the watermelon flesh from the rind. Discard the rind and cut the watermelon into chunks. You should have 5 to 6 cups total.

Place the watermelon chunks, lime juice, sugar, and a small pinch of salt in a food processor and process until smooth. Fill a set of ice-pop molds with the pureed watermelon.

Place the molds in the freezer for 8 hours or overnight. To loosen the paleta, run the mold under warm water for a few seconds. Serve immediately.

Makes 6 to 12 paletas (depending on size of molds)

GLUTEN-FREE
SOY-FREE
NO OIL
QUICK AND EASY

1 medium seedless watermelon, halved

2 tablespoons freshly squeezed lime juice

¼ cup superfine sugar

Pinch of salt

The Caribbean

Sometimes I just crave a fix of the Caribbean. Once you've had it, you know the unique flavors born of Africa, Spain, England, Holland, France, and the East Indies. The varied influences of Caribbean cooking also include the native island fruits, vegetables, and spices, such as allspice, cinnamon, ginger, and nutmeg that are used with chiles, curry powder, peppercorns, and coconuts to season many of the island dishes such as Jamaican Jerk Vegetable Skewers on page 114.

From West Africa came cassavas, sweet potatoes, and plantains, which are popular in island cooking in dishes like Spicy Plantain Fritters with Mango-Papaya Relish on page 112. Beans are called peas in the Caribbean, and black-eyed peas are a favorite. The use of rice and a colorful variety of tropical produce make island cooking vegan-friendly, and the abundance of some of the hottest chiles add a spicy accent to the food as well. This complex, satisfying cuisine calls to me, and this section features some of my favorite recipes from the region.

Spicy Plantain Fritters with Mango-Papaya Relish

Plantains, mangoes, and papayas are all synonymous with island cooking, so it's especially lovely to enjoy all three in the same dish. The refreshing relish is a perfect accent to the spicy fritters. The plantains for this recipe should be black with some yellow outside, but they should be firm and creamy white inside. If you use a gluten-free flour, this dish will be gluten free.

Relish

1 ripe papaya, peeled, seeded and diced

2 ripe mangoes, peeled, pitted, and diced

½ cup finely chopped red bell pepper

¼ cup minced scallion

¼ cup chopped fresh cilantro

2 teaspoons grated fresh ginger

2 tablespoons freshly squeezed lime juice

1 tablespoon olive oil

Salt and freshly ground black pepper

Plantains

2 ripe plantains, peeled and cut into chunks

3 scallions, chopped

2 teaspoons finely minced lime zest

2 tablespoons ground flaxseeds blended with 2 tablespoons water

½ teaspoon salt

¼ teaspoon dried oregano

⅛ teaspoon allspice

¼ teaspoon cayenne

⅛ teaspoon freshly ground black pepper

½ cup all-purpose flour, plus more as needed

2 tablespoons olive oil

To make the relish, combine the papaya, mangoes, bell pepper, scallion, cilantro, ginger, and lime juice in a bowl. Mix well and set aside.

To make the plantains, preheat the oven to 275°F. In a food processor, combine the plantains, scallions, lime zest, flaxseeds mixture, salt, oregano, allspice, cayenne, and pepper and process until smooth. Add as much of the flour as needed so that the mixture holds together when pressed in your hand, and process to mix. Shape the mixture into small fritters, using about 1 tablespoon of the mixture for each.

Heat the oil in a large skillet over medium heat. Place the fritters in the hot oil and press them lightly with a metal spatula to flatten. Fry until golden brown on both sides, 3 to 4 minutes per side. Drain on paper towels, then transfer to a baking sheet and place in the oven to keep warm until all the fritters are cooked. Serve hot with the relish.

Serves 4 to 6

GLUTEN-FREE OPTION
SOY-FREE

Roasted Corn Chowder

This chowder gets it great corn flavor by combining roasted corn kernels with pureed creamed corn. The result is out of this world delicious. Chopped roasted poblano peppers would make a great addition to this soup, too.

Preheat the oven to 400°F. Lightly oil a rimmed baking pan and set aside. If using fresh corn, shuck the corn and cut the kernels from the cobs. In a bowl, combine the corn kernels (fresh or thawed frozen) with 1 tablespoon of the oil and season with salt and pepper to taste. Toss to combine.

Spread the corn kernels evenly on the prepared pan and roast for 15 to 20 minutes, stirring and turning the kernels occasionally, until they're tender and lightly browned. Remove from the oven and set aside.

Heat the remaining 1 tablespoon of oil in a large pot over medium-high heat. Add the onion, celery, and potato. Cover and cook until softened, about 5 minutes. Stir in the vegetable broth and bring to a boil. Lower the heat to medium, add the reserved corn kernels, paprika, and salt and pepper to taste. Simmer until the vegetables are tender, about 15 minutes. While the soup is simmering, combine the creamed corn and almond milk in a blender and blend until smooth and creamy, then stir the mixture into the soup. Heat for a minute or two until hot, then taste and adjust the seasonings, if needed. To serve, ladle into bowls and sprinkle each serving with cilantro.

Serves 4 to 6

GLUTEN-FREE
SOY-FREE

4 medium ears corn or 3 cups frozen corn kernels, thawed

2 tablespoons olive oil

Salt and freshly ground black pepper

1 medium yellow onion, chopped

1 celery rib, thinly sliced

1 Yukon Gold potato, chopped

2 cups vegetable broth

½ teaspoon smoked paprika

1 (16-ounce) can creamed corn

½ cup plain unsweetened almond milk

2 tablespoons chopped cilantro or parsley

Jamaican Jerk Vegetable Skewers

I love the jerk-spiced dishes at my favorite Jamaican restaurant, the vegan-friendly Nine Mile in Asheville, North Carolina, but this recipe satisfies my jerk cravings when I'm home. Ideal for the grill, these vegetable skewers can also be roasted or broiled in the oven. If you don't like the fussiness of skewers, you can cook the vegetables in a grill basket instead.

1 teaspoon dried thyme

1 teaspoon natural sugar

1 teaspoon salt

½ teaspoon garlic powder

½ teaspoon onion powder

½ teaspoon cayenne

½ teaspoon ground allspice

½ teaspoon smoked paprika

¼ teaspoon ground nutmeg

¼ teaspoon freshly ground black pepper

1 large red onion, cut into 1½-inch pieces

2 yellow bell peppers, seeded and cut into 1½-inch pieces

2 small zucchini, cut crosswise into ¾-inch chunks

8 ounces small cremini or white mushrooms, trimmed

12 ounces cherry tomatoes

Olive oil

If using wooden skewers, soak them in water for 1 hour or overnight. (You should need about eight to twelve skewers, depending on their size.)

In a shallow bowl, combine all of the spices, stirring to mix well. Set aside.

Thread the vegetables onto skewers, either alternating different vegetables or, alternatively, skewer one type of vegetable on separate skewers for even cooking. Brush the vegetables with olive oil, then sprinkle on the spice mixture, turning to coat all over with the spices. Preheat the grill until hot.

Arrange the skewers on a lightly oiled grill and cook for about 5 minutes per side, turning once, or until the vegetables are tender and nicely browned. Serve hot.

Serves 4

GLUTEN-FREE
SOY-FREE
LOW OIL

Mojito Roasted Sweet Potatoes

Lime juice, rum, and fresh mint combine to add the flavor of mojitos to these roasted sweet potatoes. For a nonalcoholic version, omit the rum. Use coconut oil, if you have some, to add a complementary flavor to the sauce.

3 large sweet potatoes, peeled and cut into ¼-inch-thick slices (about 2 pounds)

1 large sweet yellow onion, chopped

Salt and freshly ground black pepper

1 tablespoon melted coconut oil or olive oil, plus more for drizzling

3 cloves garlic, minced

¼ cup rum

2 tablespoons agave nectar

¼ cup vegetable broth

¼ cup freshly squeezed lime juice

¼ cup chopped fresh mint

Preheat the oven to 400°F. Arrange the sweet potato slices on a lightly oiled baking sheet. Scatter the onion around the potatoes and drizzle with a little oil. Season with salt and pepper and roast until just tender, turning once, about 30 minutes total.

While the sweet potatoes are roasting, heat 1 tablespoon of the remaining oil in a small saucepan. Add the garlic and cook until fragrant, about 1 minute. Stir in the rum and agave nectar. Add the broth and bring to a boil. Decrease the heat to low and stir in the lime juice and mint. Transfer the roasted sweet potatoes to a shallow serving bowl and drizzle with the mojito sauce. Serve hot.

Serves 4

GLUTEN-FREE
SOY-FREE
LOW OIL

Red Bean Stew with Mango

Sweet and colorful pieces of mango add a sweet note to the savory ingredients in this delicious Jamaican-inspired stew. Accompany with grilled rustic bread and a fresh green salad or serve over rice, quinoa, or even pasta.

Heat the oil or water in a large pot over medium-high heat. Add the onion, bell pepper, and garlic. Decrease the heat to medium, cover, and cook until softened, about 10 minutes. Stir in the sweet potato, zucchini, chile, if using, tomatoes, tomato paste, marjoram, thyme, curry powder, and nutmeg. Add the broth and bring to a boil. Lower the heat to a simmer. Cover and cook for 20 minutes. Stir in the kidney beans and corn and season to taste with salt and pepper. Simmer, uncovered, for 12 to 15 minutes longer, or until the vegetables are soft. Stir in the mango and serve hot.

Serves 6

GLUTEN-FREE
SOY-FREE
LOW OIL

1 tablespoon olive oil or ¼ cup water

1 large yellow onion, chopped

1 green bell pepper, seeded and chopped

2 cloves garlic, minced

1 large sweet potato, peeled and diced

1 medium zucchini, diced

1 Scotch bonnet chile, seeded and minced (optional)

1 (14.5-ounce) can fire-roasted diced tomatoes, undrained

1 tablespoon tomato paste

1 teaspoon dried marjoram

1 teaspoon dried thyme

1 teaspoon yellow curry powder

¼ teaspoon ground nutmeg

1 cup vegetable broth

3 cups cooked dark red kidney beans or 2 (15.5-ounce) cans, drained and rinsed

1 cup corn kernels, fresh or frozen

Salt and freshly ground black pepper

1 large ripe mango, peeled, pitted and chopped

Piña Colada Squares

These treats aren't too sweet if you use unsweetened coconut. Alternatively, you can substitute 2 to 3 tablespoons of sweetened coconut for part of the unsweetened coconut and omit the confectioners' sugar. If you don't have dark rum, use ½ to 1 teaspoon rum extract and make up the rest of the liquid (to equal the 1 tablespoon) with pineapple juice or a little water or almond milk.

Bottom Layer

1 cup dried pineapple pieces

½ cup raw cashews or slivered almonds

½ cup old-fashioned (rolled) oats

½ cup unsweetened shredded coconut

1 tablespoon confectioners' sugar

1 tablespoon Myers' dark rum
or 1 teaspoon rum extract and
2 teaspoons water or pineapple juice

Top Layer

8 ounces vegan cream cheese, softened

¼ cup confectioners' sugar

1 tablespoon Myers' dark rum
or 1 teaspoon rum extract

1 teaspoon coconut extract (optional)

½ cup shredded coconut

½ cup fresh or canned pineapple chunks, blotted dry

To make the bottom layer, grease an 8-inch square baking pan and set aside. In a food processor, combine the dried pineapple, cashews, oats, coconut, confectioners' sugar, and rum. Pulse to chop, then process until finely chopped and well combined. The mixture should hold together easily. Press the mixture evenly into the prepared pan. Set aside.

To make the top layer, combine the cream cheese, confectioners' sugar, rum, coconut extract, if using, and ¼ cup of the shredded coconut in a food processor. Process until smooth and creamy. If the mixture is too thin, add a little more confectioners' sugar and process again. Spread the topping mixture evenly over the bottom layer. Sprinkle the top with the pineapple chunks and the remaining ¼ cup coconut. Cover and refrigerate until ready to serve. Cut into 9 squares.

Note: Be sure you use dried pineapple pieces to make the bottom layer (not fresh or canned) or it will be too wet.

Makes 9 squares

QUICK AND EASY
NO OIL

South America

Potatoes may not be the first thing you think of in regard to South America, but maybe they should be. After all, over a thousand different types of potatoes are cultivated there. Many people don't realize that the rest of the world received the potato from the Andes four centuries ago, and potatoes are now the fourth most produced vegetable in the world.

Of course, there's more to South American cooking than potatoes, and as with most areas of the world, each country in South America, and the many regions within each country, has its own cuisine, in which the influences of native peoples played an important role. Beans, corn, rice, and quinoa (a grain native to South America) are staple foods that are often flavored with chiles, onions, garlic, and tomatoes.

The recipes in this section, from Colombian Stuffed Potatoes (page 126) to Brazilian Feijoada (page 128), are the ones I return to again and again, which reflect just a sampling of several South American countries. While the flavors and styles are varied, one thing they have in common is that they are all heavily influenced by Spanish and Portuguese cooking, but still maintain the roots of their underlying indigenous cultures.

Cucumber and White Bean Ceviche

This lime-marinated salad from Peru is traditionally made with raw fish or scallops, but cannellini beans combined with thinly sliced cucumber are also well suited to the zesty marinade. This dish can make a lovely presentation on individual salad plates by fanning the cucumber slices and then spooning a mound of beans in the center. If you don't want to arrange the ingredients on separate salad plates, you can use a similar presentation for one large salad that looks great on a buffet.

¼ cup freshly squeezed lime juice

2 tablespoons olive oil

¼ teaspoon salt

2 scallions, minced

2 teaspoons chopped capers

1½ cups cooked cannellini beans or 1 (15.5-ounce) can, drained and rinsed

1 English cucumber, peeled and thinly sliced

5 cherry or grape tomatoes, thinly sliced or quartered

1 tablespoon minced fresh cilantro or parsley

Freshly ground black pepper

In a bowl, combine the lime juice, oil, salt, and scallions. Stir to combine. Add the capers and beans and toss gently to coat. Refrigerate, covered, for 1 hour.

Fan the cucumber slices in a circle in the center of a large platter or individual salad plates. Spoon the bean mixture on top of the cucumber slices. Garnish with tomatoes, sprinkle with cilantro, and top with a few grinds of black pepper.

Serves 4

GLUTEN-FREE
SOY-FREE
QUICK AND EASY

Bolivian Quinoa Pilaf

Made with ingredients popular in Bolivia, such as quinoa, corn, and beans, and imbued with the flavors of llajawa, a spicy salsa from the region, this pilaf is an homage to all things Bolivia.

1 tablespoon olive oil or ¼ cup water

1 large sweet yellow onion, finely chopped

1 red bell pepper, seeded and chopped

3 cloves garlic, minced

1 to 2 jalapeños, seeded and minced

1 teaspoon ground cumin

½ teaspoon dried oregano

½ teaspoon smoked paprika

1 cup quinoa, drained and rinsed

2 cups vegetable broth or water

Salt and freshly ground black pepper

1 cup fresh or frozen corn kernels, thawed

1 cup fresh or frozen green peas, thawed

1 fresh ripe tomato, finely chopped

1½ cups cooked dark red kidney beans or 1 (15.5-ounce) can, drained and rinsed

1 ripe Hass avocado, peeled, pitted, and diced

½ cup chopped fresh cilantro

Heat the oil or water in a large saucepan over medium heat. Add the onion, bell pepper, garlic, and jalapeño and cook for 4 minutes to soften. Stir in the cumin, oregano, and paprika. Stir in the quinoa, broth, and salt and pepper to taste and bring to a boil. Lower the heat to a simmer, cover, and cook for 15 minutes.

Stir in the corn, peas, tomato, and beans, and cook until the quinoa and vegetables are tender, about 10 minutes longer. Taste and adjust the seasonings, if needed.

Serve topped with the avocado and cilantro.

Serves 4

GLUTEN-FREE
SOY-FREE
QUICK AND EASY
LOW OIL

Aji Salsa

This uncooked salsa from Colombia can be used on everything from potatoes to plantains and in soups and stews. It's the perfect complement to the stuffed potatoes on page 126. A small amount of (nontraditional) rice vinegar is added to mellow the lime juice a bit while still keeping a nice tang. If you prefer a chunkier salsa, you can chop the vegetables by hand and mix them in a bowl.

In a blender or small food processor, combine the chiles, lime juice, water, vinegar, sugar, salt, and pepper. Process until the chiles are finely minced and the mixture is well blended. Add the scallions, tomato, and cilantro and pulse to combine. Transfer to a small bowl to serve. If not serving right away, cover and refrigerate until needed.

Makes about 1 cup salsa

GLUTEN-FREE
SOY-FREE
NO OIL
QUICK AND EASY

2 jalapeño chiles or 1 habanero chile, seeded and quartered

3 tablespoons freshly squeezed lime juice

3 tablespoons water

1 tablespoon rice vinegar

½ teaspoon sugar

½ teaspoon salt

¼ teaspoon freshly ground black pepper

4 scallions (white and green parts), minced

1 small ripe tomato, finely minced

⅓ cup chopped fresh cilantro

Colombian Stuffed Potatoes

Papas rellenas, the fried, stuffed potatoes of Colombia, are the ultimate comfort food snack. Served with spicy Aji Salsa, this popular *fritanga* (fried snack) is made by stuffing mashed potatoes with a savory filling. When cooked, the stuffed potato balls look like whole potatoes. This oven-broiled version is much lighter than the traditional batter-dipped deep-fried variety, but still loaded with flavor. A panfried variation follows this recipe that is slightly more decadent, but still much less so than the deep-fried original.

4 large russet potatoes, peeled and cut into chunks

1 tablespoon olive oil

1 medium yellow onion, chopped

3 cloves garlic, minced

2 large plum tomatoes, chopped

½ teaspoon smoked paprika

½ teaspoon ground coriander

½ teaspoon ground cumin

¼ teaspoon dried oregano

¼ teaspoon salt

¼ teaspoon freshly ground black pepper

1 cup cooked or canned pinto or kidney beans, mashed

½ cup frozen green peas, thawed

Sprinkling of paprika

Aji Salsa (page 125)

Serves 4

GLUTEN-FREE
SOY-FREE
LOW OIL

Cook the potatoes in a large pot of boiling salted water until tender, 15 to 20 minutes. Drain very well, then return to the pot. Mash well and refrigerate for several hours or overnight.

Heat the oil in a saucepan over medium heat. Add the onion and cook for 5 minutes to soften. Add the garlic and cook 2 minutes longer, then stir in the tomatoes, paprika, coriander, cumin, oregano, salt, and pepper. Add the beans and peas and continue to cook, stirring occasionally, until the vegetables are soft and the liquid is absorbed, about 10 minutes. Set aside to cool or cover and refrigerate until needed.

Divide the chilled mashed potatoes into 10 to 12 equal portions, about ⅓ cup each. Use your hands to shape each portion into round flat patties and place each of the potato patties on top of a square sheet of plastic wrap. Spoon about 2 tablespoons of the filling in the center of each one. Close up the plastic wrap to shape the potato patties around the filling, forming them into potato-shaped balls that enclose the filling completely. Chill the stuffed potato balls in the refrigerator for 1 hour or longer.

Preheat the oven to a low broil. Arrange the stuffed potatoes on a baking sheet lightly sprayed with cooking oil spray. Spray the potatoes with a little cooking oil spray and sprinkle them with a little paprika. Lightly broil for 10 minutes, then flip them and broil for another 5 to 7 minutes or until crisp and browned. To serve, transfer to a platter and serve with the salsa.

Panfried Variation: Follow the instructions up to and including the assembly of the stuffed potatoes. After chilling the stuffed potatoes, prepare the coating mixture and cook according to the directions that follow. To make this variation gluten-free, use a gluten-free flour.

Blend the ground flaxseed with the water in a shallow bowl, stirring to thicken. Set aside. In a separate shallow bowl, mix together the flour, cumin, salt, and pepper. Set aside.

In a large nonstick skillet over medium-high heat, heat a thin layer of grapeseed oil. Roll the stuffed potatoes one at a time into the flax mixture, then dredge in the flour mixture to completely coat. Carefully place the coated potatoes in the hot pan, in batches, if needed. Do not crowd. Cook the potatoes until golden brown, 4 to 5 minutes, turning halfway through. Remove from the pan and drain on paper towels. To serve, transfer to a platter and serve with the salsa.

2½ tablespoons ground flaxseed

½ cup water

¾ cup all-purpose flour

½ teaspoon ground cumin

½ teaspoon salt

¼ teaspoon freshly ground black pepper

Grapeseed oil, for cooking

Brazilian Feijoada

This hearty stew, Brazil's national dish, is typically made with a variety of beef and pork products, along with black beans. My version keeps the beans and features seitan, along with sweet potatoes, peppers, and fire-roasted tomatoes. Seasoned with chives, cumin, thyme, and cilantro, feijoada is traditionally garnished with orange slices. Serve over cooked rice or quinoa. Use coconut aminos instead of soy sauce to make this soy-free.

1 tablespoon olive oil or ¼ cup water

1 large red onion, chopped

4 cloves garlic, minced

1 red or yellow bell pepper, seeded and diced

1 small jalapeño, seeded and minced

1 teaspoon dried thyme

1 teaspoon smoked paprika

½ teaspoon ground cumin

1 large sweet potato, peeled and diced

1 (14.5-ounce) can diced fire-roasted tomatoes, undrained

1 cup vegetable broth

3 cups cooked or 2 (15.5-ounce) cans black beans, drained and rinsed

1½ cups chopped seitan, reconstituted Soy Curls, or crumbled vegan chorizo

1 tablespoon soy sauce

Salt and freshly ground black pepper

½ cup chopped fresh cilantro

1 sweet orange (such as navel or cara cara), halved and sliced

Heat the oil or water in a large pot over medium heat. Add the onion and cook until softened, about 5 minutes, Stir in the garlic, bell pepper, and jalapeño and cook another 2 minutes. Stir in the thyme, paprika, cumin, and sweet potato. Add the tomatoes and their juice and the broth and bring to a boil. Lower the heat to a simmer and stir in the beans, seitan, soy sauce, and salt and pepper to taste. Cover and cook until the vegetables are tender and the flavors have developed, about 30 minutes. Stir in the cilantro and serve hot garnished with the orange slices.

Serves 4

LOW OIL
SOY-FREE OPTION

Chimichurri-Grilled Vegetables

In addition to giving grilled vegetables a dynamic flavor, this versatile sauce can be used as a marinade for tofu or portobello mushrooms, a dipping sauce for bread, or alongside empanadas. Using a food processor makes short work of the chopping, but you can use a knife and a cutting board, if you prefer. Serve over cooked rice or quinoa.

Sauce

4 cloves garlic

2 tablespoons chopped red onion or shallot

¾ cup fresh parsley

1 teaspoon fresh marjoram

½ teaspoon salt

¼ teaspoon freshly ground black pepper

2 tablespoons freshly squeezed lemon juice

1½ tablespoons red wine vinegar

¼ cup olive oil

Vegetables

1 large red onion, cut into ½-inch slices

2 large red bell peppers, seeded and quartered lengthwise

3 small zucchini, trimmed and halved lengthwise

4 small portobello mushrooms, stemmed

3 plum tomatoes, halved lengthwise

1 tablespoon olive oil, plus more for grilling

To make the sauce, combine the garlic and onion and pulse until chopped in a food processor. Add the parsley, marjoram, salt, and pepper, and pulse until minced. Add the lemon juice, vinegar, and oil, and process until blended. Transfer to a bowl and set aside until ready to use.

To make the vegetables, first preheat the grill. Brush the onion, bell peppers, zucchini, mushrooms, and tomatoes with enough olive oil to lightly coat. Season with salt and pepper, and grill until softened and lightly browned, turning once, 3 to 8 minutes per side (depending on the vegetable). While the vegetables are cooking, gently heat the reserved sauce. To serve, transfer the vegetables to a serving platter and spoon the sauce on top, or serve the sauce on the side.

Serves 4

GLUTEN-FREE
SOY-FREE
QUICK AND EASY

Brigadiero Chocolate Fudge Truffles

These truffles are frequently served at parties in Brazil. Named for a Brazilian air force brigadier, they are traditionally coated in chocolate sprinkles.

Drain the cashews, then transfer to a food processor. Drain the dates and add them to the cashews, along with 1 tablespoon of water and blend until smooth. Add the cocoa and pulse until completely mixed. Pinch a small piece of the mixture between your fingers to see if it holds together. The mixture should be firm when pinched between your fingers. If the mixture is too dry, add an additional tablespoon of water. If the mixture is too wet, add a little more cocoa powder, 1 tablespoon at a time. If the mixture is not firm enough to roll into balls, refrigerate it for an hour.

Lightly dust your hands with cocoa or grease them with a little vegan butter. Pinch off about 1 teaspoon of the mixture and roll it between the palms of your hands to shape it into a 1-inch ball. Repeat with the remaining mixture until it is used up.

Place the chocolate sprinkles in a shallow bowl and add the truffles, a few at a time, rolling the truffles in the sprinkles to coat. Arrange the truffles on a plate or place them in small paper candy cups. Store leftovers in a tightly sealed container in the refrigerator.

Makes about 18 truffles

GLUTEN-FREE
SOY-FREE
NO OIL

1 cup raw cashews, soaked for 3 hours or overnight

1 cup pitted dates, soaked in warm water for 30 minutes

¼ cup cocoa powder

Chocolate sprinkles or unsweetened cocoa powder, for coating

CHAPTER 6

Africa

As with each region of the world, one could write a separate chapter on every country in Africa, but that would be beyond the scope of this book. However, these simplified notes will help explain at least some of the major differences, and also why I chose to share the particular recipes in this section.

The differences in the African cuisines are vast and varied. This is easily seen by comparing Moroccan cooking to that of West Africa. In Morocco, the heady spice mixtures of cumin, cinnamon, ginger, turmeric, and coriander are more like those of India. The cuisine also has a tradition of using fruit in cooking. Fragrant cilantro, marjoram, and mint combine with the delicate scents of orange flower water and rosewater to provide an intoxicating flavor palette for staples, such as chickpeas, couscous, olives, nuts, dates, oranges, lemons, and pomegranates. Long, slow cooking methods are used, in particular, the tagine (see the recipe for Vegetable Tagine on page 142), which is the name of both a Moroccan stew and the clay pot in which it is cooked.

In West Africa, chiles are used with warming spices, such as cardamom, coriander, and ginger, as well as the haunting flavors of the peanut sauces that grace so many of the dishes of Ghana, Nigeria, and Senegal, among others. Other regions of the African continent also have their plant-based dishes, including Ethiopia, Sierra Leone, and at the opposite end of the continent, South Africa. European influences are evident, since the British and Dutch settled there in the seventeenth century. Add to that the popular spicy curries brought by people from the Indian subcontinent during the nineteenth century.

Many of the mainstay ingredients in Africa include plant-based favorites, such as rice, millet, chickpeas, lentils, and peas, in recipes such as Moroccan Lentil and Chickpea Soup on page 134 or Spicy Lemon Chickpeas, page 136. African cooks also use root vegetables like yam and cassava, as well as plantains, peanuts, and fruits. Most traditional dishes that are not naturally vegan are easily adapted with plant-based ingredients.

Moroccan Lentil and Chickpea Soup

This spicy Moroccan soup known as *harira* features lentils and chickpeas. It is traditionally eaten at the end of Ramadan. Use more or less harissa, according to your own heat tolerance.

1 tablespoon olive oil or ¼ cup water

1 large yellow onion, chopped

3 cloves garlic, chopped

1 teaspoon grated fresh ginger

1 (16-ounce) can crushed tomatoes

⅔ cup dried lentils

½ teaspoon ground coriander

½ teaspoon ground cumin

¼ teaspoon ground turmeric

6 cups vegetable broth

Salt and freshly ground black pepper

1½ cups cooked chickpeas, or 1 (15.5-ounce) can, drained and rinsed

1 to 2 teaspoons Harissa Sauce, homemade (recipe follows) or purchased

2 tablespoons freshly squeezed lemon juice

2 tablespoons chopped parsley or cilantro

Heat the oil or water in a large saucepan over medium heat. Add the onion and cook for 5 minutes to soften. Stir in the garlic and ginger and cook for 30 seconds, or until fragrant. Add the tomatoes, lentils, coriander, cumin, and turmeric. Cook 5 minutes longer, then stir in the broth and season with salt and pepper to taste, depending on the saltiness of your broth. Simmer for 45 minutes, or until the lentils are tender. Stir in the chickpeas, harissa, and lemon juice and cook uncovered for 10 minutes to blend the flavors. Serve hot, sprinkled with parsley or cilantro.

Serves 4 to 6

GLUTEN-FREE
SOY-FREE
LOW OIL

Harissa Sauce

This spicy North African condiment can be added to soups, stews, and grilled vegetables. For a mild version, use ancho or other mild chiles instead of hot ones.

Break the chiles into pieces and soak in hot water for 20 minutes. Drain and transfer to a food processor. Add the garlic, oil, caraway, coriander, and salt and process to a paste. Blend in the water until smooth. Transfer to a small bowl with a tight-fitting lid and refrigerate until needed. Properly stored, it will keep for several weeks.

Makes about ½ cup sauce

GLUTEN-FREE
SOY-FREE
LOW OIL
QUICK AND EASY

6 dried hot red chiles, stemmed and seeded

3 cloves garlic

1 tablespoon olive oil

1 teaspoon ground caraway seeds

1 teaspoon ground coriander

½ teaspoon salt

3 tablespoons water

Spicy Lemon Chickpeas (Fasting Eggs)

The Ethiopian dish called *buticha* is also known as "fasting eggs" because it resembles scrambled eggs in appearance. The flavor of this addictively delicious dish is like a lemony Ethiopian-spiced hummus (only better). I first sampled it at Ethiopic, one of many great Ethiopian restaurants in Washington, DC. Scoop it up with Injera, the distinctive Ethiopian fermented flatbread (page 141), or with your favorite flatbread or crackers.

1½ cups cooked chickpeas, or 1 (15-ounce) can, drained and rinsed

½ cup minced red onion

2 tablespoons bottled chopped japaleños

1 clove garlic, minced

1 teaspoon grated fresh ginger

2 tablespoons freshly squeezed lemon juice

1 tablespoon olive oil

½ teaspoon prepared yellow mustard

½ teaspoon ground turmeric

¼ teaspoon ground cayenne

½ teaspoon salt

¼ teaspoon freshly ground black pepper

Water, as needed

In a large, shallow bowl, mash the chickpeas well with a potato masher. Add the onion, jalapeños, garlic, and ginger and mix well. Alternatively, you can combine the ingredients in a food processor and pulse until chopped, but with a little texture remaining, then transfer to a bowl.

In a separate bowl, combine the lemon juice, oil, mustard, turmeric, cayenne, salt, and pepper, stirring to mix well. Stir the mixture into the chickpea mixture, until well mixed. If the mixture is too thick, add a little water, if needed, and stir to incorporate. Cover and chill for several hours or overnight before serving to allow flavors to blend. Serve chilled or at room temperature.

Serves 4

GLUTEN-FREE
SOY-FREE
LOW OIL
QUICK AND EASY

Chickpea and Kale Wat

The Ethiopian stew known as *wat* can feature a variety of main ingredients, from collards, to red lentils, or my favorite, chickpeas, which I combine here with some kale. Serve with Injera (page 141), or on a bed of cooked rice or couscous. This is a spicy dish, so I've made the cayenne optional if you prefer less heat. You can also use less red pepper flakes, if you wish. Garam masala is a blend of ground spices that is popular in Indian cooking and other cuisines. There are many variations available in well-stocked markets and online.

Heat the oil in a large pot over medium heat. Add the onion and carrots. Cook until softened, about 5 minutes. Stir in the garlic and ginger, then add the garam masala, paprika, thyme, sugar, red pepper flakes, salt, pepper, cumin, and cayenne, if using. Stir in the tomato paste and ½ cup of the water. Add the kale and simmer for 3 to 5 minutes to wilt the kale. Add the chickpeas and the remaining 1 cup of water and bring to a boil. Decrease the heat to low and simmer, covered, until the vegetables are tender and the flavor is developed, about 20 minutes, adding a little more water, if needed, so the stew doesn't dry out or burn.

Serves 4

GLUTEN-FREE
SOY-FREE
LOW OIL
QUICK AND EASY

1 tablespoon olive oil

1 large sweet onion, finely chopped

2 carrots, chopped

3 cloves garlic, minced

1 teaspoon grated ginger

2 teaspoons garam masala (see headnote)

1 teaspoon smoked paprika

1 teaspoon dried thyme

1 teaspoon natural sugar

½ teaspoon red pepper flakes

1 teaspoon salt

¼ teaspoon freshly ground black pepper

¼ teaspoon ground cumin

¼ teaspoon cayenne (optional)

2 tablespoons tomato paste

1½ cups water

4 cups chopped kale (tough stems removed)

3 cups cooked chickpeas, or 2 (15-ounce) cans, drained and rinsed

Black-Eyed Pea Fritters (Akara)

In western Africa, black-eyed pea fritters are known variously as *akara*, *akla*, *binch*, *koose*, and *kwasi*, depending on the region. In addition to being a favorite with home cooks, these tasty fritters are also sold as "fast food" by street vendors. Traditional *akara* recipes often call for using ground soaked (uncooked) black-eyed peas in the fritters, but I find using cooked ones to be more easily digestible. If you don't have time to make the dipping sauce, you can douse them with your favorite hot sauce instead. The fritters are a bit delicate, so use a thin metal spatula to turn them. For a more decadent version, they can be deep-fried.

Dipping Sauce

¼ cup chopped yellow onion

¼ cup chopped bell pepper

¼ cup chopped fresh parsley

1 hot chile, seeded and chopped

1 to 2 ripe tomatoes, coarsely chopped

1 teaspoon hot sauce

½ teaspoon ground cumin

½ teaspoon ground coriander

Salt and freshly ground black pepper

Fritters

2 tablespoons ground flaxseeds, soaked in 1 tablespoon warm water

1½ cups cooked black-eyed peas, or 1 (15.5-ounce) can, drained and well dried

1 small onion, minced

3 cloves garlic, minced

1 hot chile, seeded and minced

½ red bell pepper, seeded and minced

1 tablespoon cornstarch or tapioca flour

½ teaspoon grated fresh ginger

1½ teaspoons ground cumin

1 teaspoon ground coriander

¼ teaspoon cayenne

¾ teaspoon salt

¼ teaspoon freshly ground black pepper

Cornmeal, for dredging

Grapeseed oil or other neutral oil, for frying

To make the dipping sauce, in a food processor, combine the onion, bell pepper, parsley, chile, tomato, hot sauce, cumin, coriander, and salt and pepper to taste. Pulse to combine. Do not overprocess, as you want the sauce to remain somewhat chunky. Transfer to a bowl and set aside while you prepare the fritters.

To make the fritters, in a food processor, combine the flaxseed mixture, black-eyed peas, onion, garlic, chile, bell pepper, cornstarch, ginger, cumin, coriander, cayenne, salt, and pepper. Pulse until well combined. Shape the mixture into 1½-inch balls and refrigerate for 20 minutes. Place the cornmeal in a shallow bowl. Dredge the fritters in the cornmeal. Preheat the oven to warm.

Heat a thin layer of oil in a nonstick skillet over medium-high heat. Add the fritters, in batches if needed, and cook until they are golden brown on both sides, turning once, about 4 minutes per side. Keep the cooked fritters warm in a warm oven until all the fritters are cooked. Serve with the dipping sauce.

Serves 4

GLUTEN-FREE
SOY-FREE

VEGETABLE TAGINE, PAGE 142

Injera

Injera is a spongy crepe-like flatbread with a distinctive sour flavor that is an important part of Ethiopian meals because it doubles as an eating utensil. It is served on a large platter, almost as an edible tablecloth, with portions of various stews and other dishes mounded on it. The injera is then torn off in pieces and used to scoop up the food to eat it. To make *injera*, you should begin a few days in advance, since the batter, made with teff flour, must ferment for at least one to three days.

Put the teff flour in the bottom of a mixing bowl. Add the yeast, then slowly stir in 1 cup of the water until smooth. Cover the bowl loosely and set aside at room temperature (around 70°F) for one to three days to allow it to ferment (longer is better).

By the third day, the batter will have a "fermented" smell and there should be small bubbles on the surface. Stir in the salt. The batter should be similar to thin pancake batter. If it's too thick, stir in as much of the remaining ⅓ cup of water as needed. Set aside.

Lightly oil a nonstick pan or cast-iron 10-inch skillet with grapeseed oil and heat over medium heat. Pour about ½ cup of batter in the center of the skillet, then tilt the skillet to coat evenly and spread the batter. Let the *injera* cook for about 1 minute, or until holes begin to form on the surface. Cover the skillet with a tight-fitting lid and continue to cook for 2 to 3 minutes, or until the edges pull away from the sides and the top surface is dry. Remove the injera from the pan and set aside for 3 to 5 minutes before serving. Repeat with the remaining batter. Injera is best eaten on the same day it is made, but if you must store it, allow it to cook completely before stacking and then wrap tightly to keep soft until needed. It can be refrigerated for up to 5 days.

Note: Teff is a tiny, nutritious grain that contains no gluten. It is available both whole and ground into flour through various online sources.

Makes 4 injera

GLUTEN-FREE
SOY-FREE
LOW OIL

1 cup teff flour (see Note)

⅛ teaspoon active dry yeast

1⅓ cups warm water (105°F)

¼ teaspoon salt

Grapeseed oil or other neutral oil

Vegetable Tagine

Fragrant spices and dried fruits are key to this Moroccan stew traditionally made in a pot by the same name. Tagine pots are typically made of clay, often painted or glazed. It has a flat circular base and a large cone-shaped cover that is designed to circulate the condensation. A Dutch oven or other large covered pot may be used instead. Serve the tagine over couscous or rice accompanied by a small bowl of Harissa Sauce (page 135) for those who like it spicy hot.

1 tablespoon olive oil or ¼ cup water

1 large yellow onion, chopped

1 carrot, chopped

1 sweet potato, peeled and diced

1 red bell pepper, seeded and chopped

3 cloves garlic, minced

1 teaspoon minced fresh ginger

1 teaspoon ground coriander

1 teaspoon ground cumin

½ teaspoon turmeric

½ teaspoon smoked paprika

½ teaspoon salt

¼ teaspoon cayenne

6 cups chopped kale (thick stems removed and discarded)

1 (15-ounce) can chickpeas, drained and rinsed

1 (14.5-ounce) can fire-roasted diced tomatoes, undrained

2 cups vegetable broth

⅓ cup dried apricots, halved or quartered

3 pitted dates, halved

½ cup frozen peas, thawed

⅓ cup pitted green olives, halved lengthwise

2 teaspoons finely grated lemon zest

1 tablespoon freshly squeezed lemon juice

2 tablespoons minced fresh cilantro or parsley

Heat the oil or water in a large pot over medium heat. Add the onion, carrot, sweet potato, bell pepper, and garlic. Cover and cook until softened, about 5 minutes. Stir in the ginger, coriander, cumin, turmeric, paprika, salt, and cayenne. Cook, stirring, for 30 seconds to bring out the flavors. Add the kale, chickpeas, tomatoes and their juice, and broth. Bring to a boil, then decrease the heat to low, cover, and simmer for 30 minutes.

While the tagine is cooking, soak the apricots for 30 minutes in hot water. Drain, cut in half, and add to the pot, along with the dates, peas, olives, and lemon zest. Cook, uncovered, for 15 minutes, or until the vegetables are tender. Stir in the lemon juice and cilantro, then taste and adjust the seasonings, if needed.

Serves 4 to 6

GLUTEN-FREE
SOY-FREE
LOW OIL

Berbere-Spiced Crackers

A popular snack in Ethiopia, *dabo kolo* are spicy crunchy crackers that are easy to make. They are fun to serve as a nibble prior to an African dinner. Because they are so flavorfully spiced, they can be enjoyed alone with a cool drink (they are especially good alongside a cold beer). These tasty crackers also make an interesting garnish for soup— they sure beat oyster crackers for flavor!

In a bowl, combine the flour, berbere, sugar, and salt. Stir in the water and oil, mixing to form a stiff dough.

Turn the dough out onto a lightly floured work surface. Knead lightly for 1 to 2 minutes, or until smooth. Cover with plastic wrap, and set aside to rest for at least 10 minutes or refrigerate for up to 24 hours at this point. (If refrigerated, bring to room temperature for 30 minutes before proceeding.) Lightly grease one or two large baking sheets, or line them with parchment paper. Set aside. Preheat the oven to 350°F.

Divide the dough into four pieces. Roll each piece under your hands into a long rope, about ¼ inch thick. Cut each dough "rope" into ½-inch pieces.

Arrange the dough pieces in a single layer on the prepared baking sheets. Bake for 20 to 25 minutes, or until crunchy and browned, stirring once about halfway through to brown evenly. Allow the baked crackers to cool completely on the pans. Transfer to a bowl to serve or an airtight container to store at room temperature until needed.

Serves 4

SOY-FREE

1 cup white whole wheat flour

1 tablespoon berbere spice blend, homemade (recipe follows) or store-bought

1 teaspoon sugar

½ teaspoon salt

¼ cup water, at room temperature

2 tablespoons olive or grapeseed oil

Berbere Spice Blend

Berbere is a popular spice blend used to season many Ethiopian dishes. In addition to using this spice blend to make the crackers on page 143, you can use it to give an exotic flavor to roasted vegetables, cooked grains, or beans. It can also be used as a zesty spice rub for seitan, tempeh, or tofu.

¼ cup cayenne

2 tablespoons paprika

2 teaspoons salt

½ teaspoon freshly ground black pepper

½ teaspoon ground ginger

½ teaspoon ground coriander

½ teaspoon ground fenugreek

¼ teaspoon onion powder

¼ teaspoon ground cinnamon

¼ teaspoon ground cardamom

¼ teaspoon ground nutmeg

⅛ teaspoon ground allspice

⅛ teaspoon ground cloves

Combine all the ingredients in a small bowl and mix well. To store, transfer to a small jar with a tight-fitting lid and keep in a cool, dry place where it will keep for several months.

Makes about ½ cup berbere spice blend

GLUTEN-FREE
SOY-FREE
LOW OIL
QUICK AND EASY

Spicy Couscous with Carrots and Chickpeas

Harissa adds heat to this easy pilaf made with quick-cooking couscous. Raisins and shredded carrots add sweetness and chickpeas provide the protein.

Heat the oil in a large saucepan or Dutch oven over medium heat. Add the garlic, carrots, scallions, harissa, and salt, and stir until fragrant, about 2 minutes. Stir in the couscous and broth and bring to a boil. Decrease the heat to low, stir in the chickpeas, raisins, and lemon juice. Cover and cook over very low heat just long enough to heat through and absorb the liquid, about 10 minutes. Taste and adjust the seasoning, adding more salt if necessary. Serve sprinkled with parsley.

Serves 4

SOY-FREE
QUICK AND EASY
LOW OIL

1 tablespoon olive oil

1 clove garlic, chopped

1 pound large carrots, coarsely shredded

5 scallions, chopped

2 teaspoons Harissa Sauce (page 135) or store-bought

½ teaspoon salt

1½ cups quick-cooking couscous

3 cups vegetable broth or water

1 (15-ounce) can chickpeas, drained and rinsed

½ cup golden raisins

2 tablespoons freshly squeezed lemon juice

¼ cup minced fresh parsley or cilantro

Falafel Pie

A universally popular street food, falafel are deep-fried patties or balls made from ground chickpeas. They are usually served in a pita pocket or wrapped in some sort of flatbread and topped with lettuce, tomato, and tahini sauce. In this recipe, the falafel mixture is transformed into a crust in this savory pie topped with the usual suspects including tomato, cucumber, lettuce, and a creamy tahini sauce. Tahini is a paste or "butter" made from ground sesame seeds and is widely available in well-stocked supermarkets, ethnic grocers, natural food stores, and online. This recipe serves four as a main dish or 6 as an appetizer.

Base

1½ cooked chickpeas, or 1 (15-ounce) can, drained and rinsed

4 scallions, chopped

1 to 2 cloves garlic, chopped

¼ cup chopped fresh parsley

2 tablespoons chopped fresh cilantro

2 tablespoons tahini

2 tablespoons freshly squeezed lemon juice

1 teaspoon ground coriander

1 teaspoon ground cumin

½ teaspoon salt

¼ teaspoon cayenne

¼ cup all-purpose flour, plus more as needed

½ teaspoon baking powder

Sauce

½ cup plain unsweetened vegan yogurt

½ cup cooked white beans

¼ cup tahini

1 teaspoon minced garlic

2 tablespoons chopped fresh parsley or cilantro

1½ tablespoons freshly squeezed lemon juice

1 teaspoon ground cumin

Salt and freshly ground black pepper

Garnish

1½ cups shredded lettuce

1 cup chopped cucumber

1 cup chopped tomatoes

To make the base, lightly oil a deep-dish pie pan or a 9-inch springform pan and set aside.

In a food processor, combine the chickpeas, scallions, and garlic. Pulse to mince well. Add the parsley, cilantro, tahini, lemon juice, coriander, cumin, salt, and cayenne. Pulse to combine.

Add the flour and baking powder and pulse to just combine. The mixture should hold together when pressed. If it is too wet, add a little more flour. Press the chickpea mixture evenly into the prepared pan and refrigerate for 30 minutes. Preheat the oven to 350°F. Bake for 45 minutes, or until firm and golden brown.

To make the sauce, combine the yogurt, white beans, tahini, garlic, parsley, lemon juice, cumin, and salt and pepper to taste in a food processor and process until very smooth. Taste and adjust the seasonings, if needed.

To assemble, spread the tahini sauce on top of the baked crust. Sprinkle with shredded lettuce, chopped cucumber, and chopped tomatoes. Serve immediately.

Serves 4 to 6

LOW OIL

Caakiri Pudding with Pineapple

Caakiri is a West African dessert that is similar to rice pudding. Traditionally it had been made using African grains such as fonio, a type of millet, but it is now mostly made with couscous. Bits of pineapple, a popular fruit in Africa, add a juicy sweetness to the pudding, while slivered almonds add crunch and fresh mint leaves make a fragrant garnish.

1 cup couscous

½ cup sugar

⅛ teaspoon salt

1½ cups vanilla vegan yogurt

¾ cup nondairy milk

½ teaspoon vanilla extract

⅛ teaspoon ground nutmeg

1 cup fresh or canned crushed pineapple

¼ cup toasted slivered almonds

1 tablespoon small fresh mint leaves

Bring 2 cups of water to a boil in a saucepan. Add the couscous, sugar, and salt. Stir, cover, and remove from the heat. Set aside for 10 minutes.

In a large bowl, combine the yogurt, nondairy milk, vanilla, and nutmeg. Stir in the reserved couscous and pineapple, mixing well to combine. Taste and add a little more sugar, if needed. Serve warm or chilled sprinkled with almonds and mint leaves.

Serves 6

QUICK AND EASY
NO OIL

AJVAR, PAGE 160

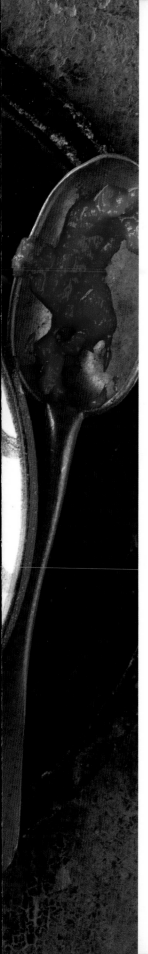

CHAPTER 7

The Middle East

The Middle East abounds with plant-based gastronomic pleasures, from familiar vegan mainstays such as hummus, falafel, and tabbouleh, to stuffed grape leaves, the eggplant dip called baba ghanoush, and *fattoush*, a hearty bread salad. There's also a luscious roasted red pepper and walnut dip called *muhammara* that begs to be served with fragrant flatbreads topped with zesty *za'atar* spices. When several of these flavorful dishes are served at the same time, the meal is called a meze. I call it vegan heaven.

From Iran, Syria, Lebanon, and Turkey, we find traditional dishes made with eggplant, tomatoes, artichokes, rice, couscous, and lentils, among other staples. Seasonings include chiles, garlic, cumin, mint, fennel, saffron, and cinnamon, as well as spice blends such as the Baharat Spice Blend on page 156.

The warm climate of the region supports a wide variety of fresh produce that includes figs, grapes, apricots, and pomegranates. Fruit is generally served with most meals, and dried fruits are enjoyed as snacks or dessert as in Stuffed Dates, Three Ways on page 162.

In addition to working culinary magic with grains and beans, cooks in this region also have a knack for preparing vegetables as evidenced by specialties such as cauliflower served with a tangy orange and tahini sauce and *batata harra*, spicy potatoes made with chiles, garlic, and cilantro. Heartier dishes include *foules mesdames*, a luscious fava bean stew, a hearty lentil soup made with chard and lemon juice, and *sleek*, a satisfying bulgur pilaf made with black-eyed peas and chard or kale, which is used as a delicious stuffing in my recipe for Sleek-Stuffed Eggplant with Pomegranate Sauce (page 158).

Muhammara

Muhammara is a Middle Eastern dip believed to have originated in Aleppo, Syria, but is also popular in Lebanon and Palestine. Made from roasted red peppers, toasted walnuts, and pomegranate syrup, it has an assertive flavor from the peppers with a slight sweetness from the pomegranate. The texture is fairly smooth, but with some texture remaining from the walnuts and bread crumbs. It makes a delicious addition to a meze platter when served as a dip with pita and raw vegetables. It also makes a great spread for a vegetable wrap and can also be used as a sauce for grilled vegetables or kebabs. Use gluten-free bread crumbs to make this gluten free.

1 tablespoon olive oil

1 small yellow onion, finely chopped

2 cloves garlic, minced

1 (7-ounce) jar roasted red peppers, drained or 3 home-roasted red bell peppers

½ cup toasted walnut pieces

½ cup panko bread crumbs

1 tablespoon pomegranate molasses

1 tablespoon freshly squeezed lemon juice

½ teaspoon red pepper flakes

½ teaspoon ground cumin

½ teaspoon salt

¼ teaspoon freshly ground black pepper

Pita triangles, for serving

Heat the oil in a small skillet over medium-high heat. Add the onion and cook until softened and lightly browned. Stir in the garlic and cook until fragrant. Remove from the heat to cool slightly.

Scrape the onion mixture into a food processor. Add the roasted peppers, toasted walnuts, panko, pomegranate molasses, lemon juice, red pepper flakes, cumin, salt, and pepper. Process, pulsing, until well mixed and smooth. Scrape the mixture into a serving bowl. Cover and refrigerate for at least 30 minutes to allow flavors to blend. Bring to room temperature to serve. Serve with pita triangles.

To toast walnuts: Place the walnuts in a dry skillet over medium heat, shaking frequently, until fragrant and lightly browned, about 5 minutes.

Makes about 2½ cups dip

GLUTEN-FREE OPTION
SOY-FREE
QUICK AND EASY
LOW OIL

Baharat-Spiced Baba Ghanoush

The popular eggplant dip known as baba ghanoush gets a flavor boost from the addition of a seasoning blend known as *baharat*. Use this dip in the same way you would use hummus: as part of a meze platter, as a dip for raw vegetables or warm pita wedges, or as a spread for a sandwich wrap. This recipe is soy free if you omit the optional yogurt or use one that is soy free.

Preheat the oven to 375°F. Using a sharp knife, make several deep cuts in the eggplant and place the garlic pieces inside. Place on a baking sheet and bake until soft, about 45 minutes. Let cool. Remove the eggplant skin and discard.

Transfer the eggplant flesh and garlic to a food processor or blender. Add the tahini, yogurt, if using, lemon juice, olive oil, and spice blend. Season with salt to taste and process until smooth. If not using yogurt, you may want to add an additional tablespoon of lemon juice.

Transfer the mixture to a serving bowl and sprinkle with the mint. Serve at room temperature.

Serves 4 to 6

GLUTEN-FREE
SOY-FREE
LOW OIL

1 large eggplant

3 cloves garlic, slivered

⅓ cup tahini (sesame paste)

⅓ cup plain vegan yogurt (optional)

1 tablespoon freshly squeezed lemon juice, plus more as needed

1 tablespoon olive oil

2 teaspoons Baharat Spice Blend (page 156) or store-bought

Salt

2 tablespoons minced fresh mint leaves

Kale-Stuffed Phyllo "Pens"

Variously known as *sigara* (cigarette) or *kalem* (pen) *böregi* (or *börek*), these delicious appetizers are believed to have originated in what is now Turkey. These small cylindrical phyllo pastries filled with a savory stuffing are popular throughout the Middle East, as well as the Mediterranean and parts of Eastern Europe. They are traditionally filled with feta cheese and sometimes vegetables or ground meat. My favorite filling is made with kale and white beans. Wrapped tightly into little phyllo "pens," they look a bit like crispy spanakopita spring rolls.

1 tablespoon olive oil, plus more to brush phyllo

1 medium yellow onion, minced

3 cloves garlic, minced

12 ounces kale, tough stems removed, finely chopped

1 teaspoon dried oregano

2 tablespoons chopped fresh dill

½ teaspoon dried mint

2 teaspoons finely grated lemon zest

1½ cups cooked white beans, or 1 (15.5-ounce) can, drained, rinsed, and mashed

Salt and freshly ground black pepper

8 (14 by 18-inch) sheets phyllo dough, thawed

¼ cup finely ground walnuts

Heat the oil in a deep skillet or Dutch oven over medium heat. Add the onion and garlic and cook until softened, about 4 minutes. Add the kale and cook, stirring, until wilted, about 5 minutes. Stir in the oregano, dill, mint, and lemon zest. Add the mashed white beans and season with salt and pepper to taste. Transfer to a bowl and mix well. Set aside or refrigerate to cool completely before using.

Place a sheet of phyllo dough on a flat work surface. Brush the sheet evenly with olive oil and top it with a second sheet of phyllo. And brush the second sheet with oil. Keep the remaining dough covered with plastic wrap or a clean towel to keep from drying out.

Use a sharp knife to cut the phyllo sheets into three strips. With the short side of the phyllo facing you, spoon a line of the filling (about 1-inch diameter) about 1 inch from the bottom edge of a strip of phyllo, about ½ inch from each side. Fold in the side ends of the phyllo toward the center, then use both hands to tightly roll up the phyllo to enclose the filling, evenly and firmly rolling it up into a tight roll, as you would a spring roll. Transfer the phyllo "pen" to a platter.

Repeat the process for the remaining phyllo until the filling is used up. When all of the *böregi* are assembled, cover tightly with plastic wrap and refrigerate for at least 30 minutes.

To bake, preheat the oven to 400°F. Arrange the *böregi* on a nonstick baking sheet. Brush the top of the phyllo rolls with any remaining oil and sprinkle with the walnuts. Bake until crisp and golden brown, 15 to 18 minutes.

Makes 1 dozen *böregi*

SOY-FREE

AJVAR, PAGE 160

Baharat Spice Blend

Baharat is the name of a spice blend used in Lebanon and throughout the Middle East and North Africa. The word means "spice," and the actual spices in the blend vary from region to region, although most feature black pepper, coriander, cloves, and cumin in the mix. Turkish style *baharat* often includes mint and cassia, whereas Tunisian *baharat* features dried rose petals. *Baharat* spice mixtures can be found at Middle Eastern grocery stores and gourmet grocers. It's a great addition to the baba ghanoush on page 153 and can also be added to bean and grain dishes, or used as a spice rub on grilled vegetables, tofu, tempeh, or seitan.

1 tablespoon freshly ground black pepper

2 teaspoons ground coriander

2 teaspoons ground cumin

1 teaspoon ground fenugreek

1 teaspoon ground cloves or ginger

½ teaspoon ground nutmeg or cinnamon

¼ teaspoon ground allspice or cardamom

In a small bowl, combine the pepper, coriander, cumin, fenugreek, cloves, nutmeg, and allspice and mix until well blended. If not using right away, store in an airtight container, where it will keep for several months.

Makes about 3 tablespoons spice blend

GLUTEN-FREE
SOY-FREE
NO OIL
QUICK AND EASY

Fattoush Wraps

The Lebanese bread salad known as *fattoush*, which combines pieces of toasted pita bread with lettuce, tomatoes, and other salad vegetables tossed in lemon juice and olive oil, is the inspiration for this recipe. These wraps put the salad inside the bread instead of putting the bread into the salad. It has all the same great flavor you'd expect from *fattoush*, but in one convenient edible package.

In a food processor, combine the garlic, chickpeas, tahini, lemon juice, olive oil, salt, and cayenne. Process until smooth and well mixed.

Transfer the mixture to a bowl, stir in the minced onion, parsley, and mint. Taste and adjust the seasonings, if needed.

Spread the mixture onto the flatbreads, dividing evenly. Sprinkle a line of cucumber, tomato, and bell pepper down one-third of each flatbread, then top each with shredded lettuce. Roll up and serve.

Serves 4

SOY-FREE
QUICK AND EASY

2 cloves garlic, crushed

1½ cups cooked chickpeas, or 1 (15-ounce) can, drained and rinsed

1 tablespoon tahini (sesame paste)

⅓ cup freshly squeezed lemon juice

3 tablespoons olive oil

½ teaspoon salt

Pinch of cayenne

⅓ cup minced red onion

⅓ cup chopped fresh parsley leaves

⅓ cup chopped fresh mint leaves

4 *lavash* or other flatbreads

1 large cucumber, peeled, seeded, and chopped

1 large ripe tomato, seeded and chopped

½ small green bell pepper, seeded and chopped

2 cups shredded romaine lettuce

Sleek-Stuffed Eggplant with Pomegranate Sauce

The stuffing, made with greens and black-eyed peas, is called sleek, *derived from the word* silek, *which is Arabic for "chard." While the stuffing is certainly delicious enough to eat on its own, it's even better baked inside an eggplant.*

Eggplant

2 medium eggplants, halved lengthwise

Sleek

½ cup medium-grind bulgur

1¼ cups vegetable broth

1 tablespoon olive oil

1 large yellow onion, finely chopped

9 ounces chard or kale, chopped

3 scallions, chopped

2 teaspoons Baharat Spice
Blend (page 156)

1½ cups cooked black-eyed peas, or
1 (15-ounce) can, drained and rinsed

2 tablespoons freshly
squeezed lemon juice

Salt and freshly ground black pepper

Sauce

1 tablespoon olive oil or ¼ cup water

1 small yellow onion, chopped

½ teaspoon ground turmeric

½ cup ground walnuts

1 cup vegetable broth

Salt and freshly ground black pepper

2 tablespoons tomato paste

2 tablespoons pomegranate
molasses (see Note)

To make the eggplant, preheat the oven to 400°F. Place the eggplant halves on a lightly oiled baking sheet, cut side down. Bake until partially softened, about 15 minutes. Remove from the oven and set aside to cool. When cool enough to handle, scoop out the inside of the eggplants, leaving ¼-inch-thick shells intact. Coarsely chop the eggplant flesh and set aside, along with the shells.

To make the sleek, place the bulgur in a bowl. Add the vegetable broth and set aside for 30 minutes. Heat the oil in a large skillet over medium heat. Add the onion and cook until soft and golden. Add the chard, scallions, spice blend, black-eyed peas, and the reserved bulgur mixture and bring to a boil. Decrease the heat to low, cover, and simmer until tender, about 10 minutes. Stir in the chopped eggplant and lemon juice and season to taste with salt and pepper. Continue cooking to blend the flavors, about 5 minutes.

Divide the stuffing among the eggplant shells and arrange them in a lightly oiled baking dish. Cover tightly and bake until the eggplant shells are tender and the filling is hot, about 20 minutes.

To make the sauce, heat the oil or water in a saucepan over medium heat. Add the onion, cover, and cook until softened, about 5 minutes. Add the turmeric, walnuts, broth, and salt and pepper. Bring to a boil, then lower the heat to a simmer and cook, stirring occasionally, until the sauce begins to thicken, about 15 minutes.

In a small bowl, combine the tomato paste, pomegranate molasses, and ½ cup of hot water. Blend well, then stir into the sauce and decrease the heat to low to keep warm.

To serve, spoon the sauce over the stuffed eggplant. Serve hot.

Note: If pomegranate molasses is unavailable, make your own: Combine ½ cup of bottled pomegranate juice (available in most supermarkets) with ¼ cup of natural sugar in a small saucepan. Bring to a boil, then decrease the heat to low, and cook until reduced by half and syrupy. Stir in 2 tablespoons of lemon juice.

Serves 4

SOY-FREE

Ajvar

This flavorful Balkan condiment (see page 150) made with red peppers can be used as a dip for pita chips or as a sandwich spread with crisp vegetables. It can also be enjoyed as a zesty accompaniment to the Kale-Stuffed Phyllo "Pens" on page 154. *Ajvar* often contains eggplant as well and can be made mild or spicy, according to taste.

1 tablespoon olive oil

3 cloves garlic, chopped

1 fresh hot chile, minced or ½ teaspoon red pepper flakes

2 plum tomatoes, seeded and chopped

2 roasted red bell peppers (jarred or home-roasted), chopped

2 teaspoons freshly squeezed lemon juice

½ teaspoon salt

Freshly ground black pepper

Heat the oil in a skillet over medium heat. Add the garlic and cook until fragrant, 30 seconds. Add the chile and tomatoes and cook for 1 minute, stirring. Add the roasted red peppers and cook for about 10 minutes, stirring occasionally, until the vegetables are softened and well blended.

Transfer the mixture to a food processor. Add the lemon juice, salt, and pepper to taste. Pulse until the mixture is finely minced and well combined. You can leave a little texture remaining or you can puree it until smooth. Transfer to a bowl to serve. Store in a tightly sealed container in the refrigerator where it will keep for up to a week.

Makes about 1½ cups ajvar

GLUTEN-FREE
SOY-FREE
LOW OIL
QUICK AND EASY

Za'atar Roasted Cauliflower

I love roasted cauliflower any way I can get it, and this fragrantly spiced Middle Eastern version, known as *zahra mekhla*, is no exception. *Za'atar* spice is available in Middle Eastern markets, natural food stores, or online. You can also make your own by combining equal amounts of dried thyme, dried marjoram, dried sumac, and sesame seeds and grind them together in a spice grinder to make a fine powder.

Preheat the oven to 450°F. Lightly oil a rimmed baking sheet and set aside.

Break up the large cauliflower slices and place the cauliflower in a bowl. Add 1 tablespoon of the oil and season with salt and pepper to taste. Toss to coat the cauliflower. Spread the cauliflower evenly on the prepared pan. Roast for 25 minutes, or until tender and nicely browned.

While the cauliflower is roasting, heat the remaining tablespoon of oil in a small saucepan over medium heat. Add the garlic and cook until softened and fragrant, about 1 minute. Decease the heat to low. Stir in the tahini, 2 tablespoons of the lemon juice, *za'atar*, cumin, and salt and pepper to taste. Stir in the water and heat over low heat, stirring, until warm. Taste and adjust the seasonings, adding more lemon juice or salt, if needed. Set aside. Top the roasted cauliflower with the sauce and sprinkle with sesame seeds. Serve hot.

Serves 4

GLUTEN-FREE
SOY-FREE

1 medium head cauliflower, cored and cut into ½-inch slices

2 tablespoons olive oil

Salt and freshly ground black pepper

3 cloves garlic, minced

½ cup tahini

2 to 3 tablespoons freshly squeezed lemon juice

1 teaspoon za'atar spice blend

½ teaspoon ground cumin

¼ cup water

Toasted sesame seeds, for garnish

Stuffed Dates, Three Ways

Dates are perfect for stuffing and are so simple to make. This recipe features three different ways to do it. Choose your favorite or make some of each. I like to use the large Medjool dates for stuffing. For the chocolate version, use your favorite dark or semisweet chocolate, depending on your preference.

Chocolate Walnut Dates

20 whole pitted dates

20 toasted walnut halves

8 ounces dark or semisweet vegan chocolate, chopped

Line a baking sheet with waxed paper, parchment paper, or aluminum foil. Stuff each date with a walnut half and set aside.

Place the chocolate in a heatproof bowl and melt in the microwave for 1 to 2 minutes, stirring every 30 seconds, or until almost melted. Stir until smooth.

Dip the stuffed dates into the melted chocolate and transfer to the prepared baking sheet. Place the baking sheet with the dates in the refrigerator for at least 3 hours before serving to allow the chocolate to firm up. Store leftovers in a tightly sealed container in the refrigerator where they will keep for up to a week.

Makes 20 dates

Pecan-Stuffed Dates

Stuff each date with one pecan half and roll them in the confectioners' sugar to coat. Arrange the dates on a serving plate and refrigerate until ready to serve. Store leftovers in a tightly sealed container in the refrigerator where they will keep for up to a week.

Makes 20 dates

20 whole pitted dates

20 toasted pecan halves

Confectioners' sugar, for dusting

Smoked Almond Dates

Stuff each date with one almond and arrange on a serving plate. Serve at once or cover and set aside or refrigerate until needed. Store leftovers in a tightly sealed container in the refrigerator, where they will keep for up to a week.

Makes 20 dates

GLUTEN-FREE
SOY-FREE
QUICK AND EASY
NO OIL

20 whole pitted dates

20 whole smoked almonds

CHAPTER 8

India

India's diverse regions have produced a variety of distinct cuisines, each one using a combination of pungent spices and fresh ingredients to create a palette of flavors unique to each area, such as the Goan tradition of cooking in coconut milk or the tandoori cooking of the Punjab region. As much of India's population is vegetarian, Indian cuisine includes a wealth of colorful vegetable and bean dishes, often served over fragrant basmati rice in the southern regions, or with a variety of tasty breads in the north, accompanied by flavorful salads, chutneys, and other condiments. To me, foods from the Indian subcontinent are a kaleidoscope of rich experiences, and I've selected my favorite go-to dishes to share.

The aromatic spices of India create seemingly ethereal flavors that seduce us with their intoxicating aromas and can transform everyday vegetables such as spinach, cauliflower, eggplant, and tomatoes into extraordinarily flavorful dishes, such as Manchurian Cauliflower (page 176) and Coconut Spinach and Lentil Dal (page 177).

Traditional Indian cooks make their own spice blends that vary for each dish, but you can also find prepared curry pastes and cooking sauces in Indian grocery stores, supermarkets, and natural food stores.

Northern Indian cooking, with its delicate, fragrantly spiced *korma*, *kofta*, and *biryani* dishes, is the type you find most often in Indian restaurants in America. There is typically a variety of vegan fare featured. Despite the hot and spicy reputation of Indian food, a good portion of its cuisine is mild yet flavorful.

To many Westerners, Indian food means "curry," but anyone who knows an *idli* from an *uttapam* will tell you that Indian food isn't just about curry, any more than Italian food is only about pizza. Among the many delights Indian food has to offer are savory snack foods called *chaat* typically sold by street vendors. *Chaat* (Hindi for "to lick or taste") is a term used throughout India to refer to small plates of savory snacks, such as Papri Chaat (page 170). The particular varieties of *chaat* vary from region to region, although the most well-known *chaat* are *pakoras* (vegetable fritters coated in a chickpea batter) and samosas, savory filled pastries believed to have originated prior to the tenth century in Central Asia, arriving in India via trade routes.

HAKKA

Hakka cuisine is neither distinctly Indian nor Chinese. It originated with the Hakka people of China, many of whom settled in Kolkata, India, and thus their own culture is reflected in a cuisine composed of elements of both China and India. This intriguing cuisine, with its elusive and captivating flavors, is popular in India, both as street food and in restaurants. The fusion of these cultures gives us, among other delights, a sublime sauce that combines tamarind with soy sauce, vinegar, and sugar, or perhaps a dish seasoned with sesame oil and ginger blended with cumin and cilantro. Uniquely Indian-Chinese dishes include various noodle and rice preparations as well as Manchurian-style dishes that are often stir-fried and can be served dry or saucy. The dish that is perhaps most well known in the West is the delectable Hakka Noodles (page 175), wherein thin wheat noodles are stir-fried with crisp vegetables and a simple yet flavorful sauce with notes of sesame, ginger, and soy sauce, which the noodles readily absorb.

NEPAL

Due to their common borders, the influence of Indian cuisine is evident in Nepalese food, with their shared fondness for curried dishes, rice, and chutneys, and seasonings of ginger, cumin, and coriander. A couple of Nepalese gems that I love include *dhal bhat tarkari*, which consists of a trio of pureed lentils (*dhal*), rice (*bhat*), and curried vegetables (*tarkari*). The dish is typically served with a spicy condiment called *achar*, often made with tomatoes and hot chiles. The influence of China and Tibet are also evident in the foods of Nepal, notably in perhaps my favorite of all Nepalese specialties, the luscious dumplings known as Vegetable Momos (page 182).

SRI LANKA

Sri Lanka, an island country off the southern coast of India, is home to a variety of culinary traditions, including those of India and Malaysia. For example, like much of India, rice and curry are quite popular in Sri Lanka, with Sri Lankan curries being especially hot and spicy. Flatbreads, such as paratha and chapati, are common as well. Among the more intriguing dishes native to Sri Lanka are hoppers, also called *appa*, which are made from a fermented batter of rice flour, coconut milk, and a little Sri Lankan palm wine. The batter is left to rise, then cooked in a woklike, rounded pan so the dough remains soft and thick on the bottom, and thin and crunchy around the edges.

Kottu is a popular Sri Lankan street food made by stir-frying pieces of *paratha* with spices and vegetables. It is often served with a side of curry sauce to add extra flavor.

Coconut milk and jackfruit are frequently featured in recipes, such as Tofu and Jackfruit Curry on page 184, and food is often served on banana leaves. Chutneys and *sambols* accompany most meals, the most popular being coconut *sambol*, made of ground coconut mixed with chiles and lime juice.

Chickpea and Potato Patties

These patties, called *chola aloo tikki*, are a favorite Indian appetizer or *chaat*. *Chaat* is Hindi for "to lick or taste." The term refers to small bites that are typically purchased from street vendors in India. *Tikki* is another word for *chaat*, and *chola aloo tikki* are particularly delicious little patties made with chickpeas, potatoes, chiles, ginger, and cilantro.

Steam the potatoes in the perforated top of a steamer pot over a saucepan of boiling water until soft, about 10 minutes.

While the potatoes are cooking, mash the chickpeas in a bowl. Add the cooked potatoes and mash them with the chickpeas. Add the chile, ginger, cilantro, lemon juice, salt, and pepper. Mix well, then taste and adjust the seasonings.

Shape the mixture into eight small patties, about ½ inch thick. If the mixture is too wet, stir in a small amount of flour until firm enough to shape into patties.

Heat a thin layer of oil in a large skillet over medium-high heat. Add the patties and cook until both sides are golden brown, turning once, about 3 minutes per side. Serve hot, drizzled with yogurt and your choice of mint-cilantro chutney or tamarind sauce.

Serves 4

GLUTEN-FREE
SOY-FREE OPTION

1 large russet potato, peeled and cut into 1-inch dice

1½ cups cooked chickpeas, or 1 (15-ounce) can, drained and rinsed

1 hot green chile, seeded and minced

1 tablespoon grated fresh ginger

1 tablespoon chopped fresh cilantro

1 teaspoon freshly squeezed lemon juice

½ teaspoon salt

¼ teaspoon freshly ground black pepper

Grapeseed oil or other neutral oil, for frying

Plain unsweetened vegan yogurt (use soy-free yogurt for soy free)

Mint-Cilantro Chutney (page 173) or Tamarind Sauce (page 172)

Papri Chaat

The word *chaat* is used broadly to describe savory snacks served from food carts in India. My favorite *chaat* is *papri* (also called *papdi*) *chaat*. It is made of crispy crackers that are typically topped with cooked potatoes, chickpeas, a drizzle of yogurt, a spicy mint or cilantro chutney, and a sweet tamarind sauce. A feast for the senses, *papri chaat* are all at once crunchy, creamy, spicy, and sweet.

Papri

1 cup white whole wheat flour

1½ tablespoons grapeseed oil or other neutral oil, plus more for frying

½ teaspoon salt

⅓ cup lukewarm water (105° to 115°F)

Toppings

1½ cups cooked chickpeas, or 1 (15-ounce) can, drained and rinsed

½ cup Mint-Cilantro Chutney (page 173) or bottled mint chutney

1 cup plain vegan yogurt (use coconut yogurt for soy free)

1 ripe tomato, finely chopped (optional)

1 teaspoon *chaat masala* (see Note)

1 cup Tamarind Sauce (recipe follows) or bottled tamarind sauce or chutney

½ cup chopped fresh cilantro

Note: *Chaat masala,* a spice mixture that is typically sprinkled on *chaat,* is available in Indian markets and online. It usually contains ground cumin, coriander, *amchur* (mango) powder, and black salt, among other spices. It adds a special flavor layer to *papri chaat,* but may be omitted if unavailable.

For the papri, combine the flour, oil, and salt in a bowl and mix well. Slowly stir in the water to make a smooth but firm dough, kneading for a minute or two to combine well. Do not overknead. Cover the bowl and set aside for 15 to 20 minutes.

Divide the dough into two equal parts. Take one piece of the dough and roll it out extremely thin, less than ¹⁄₁₆ inch thick. Once it is rolled, prick the dough with a fork. Use a 1½- to 2-inch round cookie cutter (or a small drinking glass) to cut the dough into round shapes. Repeat with the remaining half of the dough.

Heat about 1 inch of oil in a deep skillet over medium-high heat. Carefully add some of the *papri* to the hot oil and cook until light golden brown, flipping once, about 1 minute per side. Do not crowd. Be sure not to overcook or allow them to get dark. (Lower the heat if the *papri* begin to get too brown.)

Transfer the cooked papri to a paper towel–lined baking sheet to cool. Continue cooking in batches until all the *papri* are cooked. Let cool completely. The cooled *papri* can be stored at room temperature in an airtight container until needed for up to 3 weeks.

To assemble, coarsely mash the cooked chickpeas in a bowl. Stir in ¼ cup of the mint-cilantro chutney. Arrange the *papri* onto serving plates or in shallow bowls. Top each *papri* with a spoonful each of the cooked chickpea mixture. Spoon on the yogurt, top with the tomato, if using, then sprinkle on the *chaat masala.* Spoon on the remaining ¼ cup mint-cilantro chutney, tamarind sauce, and chopped cilantro. Serve immediately.

Serves 6

SOY-FREE

Tamarind Sauce

Tamarind is sold in many forms: as a paste, concentrate, and in a sticky brick of pulp that must be soaked, kneaded, and strained. For convenience, try to find it in paste or concentrate form. In addition to serving it with Papri Chaat (page 170), it also makes a delicious dipping sauce for *pakoras* or samosas.

⅓ cup tamarind paste or concentrate

⅓ cup pitted dates

1 cup warm water (105° to 115°F)

⅓ cup sugar

½ teaspoon ground cumin

½ teaspoon ground coriander

½ teaspoon ground ginger

½ teaspoon salt

In a food processor or high-speed blender, combine the tamarind paste, dates, water, sugar, cumin, coriander, ginger, and salt. Puree until smooth. Taste and adjust the seasonings, if needed. If the sauce is too thick, add more water, 1 tablespoon at a time, until your desired consistency is reached. Transfer to a bowl and set aside or cover tightly and refrigerate until ready to use. Properly stored, the sauce will keep for a week.

Makes about 1¾ cups sauce

GLUTEN-FREE
SOY-FREE
NO OIL
QUICK AND EASY

Mint-Cilantro Chutney

This fragrant fresh chutney adds a delicious flavor dimension to *papri chaat* when paired with tamarind sauce and a little vegan yogurt. This chutney can be served as a condiment with most any Indian meal.

Combine the mint, cilantro, chile, lemon juice, sugar, and salt in a blender or food processor and process to a paste. Add the water and process until blended. Transfer to a bowl and set aside or cover tightly and refrigerate until ready to use. Properly stored, the chutney will keep well for up to 5 days.

Makes about ¾ cup chutney

GLUTEN-FREE
SOY-FREE
NO OIL
QUICK AND EASY

1 cup packed fresh mint leaves

½ cup packed fresh cilantro leaves

1 serrano or other small hot green chile, seeded and chopped

2 teaspoons freshly squeezed lemon juice

½ teaspoon natural sugar

½ teaspoon salt

¼ cup water

Hakka Noodles

The texture of this dish should be dry rather than saucy, as the noodles absorb the flavorful sauce. For a less spicy dish, use less red pepper flakes and sriracha (or leave them out). For extra protein, add diced extra-firm tofu or thin strips of seitan.

Hakka noodles can be found in well-stocked Asian or Indian markets—look for Wai Wai or Ching brands. If unavailable, you can substitute angel hair pasta, rice or wheat vermicelli, or even ramen noodles. If you use coconut aminos instead of soy sauce, this recipe will be soy free.

Cook the noodles according to the package directions. Drain well, rinsing under cold water, then transfer the well-drained noodles to a bowl. Toss with the sesame oil and set aside.

Heat the grapeseed oil in a wok or large skillet over medium-high heat. Add the onion, cabbage, carrot, bell pepper, garlic, scallions, and ginger and stir-fry for 3 to 4 minutes. Sprinkle with sugar and season with salt and pepper to taste. Add the mushrooms, if using, and red pepper flakes and stir-fry for 1 to 2 minutes longer. Add the cooked noodles, soy sauce, tomato puree, sriracha, and vinegar, and stir-fry for a few minutes longer to mix well and heat through. Taste and adjust the seasonings, if needed. Serve hot.

Note: To make this dish in a flash, buy bagged shredded cabbage and carrots instead of shredding your own, and use the super-quick ramen noodles option. Dinner can be on the table in just a few minutes.

Serves 4

SOY-FREE OPTION
QUICK AND EASY

8 ounces hakka noodles (see headnote)

1 tablespoon sesame oil

1 tablespoon grapeseed oil or other neutral oil

1 small yellow onion, thinly sliced

4 cups shredded cabbage

1 small carrot, coarsely shredded

1 small red bell pepper, seeded and cut into thin strips

3 cloves garlic, minced

4 scallions, minced

1 teaspoon grated fresh ginger

½ teaspoon natural sugar

Salt and freshly ground black pepper

1 cup sliced mushrooms (optional)

½ teaspoon red pepper flakes

3 tablespoons soy sauce

2 tablespoons tomato puree or ketchup

1 teaspoon sriracha or other hot chili sauce

1½ tablespoons rice vinegar

Manchurian Cauliflower

If you enjoy the flavor profiles of Indian and Chinese cooking, chances are you'll love this unique dish, said to be developed by a Chinese community living in India. The tantalizing sauce that cloaks the cauliflower combines ginger, soy sauce, and sesame oil, with tomato puree and cilantro. To make this soy-free, use coconut aminos instead of soy sauce; for gluten free, use a gluten-free flour.

Cauliflower

1 head cauliflower, cut into bite-size florets (about 6 cups)

⅓ cup chickpea flour

⅓ cup all-purpose flour

⅓ cup cornstarch

1 teaspoon garlic powder

½ teaspoon cayenne

½ teaspoon freshly ground black pepper

2 tablespoons soy sauce

½ cup water

Grapeseed oil or other neutral oil, for frying

Sauce

1 large yellow onion, minced

2 cloves garlic, minced

2 teaspoons grated fresh ginger

3 tablespoons soy sauce

1 to 2 teaspoons hot sauce

½ cup tomato puree or ketchup

2 teaspoons toasted sesame oil

½ cup water

2 tablespoons chopped fresh cilantro, for garnish

To make the cauliflower, steam the florets in a perforated steamer pot over a saucepan of boiling water until just tender, about 4 minutes. Drain, rinse with cold water, then pat dry and set aside. Preheat the oven to 250°F.

In a bowl, combine both flours, cornstarch, garlic powder, cayenne, and black pepper. Add the soy sauce and water and mix to make a batter.

Heat a thin layer of oil in a large skillet over medium-high heat. Working in batches, dip the cauliflower pieces in the batter, then add to the hot skillet and cook until golden brown, turning gently about halfway through, 4 to 5 minutes. Transfer to a heatproof platter or baking pan and keep warm in the oven.

To make the sauce, add the onion to the same skillet (used for the cauliflower) over medium-high heat and cook until soft, about 5 minutes. Add the garlic and ginger, and cook 1 to 2 minutes. Stir in the soy sauce, hot sauce, tomato puree, and sesame oil; cook for about a minute. Gradually add the water, stirring constantly, and simmer until the sauce is thickened, about 2 minutes. Taste for seasoning.

Return the fried cauliflower to the pan and stir into the sauce; cook another minute or two to coat. Transfer to a serving bowl and garnish with the cilantro. Serve hot.

Serves 4 to 6

GLUTEN-FREE OPTION
SOY-FREE OPTION

Coconut Spinach and Lentil Dal

This recipe combines two Indian classics: lentil dal and *saag paneer*. The spinach from *saag paneer* (without the cheesy cubes of *paneer*) is paired with a protein-rich lentil dal in a creamy coconut sauce.

Combine the lentils in a large saucepan with 3 cups of water. Bring to a boil. Decrease the heat to low, add the turmeric, and simmer partially covered for 30 minutes, stirring occasionally. Uncover and continue to simmer until the lentils are soft and the liquid is absorbed, about 15 minutes.

While the lentils are cooking, heat the oil or water in a medium skillet over medium heat. Add the onion, cover, and cook until softened, about 5 minutes. Add the garlic, ginger, and chile and cook until fragrant, about 30 seconds. Add the cumin, coriander, garam masala, cardamom, if using, and tomatoes, stirring constantly for about 30 seconds longer. Stir in the spinach, coconut milk, and cilantro and simmer for 5 minutes. Add the spinach mixture to the lentils and stir well to combine. Taste to adjust the seasonings, if needed. Serve hot.

Serves 4

GLUTEN-FREE
SOY-FREE
LOW OIL

1 cup dried lentils

1 teaspoon ground turmeric

Salt

1 tablespoon grapeseed oil or other neutral oil or ¼ cup water

1 medium yellow onion, chopped

1 clove garlic, minced

2 teaspoons minced fresh ginger

1 hot green chile, seeded and minced

1 teaspoon ground cumin

1 teaspoon ground coriander

1 teaspoon garam masala

Pinch of ground cardamom (optional)

1 (14.5-ounce) can diced fire-roasted tomatoes, drained and finely chopped

8 to 10 ounces fresh or frozen spinach, steamed and chopped

1 (13.5-ounce) can unsweetened coconut milk

2 tablespoons chopped fresh cilantro leaves

Tamarind Chickpeas with Green Beans and Cauliflower

This fragrant stew features the sweet-tart flavor of tamarind along with ginger and warming spices in a creamy coconut sauce that envelopes the chickpeas and vegetables. If you wish, you may add diced sweet potatoes to add more bulk or substitute broccoli for the green beans or cauliflower. Serve over cooked brown basmati rice topped with plain vegan yogurt or mango chutney. Warm naan, an Indian flatbread traditionally baked in a tandoor oven, but now widely available in supermarkets, also makes a delicious accompaniment.

1 tablespoon olive oil or ¼ cup water

1 medium yellow onion, chopped

2 cloves garlic, minced

1 small hot green chile, seeded and minced

2 teaspoons grated fresh ginger

2 teaspoons garam masala

1 teaspoon ground cumin

1 teaspoon ground coriander

1 tablespoon tamarind paste

1 teaspoon natural sugar

½ teaspoon salt

1 (14.5-ounce) can diced fire-roasted tomatoes, undrained

6 ounces green beans, trimmed and cut into 1-inch pieces

2 cups small cauliflower florets

3 cups cooked chickpeas, or 2 (15-ounce) cans, drained and rinsed

1 (13.5-ounce) can unsweetened coconut milk

2 tablespoons chopped fresh cilantro

Heat the oil or water in a large pot. Add the onion and cook for 5 minutes to soften over medium-high heat. Lower the heat to medium and stir in the garlic, chile, and ginger and cook for 2 minutes, then stir in the garam masala, cumin, and coriander. Stir in the tamarind paste, sugar, and salt, then add the tomatoes and their juice. Add the green beans, cauliflower, and chickpeas, then add the coconut milk and bring to a simmer over medium heat. Cover and cook for 15 minutes, then uncover and continue cooking until the vegetables are tender and the flavors are well blended, about 5 minutes longer. Taste and adjust the seasonings, if needed. Garnish with cilantro and serve hot.

Serves 4

GLUTEN-FREE
SOY-FREE
LOW OIL

Carrot-Mung Bean Salad

This is a variation of a recipe for *kosambri*, a traditional South Indian salad, shared with me by a lovely Indian woman in the market many years ago. We were standing near the yellow split mung beans when I asked her how she prepares them. She promptly wrote down her family's recipe for this salad. I never saw her again, but all these years later, I'm still enjoying the salad. You can prepare this salad ahead of time, but if you do, reserve the cilantro and add just before serving.

Soak the mung beans in 3 cups of water for 3 hours or up to 8 hours. Drain the beans and place them in a large bowl. Add the carrot, cucumber, cashews, and lemon juice. Stir to combine and set aside.

Heat the oil in a small skillet over medium heat. Add the mustard seeds and cover the pan. The mustard seeds will start popping. When the popping stops, add the chile, and stir for 30 seconds to bring out the flavor, then stir in the ginger and remove from the heat to cool. Add the mixture to the salad along with the cilantro and season with salt to taste. Toss gently to combine and serve.

Note: Look for yellow split mung beans in Indian markets, natural food stores, or online.

Serves 4

GLUTEN-FREE
SOY-FREE
LOW OIL
QUICK AND EASY

⅓ cup yellow split mung beans, washed and drained (see Note)

1 large carrot, coarsely shredded

1 cup finely chopped cucumber

⅓ cup unsalted roasted cashews

2 tablespoons freshly squeezed lemon juice

2 teaspoons grapeseed oil

½ teaspoon black mustard seeds

1 hot green chile, seeded and chopped

1 teaspoon grated fresh ginger

2 tablespoon chopped fresh cilantro

Salt

Kofta Curry

Koftas are essentially Indian meatballs, and *kofta* curry are meatballs, often made with some sort of meat, in a creamy curry sauce. The koftas in this recipe are made with a chickpeas, and a variety of vegetables and seasonings. For a mild version, omit the chiles. Serve over hot basmati rice to soak up the delicious sauce. Use gluten-free bread crumbs to make this gluten-free.

Koftas

1 cup finely chopped carrot

1 cup finely chopped cauliflower

1 small russet potato, peeled and finely diced (1 cup)

1 cup cooked or canned chickpeas, blotted dry

½ cup thawed frozen green peas, blotted dry

½ cup dry bread crumbs, plus more as needed

2 tablespoons chopped fresh cilantro

1 teaspoon grated fresh ginger

1 teaspoon garam masala

1 teaspoon ground coriander

½ teaspoon ground cumin

½ teaspoon ground turmeric

¼ teaspoon cayenne

Salt and freshly ground black pepper

Grapeseed oil or other neutral oil, for frying

Gravy

1 tablespoon grapeseed oil or other neutral oil

1 medium yellow onion, chopped

3 cloves garlic, chopped

1 to 2 green chiles, seeded and chopped

1 teaspoon grated fresh ginger

2 teaspoons garam masala

1 teaspoon ground coriander

½ teaspoon sugar

1 (14.5-ounce) can crushed tomatoes

Salt and freshly ground black pepper

1 tablespoon cornstarch blended with ¼ cup water

½ cup unsweetened coconut milk or other nondairy milk

To make the *koftas*, steam the carrot, cauliflower, and potato in a steamer basket over a saucepan of boiling water until tender, then blot dry and transfer to a bowl. Add the chickpeas and mash well. Stir in the green peas, bread crumbs, cilantro, ginger, and spices. Press a small amount of the mixture together. It should hold together when pressed. If the mixture is too wet, add more bread crumbs. Use your hands to shape the mixture into 1½-inch balls or patties, pressing well so they hold together.

Heat a thin layer of oil in a large skillet over medium-high heat. Add the *kofta* balls, in batches if necessary, and sauté until golden brown all over, about 8 minutes. Remove with a slotted spoon and keep the cooked *kofta* warm in a low oven.

To make the gravy, heat the oil in a skillet over medium-high heat. Add the onion and cook until softened, about 5 minutes. Add the garlic, chile, and ginger and cook for 30 seconds, then stir in the garam masala, coriander, sugar, tomatoes, and salt and pepper to taste. Simmer, stirring, for 3 to 4 minutes to blend the flavors. Transfer the tomato mixture to a food processor or blender. Add the cornstarch mixture and blend until smooth. Return the mixture to the saucepan and bring to a boil, stirring to thicken. Decrease the heat to low, stir in the coconut milk, and keep warm until ready to serve.

To serve, transfer the koftas to a serving bowl and pour the gravy over the koftas. Serve hot.

Serves 4

GLUTEN-FREE OPTION
SOY-FREE

Vegetable Momos

Momos are filled dumplings similar to Chinese dumplings (*bāozi* or *bao*) or Japanese *gyoza*, These are popular in Nepal, Tibet, and northeast India. Traditionally filled with a variety of different meats and vegetables, depending on the region, here they are made with a vegetable filling of cabbage, carrot, and onion. *Momos* are especially delicious accompanied by a bowl of Tomato Achar (page 183). To save time, you can use vegan wonton or *gyoza* wrappers instead of making your own.

2 cups all-purpose flour

2 tablespoons grapeseed oil or other neutral oil

Salt

¾ cup hot water (115° to 120°F)

1 small yellow onion, minced

3 cloves garlic, minced

2 teaspoons grated fresh ginger

1 teaspoon curry powder

¼ teaspoon freshly ground black pepper

3 cups finely shredded cabbage

½ cup coarsely shredded carrot

½ cup minced scallions

1 cup chopped fresh cilantro

Tomato Achar (page 183), for serving

In a large bowl, combine the flour, 1 tablespoon of the oil, ¼ teaspoon of salt, and stir in the water. Mix well, kneading until the dough is smooth. Add a bit more flour if the dough is too sticky or a splash more water if it's too dry. Cover and set aside for 30 minutes.

While the dough is resting, heat the remaining 1 tablespoon of oil in a large nonstick skillet over medium heat. Add the onion and cook until softened, about 5 minutes. Stir in the garlic, ginger, curry powder, and pepper and cook for 30 seconds. Add the cabbage and carrot and stir-fry until softened, about 5 minutes. Stir in the scallions and cilantro, and season to taste with salt. Mix well and remove from the heat to cool before assembling.

When ready to assemble, flour your hands and knead the dough for 2 minutes on a lightly floured surface, then divide into 1½-inch pieces. Roll each piece of dough into a ball between your palms. Repeat with the remaining dough pieces. On a lightly floured surface, use a rolling pin to roll out the balls into flattened 4-inch circles.

Preheat a steamer, oiling the steamer rack well to prevent the dumplings from sticking. Place one wrapper on a work surface and spoon about 1½ tablespoons of the filling mixture into the center. Use your hands to bring all edges together to the center, making folds with the dough. Pinch the folds to tightly seal the stuffed dumpling. Repeat with the remaining ingredients.

Arrange the uncooked *momos* in the prepared steamer. Cover and steam until cooked through, about 10 minutes. Remove the dumplings from the steamer and arrange on a plate. Serve hot with the Tomato Achar.

Makes about 24 *momos*

SOY-FREE

Tomato Achar

Similar to chutney or salsa, *achar* is a must-have condiment for *momos*, but it's also delicious spooned over rice or grilled tofu. It's even good as a dip for tortilla chips or pita chips. If you prefer a less spicy sauce, use only one chile instead of two or three.

Prominent in Nepali cuisine, *achar* can be spicy, sour, or sweet, and can be made with a variety of ingredients, including tomatoes, radishes, and even cooked potatoes.

In a blender or food processor, combine the tomatoes, cilantro, chiles, garlic, ginger, lemon juice, cumin, curry powder, paprika, sugar, and salt. Blend until smooth, then taste and adjust the seasonings, if needed. Transfer to a bowl to serve. If not serving right away cover and refrigerate for up to a week.

Makes about 2 cups *achar*

GLUTEN-FREE
SOY-FREE
NO OIL
QUICK AND EASY

1 (14-ounce) can fire-roasted tomatoes, well drained

1 cup chopped fresh cilantro

2 to 3 fresh hot chiles, seeded and minced

2 cloves garlic, minced

1 tablespoon grated fresh ginger

2 teaspoons freshly squeezed lemon juice

½ teaspoon ground cumin

½ teaspoon curry powder

½ teaspoon smoked paprika

½ teaspoon sugar

½ teaspoon salt

Tofu and Jackfruit Curry

This curry combines the tofu of China, jackfruit of Southeast Asia, and a spice blend from Sri Lanka, making it a "curry without borders." If you don't want to make your own spice blend, you can substitute your favorite Indian curry powder. The texture of jackfruit is so similar to meat that it is sometimes called "vegetable meat" in certain parts of Asia. You can replace the tofu with seitan, chickpeas, or reconstituted Soy Curls.

14-ounces extra-firm tofu, drained and pressed

1 (20-ounce) can jackfruit, packed in water or brine, drained (see Note)

1 tablespoon grapeseed oil or other neutral oil

1 medium yellow onion, chopped

4 cloves garlic, chopped

2 teaspoons grated fresh ginger

1 hot green chile, seeded and chopped

2 tablespoons tomato paste

1 tablespoon or more Sri Lankan Curry Powder (recipe follows) or other hot curry powder

1 (13-ounce) can unsweetened coconut milk

Salt and freshly ground black pepper

2 tablespoons freshly squeezed lemon juice

4 cups cooked brown basmati rice, for serving

¼ cup roasted cashews

¼ cup chopped fresh cilantro

Cut the tofu into bite-size pieces and thinly slice the jackfruit. Set aside.

Heat the oil in a saucepan over medium heat. Add the onion, cover, and cook until tender, about 5 minutes. Remove the lid, stir in the garlic, ginger, and chile and cook for 1 minute to soften. Stir in the tomato paste and curry powder, and cook, stirring, for 1 minute. Slowly stir in the coconut milk, tofu, and jackfruit and bring just to a boil.

Lower the heat to a simmer and add salt and pepper to taste. Simmer for 15 minutes, stirring occasionally to allow the flavors to meld. Stir in the lemon juice, then taste and adjust the seasonings, if needed. Serve hot over cooked brown basmati rice sprinkled with cashews and cilantro.

Note: Canned jackfruit (packed in water or brine) is readily available at Asian markets and online. (Do not get the kind packed in syrup.) If you can't find it, substitute a favorite cooked vegetable, such as diced zucchini or broccoli florets.

Serves 4 to 6

GLUTEN-FREE
QUICK AND EASY
LOW OIL

Sri Lankan Curry Powder

Traditionally, dried curry leaves and *rampe* (or *pandan*) are used in Sri Lankan curry spice mixtures, but as they are difficult to find, this recipe doesn't call for them and is delicious without them. For a less hot curry powder, cut back on the chiles; for a spicier version, add an extra one. In addition to using in Tofu and Jackfruit Curry on page 184, you can use this curry powder in virtually any recipe calling for curry powder—or to simply jazz up cooked rice.

Toast all the ingredients in a small dry skillet over medium heat, stirring constantly until they are fragrant and lightly browned, 1 to 2 minutes. Be careful not to let them burn.

Transfer the toasted spices to a clean spice grinder, high-speed blender, or food processor and grind to a fine powder. The curry powder is now ready to use in recipes. If not using right away, allow the mixture to cool completely, then transfer to a glass jar with a tight-fitting lid and store in the refrigerator or at room temperature for up to 3 months.

Note: Fenugreek seeds are the seeds of the fenugreek plant. They are used in Indian and Sri Lankan cooking and can be found in Indian markets, well-stocked supermarkets, and online. They have a pleasantly bitter taste and should be used sparingly so as not to overwhelm a dish.

Makes about ¼ cup curry powder

GLUTEN-FREE
SOY-FREE
QUICK AND EASY
NO OIL

2 teaspoons coriander seeds

1 teaspoon cumin seeds

1 teaspoon fennel seeds

½ to 1 teaspoon fenugreek seeds (optional, see Note)

1 small cinnamon stick

¼ teaspoon whole cloves

¼ teaspoon cardamom seeds

3 dried hot red chiles

¼ teaspoon whole brown mustard seeds

¼ teaspoon whole black peppercorns

Coconut Sambol

Sri Lankan *pol sambol* is an addictively flavorful condiment made with coconut, lime juice, and ground chiles. The flavor should be a harmonious blending of spicy, sour, and salty, according to your taste. Some versions of *pol sambol* leave out the shallot, while others include a bit of Maldive fish, coarsely ground black pepper, and minced curry leaves. Use a food processor to finely chop the coconut and shallot, if desired. Enjoy *pol sambol* on its own with some flatbread to scoop it up, or alongside a rice or curry dish. It is an ideal accompaniment to Tofu and Jackfruit Curry on page 184.

1½ cups grated fresh coconut, or 1 cup dried unsweetened

2 tablespoons finely minced shallot

½ to 1 teaspoon cayenne

½ teaspoon paprika

½ teaspoon salt

1 to 2 tablespoons freshly squeezed lime juice

½ cup unsweetened coconut milk (if using dried coconut)

In a bowl, combine the coconut, shallot, ½ teaspoon cayenne, paprika, salt, and 1 tablespoon of the lime juice, or to taste. Stir to mix well. If using dried coconut, heat the coconut milk in a saucepan or in the microwave until hot. Stir the coconut milk into the coconut mixture.

Set aside the *sambol* at room temperature for 30 minutes to allow flavors to develop. Taste and adjust the seasonings, adding any or all of the additional cayenne and lime juice, as desired. If not using right away, cover and refrigerate until needed.

Makes about 1½ cups *sambol*

GLUTEN-FREE
SOY-FREE
QUICK AND EASY
NO OIL

Cardamom Chickpea Cookies

These fragrant cookies are inspired by the Indian cookie known as *laddu*, made with toasted chickpea flour and ground cardamom. Traditionally, *laddu* are rolled into small balls (*laddu* means "ball" in Sanskrit) and are not baked, but I break with tradition with this slightly flattened baked version. Chickpea flour is widely available at natural food stores, ethnic markets, and online. Toasting the chickpea flour removes any raw taste and gives it a richer nutty flavor. These flavorful cookies are especially good served with hot chai.

Spread the chickpea flour and ground almonds in a large skillet over medium heat. Cook, stirring constantly, until the flour and almonds begin to darken and become fragrant, 4 to 5 minutes. Watch carefully, so it doesn't burn. Remove from the heat and continue to cook, stirring for another minute or two to prevent scorching, until the flour has darkened completely. Transfer the toasted flour and almonds to a heatproof bowl and stir in the cardamom and sugar. Mix well to combine thoroughly. Set aside to let cool to room temperature.

Cut the vegan butter into the chickpea flour mixture. Add the almond milk and almond extract, if using, stirring until it is a workable dough, adding more almond milk if the mixture is too dry, or a little chickpea flour if it is sticky.

Dust a little chickpea flour on your work surface, then place the dough on the work surface and flatten the dough into a 6-inch square about ¾ inch thick. Wrap the dough in plastic wrap and refrigerate for 1 hour.

Preheat the oven to 300°F. Unwrap the dough, roll out the dough, and cut into desired shapes, using a knife or cookie cutters. Arrange the cookies on nonstick cookie sheets, spaced 1-inch apart. Press the crushed pistachios into the top of the cookies. Bake for about 25 minutes, or until the bottoms of the cookies are golden.

Remove from the oven, and set aside to let cool to room temperature before serving. To store, transfer to an airtight container for up to 2 weeks.

Makes about 2 dozen *laddu*

1½ cups chickpea flour

¼ cup finely ground almonds or pistachios

½ teaspoon ground cardamom

⅔ cup confectioners' sugar

¼ cup vegan butter

⅓ cup almond milk

⅛ teaspoon almond extract (optional)

¼ cup crushed pistachios

GLUTEN-FREE
SOY-FREE

CHAPTER 9

Asia

I have a particular affinity to the cuisines of Asia. It's fair to say I've never encountered a dish from that part of the world that I didn't like. I'm continually amazed at the captivating flavors that come from Asian cuisines, from the delicately seasoned cooking of Japan to the fiery dishes of Thailand, the hearty specialties of Korea and China, and the fragrant cuisines of Vietnam and Indonesia. By virtue of geography, similarities exist in the use of certain ingredients throughout the entire region, such as rice and soy sauce, but if you are like me, you love to discover each unique cuisine and regional specialties within each country.

Like the chapter devoted to the food of India, recipes from the countries of China, Japan, Korea, Thailand, Vietnam, and Indonesia could easily fill their own chapters. Since that would be beyond the scope of this book, I've endeavored to choose some representative recipes from each of these countries for this section.

China

The recipes in this book are my personal snapshot of cuisines from around the world, shown through the subjective lens of my personal preferences. But some countries are so rich in regional variety, a snapshot barely scratches the surface. China is a great example of this.

In a country that more than 1.35 billion people call home, cooking has been an art form for a millennia before France was France. Meal preparation reflects table etiquette, appearance, and taste as described by Confucius, a Chinese philosopher, and nutrition and balance found in Taoism, an ancient religious philosophy that emphasizes harmonious living.

The regional cuisines of China are distinctive, even from each other. When Westerners speak of Chinese food, they usually refer to Cantonese cuisine, owing to the immigration of workers from Guangdong in the nineteenth century. Others include Hunan and Szechuan, the "spicy" cuisines of China. Hunan is known for its use of oil, rich colors, and cooking techniques that produce a variety of textures as well as the savory and spicy flavors and seasonal menus. Szechuan cuisine is known for its bold flavors and skillful cooking, claiming thirty-eight different cooking methods. It features pungent seasonings including the "three peppers" (prickly ash, black pepper, and hot red chile), "three aromas" (shallot, ginger, and garlic), "seven tastes" (sweet, sour, tingling, spicy, bitter, piquant, and salty), and "eight flavors" (fish-flavored, sour with spice, pepper-tingling, odd flavor, tingling with spice, red spicy oily, ginger sauce, and home cooking). Some of these features are evident in Kung Pao Seitan and Eggplant (page 194) and Szechuan Bok Choy (page 199).

I can only include a small number of the many Chinese dishes that I enjoy, and I offer here the dishes that I love to make at home, such as Stay-in Vegetable Fried Rice (page 193) and Sesame Noodles with Tofu (page 196), when the desire for Chinese food strikes.

Lettuce Wraps

What's not to love about lettuce wraps? Made famous by a popular Chinese/American restaurant chain, they're loaded with great flavors and textures, filled with healthy and delicious ingredients, easy to make, and fun to eat! They can be served as a light lunch, or enjoy them as an appetizer, by spooning the filling into smaller lettuce cups. Here they are filled with a savory tofu and vegetable mixture, while in restaurants, you're more likely to find a chicken or shrimp filling.

Sauce

3 tablespoons soy sauce

3 tablespoons rice vinegar

1 tablespoon peanut butter

1 tablespoon agave nectar

1 teaspoon Asian garlic-chili sauce

1 teaspoon grated fresh ginger

1 teaspoon toasted sesame oil

Filling

3 tablespoons hoisin sauce

3 tablespoons soy sauce

2 teaspoons rice vinegar

1 teaspoon Asian garlic-chili paste

2 teaspoons toasted sesame oil

½ cup minced yellow onion

1 carrot, coarsely shredded

1 cup chopped white or shiitake mushrooms

1 teaspoon grated fresh ginger

14 ounces extra-firm tofu, drained, pressed, and crumbled

4 scallions, chopped

1 head Bibb or Boston lettuce, leaves separated

¼ cup chopped or crushed roasted peanuts

To make the sauce, combine the soy sauce, vinegar, peanut butter, agave, garlic-chili sauce, ginger, and sesame oil in a bowl or a blender and stir or blend until smooth and well mixed. Set aside.

To make the filling, combine the hoisin, soy sauce, vinegar, and chili paste in a bowl, stirring to mix well. Set aside.

Heat the oil in a large skillet over medium heat. Add the onion, carrot, mushrooms, and ginger and stir-fry for 3 minutes to soften. Stir in the tofu, scallions, and the reserved hoisin mixture and cook for 5 minutes to blend flavors and heat through, stirring to evaporate any liquid.

To serve, spoon the tofu mixture into the lettuce leaves, drizzle with the reserved sauce, and sprinkle with peanuts. Serve immediately.

Serves 4

GLUTEN-FREE
QUICK AND EASY

Stay-in Vegetable Fried Rice

A staple of Chinese restaurants in the United States, take-out fried rice can be too oily, contain not enough vegetables, and be flavorless. It also generally contains scrambled egg, which I've replaced with crumbled tofu. With this recipe you can stay in and make it yourself, using less oil, adding more vegetables, and seasoning it just the way you like it.

Heat the grapeseed oil in a large skillet or wok over medium-high heat. Add the onion and carrot and stir-fry for 3 minutes. Add the scallions, garlic, and ginger and stir-fry for 1 minute longer. Stir in the tofu, peas, and rice, then add the soy sauce, vinegar, sugar, and sesame oil. Stir-fry to mix well and heat through until hot, about 5 minutes. Serve hot.

Serves 4

GLUTEN-FREE
QUICK AND EASY

2 tablespoons grapeseed oil or other neutral oil

1 medium yellow onion, chopped

1 large carrot, coarsely shredded

5 scallions, chopped

2 cloves garlic, minced

1½ teaspoons grated fresh ginger

8 ounces extra-firm tofu, well-drained and crumbled

¾ cup frozen green peas, thawed

3 cups cold cooked long-grain rice

¼ cup soy sauce

2 tablespoons rice vinegar

½ teaspoon natural sugar

1 teaspoon dark sesame oil

Kung Pao Seitan and Eggplant

This spicy Szechuan stir-fry traditionally made with chicken is a fixture on American Chinese restaurant menus. Eggplant and seitan replace the chicken in this version, although you could instead use tempeh, extra-firm tofu, reconstituted Soy Curls, or sliced mushrooms. Instead of snow peas (or in addition) you can add other vegetables such as thinly sliced carrot or Chinese cabbage.

1 tablespoon cornstarch

2 teaspoons natural sugar

1 teaspoon red pepper flakes

⅓ cup soy sauce

2 tablespoons dry sherry or rice wine

1 tablespoon toasted sesame oil

1 teaspoon hoisin sauce

½ cup water

1 tablespoon grapeseed oil
or other neutral oil

1 medium yellow onion, chopped

8 ounces seitan, cut into 1-inch dice

8 ounces eggplant, peeled
and cut into ½-inch dice

2 cloves garlic, minced

1 teaspoon grated fresh ginger

1 large red bell pepper,
seeded and diced

2 ounces snow peas, trimmed

3 tablespoons dry-roasted
unsalted peanuts or cashews

3 to 4 cups hot cooked long-grain rice

In a bowl, combine the cornstarch, sugar, red pepper flakes, and soy sauce, stirring to blend well. Stir in the sherry, sesame oil, hoisin, and water, mixing well. Set aside.

Heat the grapeseed oil in a wok or large skillet over medium-high heat. Add the onion and stir-fry for 3 minutes. Add the seitan and eggplant and stir-fry until lightly browned, about 5 minutes. Add the garlic, ginger, bell pepper, and snow peas and stir-fry for 1 minute. Stir in the reserved soy sauce mixture and bring to a boil. Lower the heat to a simmer and cook until the vegetables are crisp-tender and the sauce is thickened, 2 to 3 minutes longer. Stir in the peanuts and serve hot over rice.

Serves 4

QUICK AND EASY

Sesame Noodles with Tofu

This luscious stir-fry is inspired by the classic Taiwanese sesame noodle dish called *ma jiang mian*. I like to combine the chewy noodles with lots of crisp vegetables and diced tofu, all cloaked with a delicious sauce made creamy with sesame paste. Black vinegar is traditional to the original, but rice vinegar may be substituted. For a spicier sauce, add more sriracha. Some Chinese noodles contain eggs, so be sure to check the ingredient lists before you buy them. Regular linguine makes a good substitute. Use rice noodles or other gluten-free noodles to make this gluten-free.

3 tablespoons soy sauce

3 tablespoons sesame paste

2 tablespoons black vinegar or rice vinegar

1 tablespoon vegan oyster sauce

1 teaspoon sugar

½ teaspoon sriracha sauce

⅓ cup hot water

12 ounces vegan Chinese noodles or linguine

2 teaspoons toasted sesame oil

2 tablespoons grapeseed oil or other neutral oil

8 ounces extra-firm tofu, drained and cut into ½-inch dice

3 cups shredded napa cabbage

1 carrot, coarsely shredded

2 cloves garlic, minced

2 teaspoons grated fresh ginger

4 scallions, chopped

2 ounces snow peas, trimmed and cut diagonally into 1-inch pieces

2 tablespoons toasted sesame seeds

In a small bowl combine the soy sauce, sesame paste, vinegar, oyster sauce, sugar, and sriracha. Stir to blend well, then stir in the water and set aside.

Cook the noodles according to the package directions. Drain and return to the pot. Add the sesame oil and toss to coat. Set aside.

Heat 1 tablespoon of the grapeseed oil in a large skillet or wok over medium-high heat. Add the tofu and stir-fry until it is golden brown all over, about 4 minutes. Remove the tofu from the skillet and set aside.

Reheat the skillet with the remaining 1 tablespoon of grapeseed oil. Add the cabbage and carrot and stir-fry for 1 minute to soften. Add the garlic, ginger, scallions, and snow peas, and stir-fry for 1 minute. Add the reserved tofu, noodles, and sauce and stir-fry until hot and well combined. Taste and adjust the seasonings, if needed. Serve hot sprinkled with sesame seeds.

Serves 4

GLUTEN-FREE OPTION
QUICK AND EASY

Red-Cooked Tempeh

Red cooking, or *hong shao*, is a method of braising in soy sauce and rock sugar that produces deeply savory dishes with a rich mahogany hue. A specialty of Shanghai, tempeh, tofu, or seitan all do well made this way. The soy sauce thickens during cooking while the sugar caramelizes, producing a glaze-like sauce. Traditionally aromatics like ginger, star anise, and citrus peel are used for depth of flavor, but I find that a little hoisin sauce works well, with less fuss, and adds to the color.

In a small bowl, combine the soy sauce, sherry, vinegar, hoisin, chili paste, and ½ cup of the water, stirring to blend. Set aside.

Heat the oil in a deep skillet or wok over medium-high heat. Add the sugar, stirring to dissolve. Add the tempeh, mushrooms, and garlic, and stir-fry for 1 minute. Add the soy sauce mixture and stir-fry for 2 to 3 minutes, stir-frying to coat the tempeh. Stir in the remaining ½ cup of water and bring to a boil. Decrease the heat to low and simmer for 20 minutes, or until the sauce has thickened, stirring occasionally. If the sauce hasn't thickened enough, turn up the heat to reduce the liquid further, until the desired consistency is reached. Taste and adjust the seasonings, if needed. Serve hot sprinkled with scallions.

Serves 4 to 6

GLUTEN-FREE
LOW OIL

2 tablespoons soy sauce

2 tablespoons dry sherry

1 tablespoon rice vinegar

1 tablespoon hoisin sauce

1 teaspoon Asian chili paste (such as sambal oelek)

1 cup water

1 tablespoon grapeseed oil or other neutral oil

1 teaspoon natural sugar

1 pound tempeh, steamed for 15 minutes, then cut into ½-inch dice

6 ounces fresh shiitake mushrooms, stemmed and halved

2 cloves garlic, minced

4 scallions, thinly sliced diagonally

Szechuan Bok Choy

This easy but flavorful stir-fry is typical of the cuisine of the Szechuan province of China. Made with bok choy, it's a delicious side dish but you could add strips of tofu or seitan and serve it over rice to make it a satisfying meal. This stir-fry is also delicious made with broccoli, green beans, or asparagus.

Heat the grapeseed oil in a wok or large skillet over medium-high heat. Add the bok choy and shallots and stir-fry for 2 to 3 minutes, or until almost tender. Add the garlic, ginger, and scallions and stir-fry until fragrant, about 30 seconds. Add the soy sauce, sesame oil, mirin, red pepper flakes, and sugar and stir-fry until the bok choy is tender and nicely coated with the sauce, 1 to 2 minutes.

Serves 4

GLUTEN-FREE
QUICK AND EASY

1 tablespoon grapeseed oil or other neutral oil

1½ pounds baby bok choy, trimmed and halved lengthwise

3 shallots, minced

2 cloves garlic, minced

2 teaspoons grated fresh ginger

4 scallions, minced

3 tablespoons soy sauce

1 tablespoon toasted sesame oil

1 tablespoon mirin

1 teaspoon red pepper flakes

1 teaspoon natural sugar

Almond Cookies

Almond cookies are a Chinese New Year's tradition because they are believed to symbolize coins and abundance in the new year. They are typically made with egg and sometimes lard, but this version assures that you don't have to miss out. If you need another reason to make a batch of these crisp chewy cookies, April 9 is Chinese Almond Cookie Day. A soy-free vegan butter will make this recipe soy free.

2 cups all-purpose flour

1 cup finely ground almonds (almond meal)

1 cup natural sugar

1 teaspoon baking soda

½ teaspoon salt

¾ cup vegan butter

2 tablespoons almond milk

1 teaspoon almond extract

1 teaspoon vanilla extract

24 whole blanched almonds

In a food processor, combine the flour, ground almonds, sugar, baking soda, and salt. Pulse to mix. Add the vegan butter, almond milk, almond extract, and vanilla and process just long enough to incorporate the butter. Do not overprocess. If the dough is too dry, add 1 additional tablespoon of almond milk.

Shape the dough into a 2-inch diameter log, wrap it tightly in plastic wrap, and refrigerate for 1 hour or longer to chill. Preheat the oven to 350°F. Line two baking sheets with parchment paper.

Slice the chilled dough into ½-inch slices. Arrange the cookies on the prepared baking sheets, about 2 inches apart. Gently press an almond into each cookie. Bake for 18 to 20 minutes, or until the bottoms and edges start to turn golden brown. Let the cookies cool on the pan for several minutes, then transfer them to a wire rack to cool completely. Once completely cool, the cookies may be stored in an airtight container.

Makes about 2 dozen cookies

SOY-FREE OPTION

Thailand

The subtle flavor balance of hot, sweet, sour, bitter, and salty at the same time make Thai food a sensory marvel. Rice and noodles are both enjoyed in Thailand, and often prepared with a variety of vegetables, seasonings, and sauces. Thai food is hot —not just burn-your-tongue "hot," but also hot as in trendy. No wonder. The intoxicating flavors and aromas combine to create dishes that many people find almost addictive. Some say the quality comes from the quasi-euphoric feeling you can experience while eating an especially hot Thai meal. It seems that the brain's pain sensors release the high-inducing endorphins because the brain thinks the tongue has been "injured."

Despite Thai food's hot and spicy reputation, you don't need an asbestos tongue to sample all Thai fare. Some dishes, such as the classic noodle dish, pad thai, are quite mild. And while the red and green curries can fly off the heat chart, the flavorful yellow Masaman curry, studded with chunks of pineapple, is often more sweet than spicy. Keep in mind that when you cook Thai, you can temper the degree of heat in recipes by simply using fewer chiles.

While Thai food has some similarities to Vietnamese, Chinese, and even Indian cooking, there is no mistaking this distinctive cuisine and its skillful blending of piquant ingredients. The home cook can find many Thai ingredients in Asian markets and well-stocked supermarkets. Look for Thai basil, chiles, lemongrass, coconut milk, and vegetarian oyster sauce. If you can't find fresh Thai basil, consider growing your own—one taste will tell you it's worth the effort. If Thai chiles are unavailable, crushed red pepper flakes are an easy substitute. Store a generous supply of jasmine rice along with dried rice noodles and you'll always have a base for a wonderful meal any time you want to experience the seductively complex flavor harmonies of Thai cuisine.

Tom Yum Soup

The intoxicating fragrance and flavors of lemongrass, ginger, and cilantro mingle with chili heat, chewy mushrooms, and sweet tomatoes and green peas for a bracingly delicious soup. If you're enjoying this as a first course, you can keep it lighter by eliminating the tofu and serving smaller portions. For a main dish soup, keep in the tofu (or use seitan or Soy Curls) and add some cooked noodles when ready to serve. For extra heat, add more chili paste, or drizzle in a little hot chili oil.

1 medium yellow onion or 3 shallots, halved lengthwise, then thinly sliced

1 tablespoon minced fresh lemongrass (white part only)

2 teaspoons grated fresh ginger or sliced galangal (see Note)

5 tablespoons soy sauce

2 teaspoons Asian chili paste

6 cups water

6 ounces shiitake mushroom caps, thinly sliced

4 scallions, coarsely chopped

8 ounces extra-firm tofu, cut into ½-inch dice

8 cherry or grape tomatoes, halved lengthwise

½ cup frozen green peas

¼ cup chopped fresh cilantro

1 tablespoon freshly squeezed lime juice

½ teaspoon natural sugar

Salt and freshly ground black pepper

In a large pot, combine the onion, lemongrass, ginger, and soy sauce. Stir in the chili paste, then add the water and bring to a boil. Lower the heat to a simmer and cook for 30 minutes. Add the mushrooms, scallions, tofu, tomatoes, peas, cilantro, lime juice, and sugar. Season with salt and pepper to taste. Simmer 10 minutes longer, then taste and adjust the seasonings if needed. Serve hot.

Note: Galangal is commonly used in Thai cooking. Galangal's flavor is similar to that of ginger, but more intense. Look for galangal in Asian markets. If unavailable, ginger root is a reasonable alternative.

Serves 4

GLUTEN-FREE
NO OIL

Miang Kam

I first encountered the sublime Thai appetizer known as *miang kam*, many years ago at Arun's restaurant in Chicago, where individual wild pepper leaves held tiny mounds of toasted coconut, crunchy peanuts, pungent ginger, zesty lime, and spicy chiles. To eat it, you pick up a leaf with its toppings and pop it in your mouth—it's a delicious flavor explosion that brings everything you like about Thai food into one bite. Serve this easy and unusual appetizer before a Thai meal. Wild pepper leaves (*bai cha plu*) can be found in Asian markets, but Belgian endive or baby spinach leaves provide more accessible alternatives.

To make the sauce, in a small saucepan, combine the coconut, peanuts, soy sauce, sugar, scallion, ginger, and water. Bring to a boil.

Lower the heat to low and simmer for 10 minutes to thicken. Remove from the heat and set aside to cool slightly. Transfer to a blender or food processor and blend until smooth. Transfer to a small serving bowl and place on a large serving platter.

On the same serving platter, arrange the leaves and a small amount of each of the filling ingredients in a mound on each leaf. Alternatively, arrange six leaves with a mound of the filling ingredients on individual salad plates. Top each with a small amount of sauce or serve the sauce alongside in a separate small bowl. To eat, place a filling-topped leaf in your hand, top with a small spoonful of sauce, and eat it in one bite. Repeat.

Note: Use coconut aminos instead of soy sauce to make this soy-free.

Serves 4

GLUTEN-FREE
SOY-FREE OPTION
NO OIL
QUICK AND EASY

Sauce

½ cup shredded unsweetened coconut, toasted

¼ cup unsalted roasted peanuts

3 tablespoons soy sauce

2 tablespoons palm sugar or other natural sugar

1 tablespoon minced scallion

1 teaspoon grated fresh ginger

½ cup water

Leaves

24 Belgian endive leaves (or spinach, leaf lettuce, or wild pepper leaves; see headnote)

Filling

3 small Thai chiles, cut into very thin rounds

1 fresh lime, sliced and finely chopped, including peel

½ cup roasted peanuts, crushed

½ cup unsweetened shredded coconut, toasted

¼ cup finely minced scallion

2 tablespoons grated fresh ginger

⅓ cup chopped fresh cilantro leaves

Eggplant Satays

A popular Thai appetizer, satays are usually made with meat, but there are lots of plant-based ingredients that are ideal candidates for this skewered and sauced treat. If you're not a fan of eggplant, you can use portobello mushrooms or seitan instead. Be sure to soak the bamboo skewers in cold water for 30 minutes to prevent them from burning. Instead of grilling or broiling, you can roast the satays in a 425°F oven. Use coconut aminos instead of soy sauce to make this soy free.

To make the peanut sauce, combine the coconut milk, peanut butter, ginger, garlic, sugar, soy sauce, and lemon juice in a bowl or food processor. Blend until smooth. Transfer to a saucepan and simmer over low heat until slightly thickened, stirring frequently, about 10 minutes. Set aside.

In a small bowl, combine the coriander, cumin, sugar, salt, and cayenne. Set aside.

Preheat the broiler or grill. Place the eggplants in a large bowl and drizzle with the oil. Toss to coat. Sprinkle the eggplants with the reserved spice mixture, tossing to coat. Press any remaining spice mixture from the bottom of the bowl into the eggplants so the spices adhere.

Thread the eggplants onto the skewers and place them under the broiler or on the grill until softened and well browned, 5 to 7 minutes per side.

Arrange the skewered eggplants on plates lined with the shredded lettuce. Drizzle the skewers with some of the peanut sauce and divide the reserved peanut sauce among four small dipping bowls and place them on the plates with the skewered eggplants. Serve at once.

Serves 4

GLUTEN-FREE
SOY-FREE OPTION
QUICK AND EASY

Peanut Sauce

¾ cup unsweetened coconut milk

2 tablespoons peanut butter

1 tablespoon minced fresh ginger

1 clove garlic, minced

1 tablespoon natural sugar

1 tablespoon soy sauce

1 tablespoon freshly squeezed lemon juice

½ teaspoon ground coriander

½ teaspoon ground cumin

¼ teaspoon natural sugar

¼ teaspoon salt

¼ teaspoon cayenne

4 Japanese eggplants, halved or quartered lengthwise and cut into 1-inch slices

2 tablespoons toasted sesame oil

Shredded lettuce, for serving

Thai Hangover Noodles with Tofu and Thai Basil

Also known as drunken noodles, the combination of hot chiles, fragrant Thai basil, chewy noodles, and a delicious sauce, make this my favorite Thai dish. It has much more complexity of flavor than the more familiar pad Thai. I even grow my own Thai basil, just so I can make this dish at home. If hot Thai chiles are unavailable, substituted red pepper flakes to taste.

14 ounces extra-firm tofu, drained and pressed

8 ounces rice noodles

2 teaspoons sesame oil

1 tablespoon grapeseed oil or other neutral oil

1 medium yellow onion, thinly sliced

1 red bell pepper, seeded and cut into ¼-inch strips

2 cloves garlic, minced

1 teaspoon grated fresh ginger

1 or 2 hot Thai chiles, seeded and minced

2 tablespoons soy sauce

2 tablespoons vegan oyster sauce or Golden Mountain Seasoning Sauce (see Note)

1 teaspoon natural sugar

1 cup loosely packed Thai basil leaves

6 grape or cherry tomatoes, halved lengthwise

Cut the tofu into 1-inch slices and arrange on a baking sheet lined with several thicknesses of paper towels. Top the tofu with another layer of paper towels and press on the slices to expel any excess water. Cut the pressed tofu slices into 1-inch cubes and set aside.

Cook the rice noodles according to the package directions. Drain well, toss with the sesame oil, and set aside.

Heat the oil in a large skillet or wok over medium-high heat and add onion and bell pepper, and stir-fry for 1 to 2 minutes to soften the vegetables. Add the garlic, ginger, chile, soy sauce, oyster sauce, and sugar. Add the reserved tofu and stir-fry for 2 minutes, or until the tofu is golden brown. Add the reserved noodles, basil, and tomatoes and stir-fry a few minutes, long enough to heat through and coat the noodles. Serve hot.

Note: Look for Golden Mountain Seasoning Sauce (the "secret" ingredient of Thai stir-fries) in Asian markets. You can certainly make a tasty Thai dish without it, but if you can find it, it will make your food taste more authentic.

Serves 4

GLUTEN-FREE
QUICK AND EASY

Panang Vegetable Curry

Of all the Thai curries, it is the vibrant Panang curry that gets my vote as most flavorful. Typically milder than other Thai curries (with the exception of the sweet Masaman curry), Panang curry has a more multifaceted flavor profile than green, red, or yellow Thai curries. Panang curry paste itself is a sublime blending of galangal, peanuts, lemongrass, shallots, chiles, coriander, and garlic, which is combined with coconut milk, sugar, and Thai basil leaves to make the sauce which provides a flavor and aroma that is unsurpassed.

In a food processor, combine the chiles, shallot, garlic, lime zest, lemongrass, and ginger and process to a paste. Add the chili paste, peanut butter, soy sauce, sugar, and coriander and process until smooth. Add the coconut milk and process until smooth and creamy.

Heat the oil in a large saucepan. Add the bell pepper, mushrooms, and jackfruit and cook, stirring, for 5 minutes. Stir in the broth, then add the reserved sauce and bring just to a boil. Decrease the heat to a low simmer and cook for 10 minutes to blend the flavors. Stir in the peas and basil leaves and cook 5 minutes longer to heat the peas. Taste and adjust the seasonings if needed. Serve hot over rice.

Note: Use coconut aminos instead of soy sauce to make this soy-free.

Serves 4

GLUTEN-FREE
SOY-FREE OPTION
QUICK AND EASY

1 or 2 dried red chiles, seeded, soaked, and drained

1 shallot, coarsely chopped

1 clove garlic, pressed

1 teaspoon finely grated lime zest

1 teaspoon minced fresh lemongrass (white part only)

1 teaspoon grated ginger or galangal

1 teaspoon Asian chili paste

1 tablespoon peanut butter

1 tablespoon soy sauce

1 teaspoon natural sugar

1 teaspoon ground coriander

1 (13-ounce) can unsweetened coconut milk

1 tablespoon grapeseed oil or other neutral oil

1 red or green bell pepper, seeded and cut into thin strips

8 ounces small white mushrooms, sliced

1 (15-ounce) can young or green jackfruit in water or brine (not syrup), drained, rinsed, and roughly chopped

1 cup vegetable broth

¾ cup frozen green peas, thawed

1 cup Thai basil leaves

3 to 4 cups hot cooked jasmine rice, for serving

Pineapple Fried Rice with Edamame

Refreshing pineapple, protein-rich edamame, and fragrant Thai basil are the stars of this fried rice dish dotted with colorful vegetables. If you don't want it spicy, omit the Thai chili sauce. Canned pineapple may be substituted for fresh, if necessary, and if you're not a fan of fruit in savory dishes, just omit the pineapple entirely. Use coconut aminos instead of soy sauce to make this soy-free.

1½ cups fresh or frozen shelled edamame

3 tablespoons soy sauce

2 tablespoons rice vinegar

2 teaspoons Thai chili sauce

¼ cup water

1 tablespoon grapeseed oil or other neutral oil

1 small red onion, halved and thinly sliced

1 carrot, coarsely shredded

1 red or green bell pepper, seeded and chopped

2 cloves garlic, minced

2 teaspoons grated fresh ginger

2 cups fresh pineapple, cut into ½-inch chunks

1 tablespoon palm sugar or light brown sugar

3 cups cold cooked brown rice

3 tablespoons fresh Thai basil leaves, mint, or cilantro

1 tablespoon toasted sesame seeds

Cook the edamame in a saucepan of boiling salted water until tender, about 5 minutes. Drain and set aside.

In a bowl, combine the soy sauce, vinegar, and chili sauce. Add the water, stir to mix well, and set aside.

Heat the oil in a large nonstick skillet or wok over medium-high heat. Add the onion and stir-fry for 3 minutes. Add the carrot, bell pepper, garlic, and ginger and stir-fry for 1 to 2 minutes. Add the pineapple chunks and sugar and stir-fry until golden brown. Add the reserved soy sauce mixture to the skillet and stir-fry to combine. Add the cooked rice, reserved edamame, and basil, and stir-fry gently until the mixture is hot and well combined. Serve hot sprinkled with toasted sesame seeds.

Serves 4

GLUTEN-FREE
SOY-FREE OPTION
LOW OIL
QUICK AND EASY

Bangkok Street Cart Noodles

Inspired by the popular noodle dish pad thai (but without the egg and with a whole lot of extra flavor-makers), this recipe combines rice noodles with ginger, rice vinegar, chili sauce, soy sauce, and more. If tamarind paste is unavailable, the lime juice will help lend a refreshing tart flavor. For a more substantial dish, add diced tofu. Use coconut aminos instead of soy sauce to make this soy-free.

Cook the noodles according to the package directions. Drain and return to the pot. Toss with the sesame oil and set aside.

In a small bowl, combine the chili sauce, hoisin, peanut butter, tomato paste, cornstarch, and sugar. Stir in the soy sauce, vinegar, tamarind paste, and water. Mix well, then set aside.

Heat the grapeseed oil in a large skillet or wok over medium-high heat. Add the bell pepper and broccoli and stir-fry for 2 minutes to soften. Add the garlic, scallions, and ginger, and stir-fry for 1 minute, adding a few drops of water if needed so the vegetables do not burn.

Stir in the reserved sauce mixture, then add the reserved noodles and stir-fry until they are hot and coated with the sauce, about 2 minutes. Serve immediately topped with the peanuts and cilantro.

Serves 4

GLUTEN-FREE
SOY-FREE OPTION
QUICK AND EASY

8 ounces dried rice noodles

1 teaspoon toasted sesame oil

1 teaspoon sweet chili sauce

1 teaspoon hoisin sauce

1 teaspoon peanut butter

1 teaspoon tomato paste

2 teaspoons cornstarch

1 tablespoon natural sugar

¼ cup soy sauce

2 tablespoons rice vinegar

1 to 2 tablespoons tamarind paste or concentrate, or freshly squeezed lime juice

½ cup water

1 tablespoon grapeseed oil or other neutral oil

1 small red bell pepper, seeded and cut into thin strips

2 cups small broccoli florets

2 garlic, minced

5 scallions, sliced diagonally

2 teaspoons grated fresh ginger

½ cup roasted peanuts, chopped

½ cup chopped fresh cilantro or Thai basil

Mango and Rice Verrines

These luscious rice pudding parfaits were inspired by my favorite rice dessert: the mango and sweet sticky rice of Thailand. Traditionally, this dessert is served on a plate with a scoop of coconut-infused rice surrounded by slices of mango. My version opts for a more unusual presentation, by layering the ingredients in clear glass dessert or parfait bowls or wineglasses. *Verrine* originally referred to a small glass container with no base that could hold a layered appetizer or dessert, which allows for a vertical and visually appealing presentation.

1 (13.5-ounce) can unsweetened coconut milk

½ cup natural sugar (try organic coconut sugar)

2½ cups cooked jasmine rice

1½ teaspoons vanilla extract

⅛ teaspoon salt

2 to 3 ripe fresh mangos, peeled, pitted, and finely chopped

¼ cup roasted unsalted peanuts or cashews, crushed

In a large saucepan, combine the coconut milk and sugar, and bring almost to a boil, stirring to dissolve the sugar. Add the cooked rice, vanilla, and salt, and simmer over medium-low heat for 15 minutes, or until desired consistency is reached, stirring occasionally. Set aside to cool. Spoon a small amount of the rice into the bottom of 4 clear dessert or parfait glasses (wineglasses are good for this). Top each with a layer of chopped mango, followed by another layer of rice, until the ingredients are used up (or the glasses are nearly full). Sprinkle the tops with the crushed nuts. Refrigerate until serving time. Serve chilled.

Serves 4

GLUTEN-FREE
SOY-FREE
QUICK AND EASY
NO OIL

Japan

Japanese food is deliberately elegant, spare, and harmonious in appearance and flavor. Whether you're enjoying the soothing simplicity of delicate miso soup or the artistic beauty of a vegetable sushi platter, Japanese food can be a calming refuge from the bold flavors of other cuisines.

This sublime cuisine has spawned a variety of dishes tailor-made for the vegan. Favorites include vegetable tempura, *yakisoba* (buckwheat noodles with stir-fried vegetables) (page 222), *gomai* (spinach with sesame paste) served as a topping for *donburi* on page 221, and various preparations of the esteemed soy food family such as edamame (whole fresh soybeans in the pod), soothing and restorative miso soup, and, of course, the eminently versatile tofu, as featured in Tofu Tonkatsu on page 223. Japanese cuisine tends to be less spicy than other Asian cuisines, but with seasonings ranging from soy, sesame, and sake, it is nonetheless richly flavored.

Until recent years, Japanese ingredients were available only in Asian markets or natural food stores, but these days, everything from tofu and edamame to soba noodles and shiitake mushrooms can be found in your local supermarkets.

Temple Soup

This wholesome and delicious vegetable soup, known as *kenchinjiru*, is an example of *shojin ryori*, or Buddhist temple food, a vegetarian diet based on the Buddhist teaching of compassion for all living creatures. *Shojin ryori* cooking features seasonal vegetables (except for members of the onion family), as well as tofu and other soy foods, wheat gluten, beans, sea vegetables, and nuts and fruits. This soup typically contains crumbled tofu, root vegetables, and sesame oil for a rich, satisfying flavor.

12 ounces firm tofu, drained and crumbled

3 tablespoons soy sauce

1 tablespoon dark sesame oil

1 tablespoon grapeseed oil or other neutral oil

2 medium carrots, sliced

12 ounces butternut or kabocha squash, peeled and cut into 1-inch chunks

1 Yukon Gold potato or sweet potato, peeled and cut into 1-inch chunks

1 (6-inch) piece of daikon radish, peeled and thinly sliced

6 shiitake mushrooms, stems removed

¼ cup mirin

1 cup fresh or frozen shelled edamame

6 cups water

1 piece kombu seaweed (optional)

1 teaspoon salt

8 ounces fresh spinach, coarsely chopped

2 tablespoons white or chickpea miso paste

1 tablespoon sesame seeds, for garnish (black, if available)

Place the crumbled tofu in a bowl with 1 tablespoon of the soy sauce and the sesame oil. Mix well, then set aside to marinate for a few minutes.

Heat the grapeseed oil in a soup pot over medium-high heat. Add the carrots, squash, and potato. Stir-fry for 2 to 3 minutes, then add the daikon and mushrooms. Stir-fry for 2 minutes, then stir in the tofu mixture. Add the mirin and edamame and stir-fry for 1 minute, then add the water, kombu, if using, and salt. Bring to a boil, then lower the heat to a simmer and cook for 20 to 30 minutes, or until the vegetables are tender. Stir in the spinach and the remaining soy sauce, along with extra water if more broth is needed. Ladle ½ cup of the broth into a small bowl, stir in the miso paste until smooth. Add the miso mixture to the soup, then taste and adjust the seasonings, if needed. Serve hot in large soup bowls and sprinkle with sesame seeds.

Serves 4

GLUTEN-FREE

Chilled Somen Salad

The thin white wheat noodles called *somen* are usually served cold. They are especially delicious in this salad combined with edamame and tofu, and crisp lettuce, carrots, and scallions, and topped with a flavorful sesame-soy dressing. If *somen* noodles are unavailable, substitute angel hair or vermicelli noodles, soba noodles, or thin rice noodles.

8 ounces somen noodles

8 ounces baked marinated tofu, cut into thin strips

3 cups shredded romaine lettuce

1 large carrot, coarsely shredded

1 cup cooked shelled edamame

3 scallions, minced

2 tablespoons toasted sesame seeds

3 tablespoons soy sauce

3 tablespoons rice vinegar

1 tablespoon toasted sesame oil

1 tablespoon mirin

1 teaspoon sugar

Salt and freshly ground black pepper

Cook the somen noodles according to the package directions. Drain, rinse in cold water, then drain again.

Transfer the noodles to a shallow serving bowl. Arrange the tofu, lettuce, carrot, and edamame on top of the noodles. Sprinkle with scallions and sesame seeds. Cover and refrigerate for at least 30 minutes or until ready to serve.

In a bowl, combine the soy sauce, vinegar, sesame oil, mirin, sugar, and salt and pepper to taste. Mix well. Just before serving, drizzle the dressing over the salad. Serve chilled.

Serves 4

LOW OIL
QUICK AND EASY

Eggplant Kabayaki

Classic *unagi kabayaki* is a Japanese dish made of broiled or grilled eel glazed with a sweet soy-based sauce. This plant-based version uses eggplant instead of eel on which to douse the luscious *kabayaki* sauce. The texture of the eggplant and its ability to absorb the sauce make it an ideal substitute for the eel. Instead of eggplant, you can substitute sliced portobello mushrooms or seitan. In this recipe, the eggplant is partially cooked before glazing with the sauce to prevent the sauce from burning. Use coconut aminos instead of soy sauce to make this soy free.

Preheat the oven to 425°F. Arrange the eggplant slices on a lightly oiled baking sheet. Roast the eggplant until just softened, turning once, about 10 minutes total. Remove from the oven and set aside.

In a small saucepan, combine the soy sauce, sake, and agave nectar. Cook, stirring, over medium heat to allow the flavors to blend, about 5 minutes. Preheat the grill or broiler.

Spoon or brush the sauce over the eggplant and grill or broil until hot and nicely glazed, turning and adding more sauce as needed. Serve over the rice and top with any remaining sauce. Garnish with sesame seeds or *sansho*.

Makes 4 servings

GLUTEN-FREE
SOY-FREE OPTION
NO OIL
QUICK AND EASY

3 small Japanese eggplants, cut into ¼-inch slices (about 2 pounds)

½ cup soy sauce

⅓ cup sake or mirin (sweet rice wine)

3 tablespoons agave nectar or sugar

3 cups hot cooked rice

Toasted sesame seeds or *sansho* (Japanese pepper), for garnish

Sesame-Spinach Donburi

I've been a fan of *donburi* since I first tasted it when a friend brought me to a small Japanese restaurant in New York City. The restaurant, more of a lunchroom, had no sign and was on the second floor above some shops. The room contained several long tables that were filled with Japanese people enjoying their lunch: the rice bowl dish known as *donburi*. A kind of Japanese fast food, traditional *donburi* is boiled rice topped with fish, meat, eggs, or vegetables simmered in a dashi broth made with soy sauce and mirin.

In a small bowl, combine the coconut milk, 2 tablespoons of the soy sauce, and tahini, stirring until blended. Set aside.

Heat the oil or water in a large skillet over medium heat. Add the onion and cook until soft, about 5 minutes. Add the mushrooms and ginger, and cook for 30 seconds. Add the spinach and stir-fry until wilted, about 2 minutes. Stir in the reserved coconut milk, soy sauce, and tahini mixture, and salt and pepper to taste. Simmer, stirring frequently, until hot and creamy, 5 minutes.

Heat the sesame oil in a large skillet or wok over medium heat. Add the tofu, scallions, and the remaining tablespoon of soy sauce and cook, stirring to coat. Add the cooked rice and sesame seeds, and season with salt and pepper to taste. Toss to combine and heat through. Spoon the rice mixture among individual bowls, top each with the spinach mixture and serve hot.

Serves 4

GLUTEN-FREE
QUICK AND EASY

¾ cup unsweetened coconut milk

3 tablespoons soy sauce

3 tablespoons tahini (sesame paste)

1 tablespoon grapeseed oil or other neutral oil or ¼ cup water

1 medium yellow onion, finely chopped

8 shiitake mushrooms, stemmed and thinly sliced

1 teaspoon grated fresh ginger

10 ounces fresh spinach, well washed and coarsely chopped

Salt and freshly ground black pepper

2 teaspoons toasted sesame oil

8 ounces extra-firm tofu, drained and crumbled

3 scallions, minced

3 cups cooked brown rice

2 tablespoons toasted sesame seeds

Yakisoba

The popular Japanese fried noodle dish *yakisoba* has its roots in China and is similar to lo mein. There are countless variations on *yakisoba*, but all contain noodles and vegetables, and usually some protein. The dish is always fried in a pan and finished with a somewhat sweet sauce that is put together quickly from condiments. Interestingly, *yakisoba* isn't traditionally made with soba noodles (although they do work well in this dish). The classic noodle used is called chukamen, but it is made with eggs. I usually use linguine or, oddly enough, soba noodles. Sometimes I use ramen noodles, which are similar to chukamen.

12 ounces linguine or soba noodles

1 tablespoon sesame oil

1 tablespoon grapeseed oil
or other neutral oil

3 cloves garlic, minced

1 tablespoon grated fresh ginger

8 ounces baked marinated tofu,
cut into matchstick julienne

4 cups shredded napa cabbage

2 carrots, coarsely shredded

¼ cup soy sauce

2 tablespoons vegan oyster sauce

2 tablespoons mirin

½ teaspoon sriracha sauce

1 bunch scallions, minced

½ teaspoon natural sugar

Salt and freshly ground black pepper

Cook the noodles in a pot of boiling water according to the package directions. Drain and rinse under cold water, then return to the pot. Drizzle with sesame oil and toss to coat. Set aside.

In a small bowl, combine the soy sauce, mirin, oyster sauce, sugar, and sriracha.

Heat the grapeseed oil in a wok or large skillet over medium-high heat. Add the garlic and ginger and stir-fry until fragrant, about 30 seconds. Add the cabbage and carrots and stir-fry for 2 to 3 minutes to soften. Add the tofu, noodles, scallions, and sauce mixture. Continue to stir-fry to heat through and coat the noodles and vegetables with the sauce. Taste and adjust the seasonings, adding a little salt and pepper to taste. Serve hot.

Note: Use gluten-free noodles to make this gluten-free.

Serves 4

GLUTEN-FREE OPTION
QUICK AND EASY

Tōfu Tonkatsu

The name *tonkatsu* means "pork cutlets," but this tasty dish is fabulous made with tofu, coated with panko and topped with the traditional zesty sauce. It's especially good paired with this crunchy slaw, as is traditional.

To make the sauce, combine the ketchup, soy sauce, agave, Worcestershire sauce, applesauce (if using), and mustard in a bowl. Stir to mix well. Set aside.

To make the slaw, combine the cabbage, carrot, vinegar, agave, ginger, and sesame oil in a large bowl. Season with salt and pepper to taste. Toss to combine well. Cover and refrigerate until needed.

To prepare the tofu, place the almond milk, flour, and panko crumbs in three separate shallow bowls. Dip the tofu into the almond milk, then dredge them in the flour and then back into the almond milk, followed by dredging in the panko crumbs. Repeat with the remaining tofu until all the pieces are coated.

Heat a thin layer of oil in a large skillet over medium-high heat. Add the tofu to the skillet, in batches if needed. Cook until golden brown, turning once, about 4 minutes per side. Do not overcrowd. Keep warm in a low oven until all the tofu is cooked. Arrange a bed of slaw on four plates and top with the tofu, dividing evenly. Spoon the sauce over the tofu and serve.

Serves 4

Sauce

½ cup ketchup

¼ cup soy sauce

2 tablespoons agave nectar

2 tablespoons vegan Worcestershire sauce

1 tablespoon unsweetened applesauce (optional)

2 teaspoons spicy brown mustard

Slaw

6 cups shredded cabbage (1 small head)

1 large carrot, coarsely shredded

3 tablespoons rice vinegar

2 teaspoons agave nectar

1 teaspoon grated fresh ginger

1 teaspoon dark sesame oil

Salt and freshly ground black pepper

Tofu

12 ounces extra-firm tofu, drained, pressed, and cut into ½-inch slices, then cut each slice in half, lengthwise

½ cup plain unsweetened almond milk

½ cup all-purpose flour

1 cup panko bread crumbs

Grapeseed oil or other neutral oil, for frying

Sesame Mochi

The Japanese confections known as *daifuku mochi* are small, smooth rice cakes or balls stuffed with a sweet filling. *Mochi* are made with *mochiko*, a flour made from ground sweet glutinous rice called *mochigome*. For *daifuku mochi*, the rice is pounded into paste, stuffed with a filling (usually sweet red bean paste), and molded into various shapes. They are often coated in a fine layer of cornstarch, potato starch, or confectioners' sugar to keep them from sticking. These treats are eaten year-round, but are also a traditional food for the Japanese New Year.

1¼ cups glutinous rice flour (*mochiko*) (see headnote)

⅓ cup sugar

Pinch of salt

1¼ cups almond milk

⅓ cup sesame paste

⅓ cup cooked white beans

2 tablespoons confectioners' sugar

2 tablespoons toasted sesame seeds

Coconut flour or finely ground unsweetened coconut, for dusting

In a heatproof bowl, combine the flour, sugar, and salt. Stir in the almond milk and mix well. Cover with plastic wrap and microwave for 5 minutes, then uncover and set aside to cool for 5 minutes. Cut into twelve pieces.

In a food processor, combine the sesame paste, white beans, confectioners' sugar, and sesame seeds and mix well. Set aside.

Dust your hands with the coconut flour, then flatten each piece of *mochi* into a small disk. Place 1½ teaspoons of the sesame mixture in the center of each piece of *mochi*. Pinch closed to seal, then lightly roll it into a ball, using both palms. Repeat with the remaining *mochi* and filling.

Pour about ½ cup of coconut flour into a shallow bowl. Roll the balls in the coconut flour to keep the *mochi* from sticking. Transfer to a plate and serve. *Mochi* will keep for up to 2 days at room temperature. If not using right away, they will keep in the freezer for up to 2 weeks. Do not refrigerate, or they will become hard.

Note: Glutinous rice flour, also called *mochiko*, is available at Asian markets or online.

Makes 12 *mochi*

GLUTEN-FREE
SOY-FREE
NO OIL

Korea

One of the spiciest cuisines of Asia, Korean cooking has been influenced by the cuisine of China, although it is generally spicier due to the prevalence of hot red chiles, black pepper, garlic, and spicy red chili paste (*kochujang*) in many of the dishes. Other seasonings common to Korean cuisine are soy sauce, green onions, ginger, sesame oil, sesame seed, and a bean paste, called *dhwen-jang*, which is similar to Japanese miso. Vegetables are categorized by their cooking method, which include salads (*muchim*), cooked vegetable dishes (*namul*), braised or simmered vegetables (*chorim*), and fermented vegetables (*kimchi*).

Thanks to a Korean neighbor, I've received some helpful cooking tips and enjoyed many stellar home-cooked Korean meals, all the while making mental notes to enable me to re-create the dishes at home. A typical Korean meal includes rice, soup, vegetables, a main dish, and, of course, the ubiquitous fermented vegetable mixture known as kimchi (page 230). In general, Koreans eat more vegetables than meat with their rice, and the vegetable dishes are varied and plentiful. Rice is served at every meal, sometimes in combination with barley and adzuki beans or bean curd, or tofu, which they call *tubu*. Many traditional Korean recipes combine a variety of textures and a balance of spicy, bitter, hot, cool, and sweet flavors—all in the same dish, such as Bibimbap (page 235) or Easy Chapchae (page 232). Ingredients in a Korean meal are often chosen to include five colors—green, white, yellow, red, and black.

Sesame Cucumber Salad

This crunchy salad makes a refreshing accompaniment to a Korean meal. It is especially popular in Korea during the summer. This recipe calls for English cucumber, since it's readily available, but the small Korean cucumbers would be traditional, if you can find them. I usually just add a pinch of red pepper flakes (or none at all) since the rest of the meal is typically quite spicy-hot, but if you want extra heat, just add more red pepper flakes.

3 tablespoons rice vinegar

3 tablespoons toasted sesame oil

1 teaspoon grated fresh ginger

½ teaspoon minced garlic

½ teaspoon sugar

⅛ teaspoon salt

⅛ teaspoon red pepper flakes (optional)

1 English cucumber, peeled
and thinly sliced

3 minced scallions

1 tablespoon toasted sesame seeds

In a small bowl combine the vinegar, oil, ginger, garlic, sugar, salt, and red pepper flakes, if using. Mix well. Place the cucumber slices and scallions in a bowl. Add the dressing and toss lightly to combine. Spoon the salad into small individual bowls and sprinkle with the sesame seeds.

Serves 4

GLUTEN-FREE
SOY-FREE
QUICK AND EASY

Kimchi Pancakes

Korean pancakes, or *jeon*, are enjoyed at all meals of the day as a side dish or appetizer, as well as a snack served with drinks. Jeon can be made with a variety of different fillings, including different types of meat and seafood as well as vegetables. Among the most popular jeon are *pajeon*, made with green onions and *kimchijeon*, made with kimchi. This recipe makes four to five large pancakes, but you could use the batter to make several smaller pancakes, if you prefer. Use the kimchi recipe on page 230 or, to save time, you can buy prepared kimchi at an Asian market. Use coconut aminos instead of soy sauce to make this soy free.

To make the dipping sauce, combine the chile, scallion, sesame seeds, sugar, red pepper flakes, soy sauce, vinegar, water, sake, and sesame oil in a small bowl and mix well. Set aside. Preheat the oven to 250°F.

To make the pancakes, combine the flours, salt, and sesame seeds in a medium bowl. Stir in the water and mix until blended. Stir in the kimchi and scallions and mix well.

Heat 1 tablespoon of the grapeseed oil in a large nonstick skillet over medium heat. Ladle about ½ cup of the batter into the hot skillet, spreading to form a thin pancake. Cook until firm and nicely browned, about 4 minutes. Flip the pancake to cook the other side for 2 to 3 minutes or until browned. Slide the pancake onto a baking sheet and keep warm in the oven while you cook the remaining pancakes, adding more oil to the pan as needed. Serve hot with the sauce on the side.

Serves 4

SOY-FREE OPTION

Dipping Sauce

1 hot green chile, minced

1 scallion, minced

1 tablespoon sesame seeds

1 teaspoon sugar

¼ teaspoon red pepper flakes

¼ cup soy sauce

3 tablespoons rice vinegar

2 tablespoons water

2 tablespoons sake or mirin

1 tablespoon toasted sesame oil

Pancakes

½ cup all-purpose flour

¼ cup rice flour

¼ cup tapioca flour

½ teaspoon salt

1 teaspoon sesame seeds

1 cup water

1½ cups finely chopped kimchi (recipe follows), or store-bought

2 tablespoons minced scallions

Grapeseed oil or other neutral oil, for frying

24-Hour Kimchi

If you go to an Asian market to buy kimchi, the fermented vegetable side dish, be ready for a lot of choices. In addition to several prepared varieties sold in jars, vendors often sell their own homemade kimchi from large tubs, each batch as unique as the cook who made it. Cabbage dominates in the most familiar versions, but other ingredients such as daikon radish, carrots, and other vegetables may be included as well, with varying degrees of spiciness. With all those choices, it may be easier to make your own.

5 cups coarsely chopped napa cabbage

1 carrot, peeled and thinly sliced

½ cup chopped scallions

2 teaspoons salt

4 cups water

3 cloves garlic

1 teaspoon grated fresh ginger

1 tablespoon cayenne or 2 tablespoons *kochijan* paste combined with 1 tablespoon hot water

2 tablespoons rice vinegar

¼ teaspoon freshly ground black pepper

In a large bowl, combine the cabbage, carrot, and scallions. Add the salt and water. Place a plate inside the bowl to hold the vegetables under water. Cover and set aside for 4 hours.

Drain well and discard the salt water. Rinse the vegetables well and drain again, squeezing out any remaining liquid.

In a small bowl, combine the garlic, ginger, cayenne mixture, vinegar, and pepper. Mix well. Add to the reserved vegetables and mix well to coat.

Cover tightly and set aside on the kitchen counter to ferment overnight. Taste and adjust the seasonings, if needed. Store in an airtight container in the refrigerator where it will continue to ferment at a slower rate. Properly stored, the kimchi will keep in the refrigerator for several weeks.

Makes about 4 cups kimchi

GLUTEN-FREE
SOY-FREE
NO OIL

Easy Chapchae

Also spelled *japchae*, *chapchae* combines cellophane noodles (made from sweet potato starch or mung bean) seasoned with garlic, soy sauce, and sesame oil with a variety of vegetables. In addition to (or instead of) the shiitake mushrooms, spinach, and red bell pepper used here, you can add broccoli, asparagus, or carrots. Another popular addition is *bulgogi*, so if you have any leftover seitan *bulgogi* in the fridge, this is a delicious way to use it up. Just replace the tofu with the *bulgogi*.

1 (8-ounce) package cellophane noodles

2 tablespoons dark sesame oil

5 tablespoons soy sauce

½ teaspoon natural sugar

14 ounces extra-firm tofu, drained, pressed, and cut into small dice

Salt and freshly ground black pepper

1 medium yellow onion, halved lengthwise, then thinly sliced

1 red bell pepper, seeded and cut into thin strips

2 cups sliced shiitake mushrooms

1 tablespoon rice vinegar

8 cups baby spinach

2 teaspoons sesame seeds

Prepare the noodles according to the package directions. Drain well and transfer to a large bowl. Drizzle 2 teaspoons of the sesame oil on the noodles and toss to coat. Add 2 tablespoons of the soy sauce and the sugar and toss to combine. Set aside.

In a separate bowl, combine the tofu with 2 tablespoons of the soy sauce, 1 teaspoon of the sesame oil, and salt and pepper to taste. Set aside to marinate for 20 minutes.

In large skillet, heat 1 tablespoon of sesame oil over medium-high heat. Add the onion and stir-fry for 3 to 4 minutes. Add the bell pepper and mushrooms and stir-fry for 1 minute. Add 1 tablespoon of the soy sauce and the vinegar, and stir-fry for 1 minute. Add the reserved tofu and stir-fry for 2 minutes. Stir in the noodle mixture, then add the spinach, cover, and cook for 3 minutes or until the spinach is wilted. Season to taste with salt and pepper and toss to combine. Taste and adjust the seasonings, adding a little more sugar or soy sauce to taste, if needed, and stir-fry until well mixed. Serve hot topped with sesame seeds.

Serves 4 to 6

GLUTEN-FREE

Seitan Bulgogi

Bulgogi is a popular Korean dish that is traditionally made with thinly sliced beef. I make it with seitan that has a smoky sweet flavor and is delicious served over rice. It can also be used to make Korean "sushi" rolls (*kimbap*) or stir-fried noodles (*chapchae*). *Bulgogi* is frequently served in lettuce leaves to make lettuce cups and accompanied with spicy red chili paste (*kochujang*). Use coconut aminos instead of soy sauce to make this soy-free.

In a bowl, combine the soy sauce, sugar, sesame oil, vinegar, red pepper flakes, and black pepper. Stir to mix well. Add the scallions, garlic, ginger, and seitan and mix well to coat the seitan. Set aside to marinate for 30 minutes or cover and refrigerate for 1 hour.

Heat the oil in a large skillet or wok over medium-high heat. Working in batches, add a single layer of seitan and cook until browned on both sides, turning once, about 3 minutes per side. Repeat with the remaining seitan. Serve hot sprinkled with sesame seeds and a small bowl of *kochujang* if desired.

Serves 4

SOY-FREE OPTION
QUICK AND EASY

⅓ cup soy sauce

2 tablespoons sugar

2 teaspoons dark sesame oil

1 tablespoon rice vinegar

¼ teaspoon red pepper flakes

¼ teaspoon freshly ground black pepper

4 scallions, thinly sliced diagonally

3 cloves garlic, minced

1 teaspoon grated fresh ginger

1 pound seitan, very thinly sliced

1 tablespoon grapeseed oil or other neutral oil

1 tablespoon toasted sesame seeds

Kochujang paste (Korean chili paste), for serving

Bibimbap

Bibimbap, literally "stirred or mixed rice," features a variety of vegetables and is flavored with the spicy Korean chili paste known as *kochujang*. This dish is typically made with white sticky rice, but I prefer to use brown rice because it is more nutritious. *Bibimbap* is frequently served topped with a fried egg, which is obviously omitted from this vegan version. Swapping coconut aminos for the soy sauce will make this recipe soy free.

In a bowl, combine the *kochujang* paste, soy sauce, sesame oil, vinegar, and agave. Stir to mix well. Set aside.

Heat the grapeseed oil in a large skillet or wok over medium-high heat. Add the onion, bell pepper, and garlic and stir-fry for 2 minutes. Add the cabbage and carrots and stir-fry for 2 minutes longer. Stir in the mushrooms and stir-fry for 1 minute, then add the reserved sauce and cook, stirring to coat. Add the cooked rice and cook, stirring, until well mixed and heated through. To serve, spoon the rice and vegetable mixture into bowls and top with cucumber and sesame seeds. Serve extra *kuchujang* sauce and soy sauce on the side.

Serves 4

GLUTEN-FREE
SOY-FREE OPTION
QUICK AND EASY

3 tablespoons kochujang paste (Korean chili paste)

1 tablespoon soy sauce

1 tablespoon dark sesame oil

1 teaspoon rice vinegar

1 teaspoon agave nectar

1 tablespoon grapeseed oil or other neutral oil

1 large yellow onion, chopped

1 red bell pepper, seeded and cut into matchsticks

2 cloves garlic, minced

3 cups shredded green cabbage

1 carrot, coarsely shredded

1 cup thinly sliced white or shiitake mushrooms

3 cups cooked brown rice

½ English cucumber, peeled and cut into matchsticks

1 tablespoon toasted sesame seeds

Sweet Potato Dessert

When my Korean neighbor, Sung Hee, first served us this unusual dessert, called *goguma mattang*, we were surprised at the idea of sweet potatoes for dessert. But after one taste, we were hooked. Made with Korean or Japanese sweet potatoes, it tastes the best when served while still warm.

1 tablespoon grapeseed oil or other neutral oil

5 to 6 Korean sweet potatoes, peeled and cut into 1-inch dice (about 3 cups) (see Note)

¼ cup natural sugar

3 tablespoons agave nectar

3 tablespoons water

1 tablespoon black sesame seeds

Heat the oil in a large skillet over medium heat. Add the diced sweet potatoes. Cover and cook, stirring occasionally, until tender, about 15 minutes. Transfer the potatoes to a serving bowl.

In a small saucepan over medium-high heat, combine the sugar, agave, and water, stirring to mix. When the syrup begins to bubble, decrease the heat to low and cook for another 2 minutes to thicken slightly. Add the hot syrup to the cooked potatoes and toss gently to combine. Serve immediately, sprinkled with the sesame seeds.

Note: Korean sweet potatoes (*goguma*) are sweeter and drier in texture than American sweet potatoes. They have a deep purple skin and a pale yellow interior that turns brighter yellow when cooked. Their texture and flavor reminds me a bit of chestnuts, only sweeter. Look for them at Asian markets. If unavailable you can substitute 2 or 3 American sweet potatoes, although the flavor will be somewhat different.

Serves 4 to 6

GLUTEN-FREE
SOY-FREE
LOW OIL

Vietnam

I like to explain my love of Vietnamese cuisine by comparison: Thai food excites my senses, while Japanese cuisine has a calming effect. Chinese dishes offer comfort and familiarity, but for me, Vietnamese food has an uncanny ability to do it all. While there are elements of other cuisines apparent in Vietnamese food, the end result is a unique cuisine with its own distinct qualities. The curries of Vietnam, for example, are nothing like the heady curries of India or the fiery Thai curries, yet they command attention.

Vietnamese cuisine differs from Chinese by, among other ways, the addition of tropical ingredients such as lemongrass and citrus fruits, which are indigenous, in recipes such as Lemongrass Asparagus and Edamame Stir-Fry on page 247 and Vietnamese Noodle Salad on page 244. Vietnamese cooking is, perhaps, most similar to Thai and although some dishes can be spicy, the food is not dominated by hot seasonings. The hottest dishes are found in the southern part of the country, where there is a more liberal use of chiles than in the north.

"Fresh" and "healthy" are common descriptors of Vietnamese food, owing to a liberal use of raw vegetables such as cucumbers, carrots, and lettuce; bean sprouts; fresh herbs, such as cilantro; and seasonings such as lime juice and chiles. Such ingredients are often served alongside many soup and noodle dishes for you to add as desired, as in Pho Chay on page 242.

Banh Mi Spring Rolls

Inspired by the flavors of the *bánh mì* sandwich, these spring rolls, called Banh Mi Goi Cuon, give you the same filling ingredients but without the baguette. Wrapped in rice paper and dipped in a savory hoisin-peanut sauce, these refreshing spring rolls are a great way to enjoy a light and gluten-free interpretation of bánh mì.

¼ cup vegan mayonnaise

3 tablespoons hoisin sauce

2 tablespoons soy sauce

1 teaspoon sriracha sauce

8 sheets rice paper wrappers

1½ cups fresh cilantro, mint, or Thai basil leaves

8 ounces baked extra-firm tofu, cut into thin strips

1 large carrot, coarsely shredded

½ English cucumber, peeled and cut into thin strips

¼ cup chopped pickled jalapeños

Hoisin-Peanut Dipping Sauce (recipe follows)

In a bowl, combine the mayonnaise, hoisin, soy sauce, and sriracha, stirring to blend. Set aside.

Pour warm water into a wide shallow bowl or pan and set a clean dish towel next to it. Dip a rice paper wrapper into the water for a few seconds to soften, then remove it from the water and place it on the towel.

Transfer the softened rice paper to a flat work surface. Arrange a row of cilantro leaves on the rice paper, near the end closest to you. On top of the cilantro, arrange a row of tofu strips, drizzle with the reserved sauce mixture, then top with shredded carrot, cucumber strips, and sprinkle with jalapeños. Do not overfill. Fold the edge of the rice paper closest to you over the filling, then fold the sides over and roll it up, away from you, to form a neat roll. Repeat with the remaining ingredients. Serve with the dipping sauce.

Makes 8 rolls

GLUTEN-FREE
NO OIL

Hoisin-Peanut Dipping Sauce

This sauce is absolutely dreamy with spring rolls, but it's also great with chunks of baked tofu or even steamed or roasted vegetables such as asparagus and broccoli.

Combine the hoisin, peanut butter, vinegar, soy sauce, and sriracha in a small bowl and stir to combine. Taste and adjust the seasonings. Add a little water if a thinner sauce is desired. Serve as a dipping sauce for the spring rolls. If not using right away, cover tightly and refrigerate. Properly stored, the sauce will keep for a week or longer. The recipe is easily doubled.

Makes about 1 cup sauce

GLUTEN-FREE
QUICK AND EASY
NO OIL

½ cup hoisin sauce

¼ cup peanut butter

1 tablespoon rice vinegar

2 teaspoons soy sauce

1 teaspoon sriracha sauce

Pho Chay

Pho (pronounce *fuh*) is a rich Vietnamese noodle soup usually made with beef. The meatless version is called *pho chay*. A popular street food in Vietnam, pho is traditionally eaten for breakfast in the southern part of the country, but is also enjoyed at other times of day in the north. I like to enrich this hearty soup with dark miso paste and strips of seitan, although you can leave out the seitan (or add tofu) and still have a delicious soup. Chewy rice stick noodles are traditionally used in this soup, but I've also made it with linguine and ramen noodles, depending on what's on hand.

8 ounces dried rice noodles

6 cups vegetable broth or water

3 shallots or 1 small yellow onion, chopped

1 cup thinly sliced shiitake mushroom caps

1 tablespoon grated fresh ginger

⅓ cup hoisin sauce

2 tablespoons soy sauce

1 tablespoon grapeseed oil or other neutral oil

8 ounces seitan, drained and cut into strips

2 tablespoons freshly squeezed lime juice

2 tablespoons dark miso paste

1 teaspoon sriracha sauce

1 cup fresh bean sprouts, blanched

4 scallions, thinly sliced

1 cup fresh cilantro leaves

Lime wedges, for serving

Cook the noodles according to the package directions. Drain and set aside.

Bring the broth to a boil in a large pot. Add the shallots, mushrooms, ginger, hoisin sauce, and soy sauce. Decrease the heat to low and simmer for 15 minutes.

Heat the oil in a large skillet over medium-high heat, add the seitan and brown on all sides, about 5 minutes. Remove from the heat and set aside.

Stir the lime juice into the broth. Remove ½ cup of the hot liquid to a small bowl. Add the miso paste to the liquid in the bowl and stir to blend well. Transfer the blended miso paste into the soup along with the sriracha. Do not boil. Stir in the reserved seitan and noodles.

Divide the soup among individual bowls. Top with the bean sprouts, scallions, and cilantro. Serve at once with the lime wedges and additional sriracha to add at the table.

Serves 4

LOW OIL
QUICK AND EASY

Sizzling Saigon Crepes

Known as *banh xeo* in Vietnamese (literally "sizzling cake"), these lacy yellow crepes, made with rice flour, coconut milk, and turmeric for color, are traditionally filled with pork or shrimp. They have a crisp and delicate texture and a flavor that is simply delicious. My version uses tofu and mushrooms and is served with soy sauce for dipping.

In a large bowl, whisk together the rice flour, salt, and turmeric. Add the water and coconut milk and whisk until the mixture is smooth. Let the batter rest for 30 minutes.

Heat 1 tablespoon of the oil in a large nonstick skillet over medium-high heat. Add one-fourth of the onion, scallions, and mushrooms. Stir-fry for 2 to 3 minutes, then add one-fourth of the tofu and stir-fry a minute longer. Ladle ½ cup of the reserved batter into the pan, swirling to spread evenly. Add one-fourth of the bean sprouts and basil onto one side of the crepe and lower the heat to medium. Cover the skillet and cook for 1 minute. Uncover and continue to cook until the edges begin to brown, about 2 minutes longer. Loosen the crepe from the bottom of the pan with a spatula. When the bottom turns light brown and crispy, fold the crepe in half to enclose the bean sprouts. Transfer to a plate. Repeat with the remaining ingredients to make 4 crepes. Serve sprinkled with basil, cilantro, or mint and accompanied by soy sauce for dipping.

Serves 4

GLUTEN-FREE

Batter

2 cups rice flour

½ teaspoon salt

¼ teaspoon ground turmeric

1½ cups water

¾ cup canned coconut milk

Filling

Grapeseed oil or other neutral oil

1 small yellow onion, very thinly sliced

3 scallions, thinly sliced diagonally

1 cup thinly sliced white or shiitake mushrooms

8 ounces baked tofu, homemade or store-bought, finely chopped

1½ cups fresh bean sprouts, trimmed

⅓ cup Thai basil, cilantro, or mint leaves

¼ teaspoon salt

1 to 2 medium long red chiles, sliced thinly into rings, about ⅛ inch thick

Soy sauce, for serving

Vietnamese Noodle Salad

This southern Vietnamese noodle salad known as *bun bo xao*, contains many of the elements I like most about Vietnamese cooking: fragrant herbs and seasonings, chewy noodles (*bun*), and crisp vegetables. Traditionally, this dish also features stir-fried (*xao*) beef (*bo*), but this version calls for your choice of seitan or tofu to boost the protein. Serve chilled or at room temperature with sriracha and *nuoc cham* on the table for people to add as desired.

8 ounces rice vermicelli

2 teaspoons toasted sesame oil

1 tablespoon grapeseed oil

2 shallots, minced

2 cloves garlic, minced

2 tablespoon minced lemongrass

8 ounces seitan, cut into thin strips or extra-firm tofu, drained, pressed, and cut into ½-inch dice

2 tablespoons sugar

2 tablespoons soy sauce

2 tablespoons freshly squeezed lime juice or rice vinegar

1 large carrot, coarsely shredded

1 English cucumber, peeled and chopped

2 cups shredded romaine lettuce

1 cup fresh bean sprouts, trimmed and blanched

1 cup crushed unsalted roasted peanuts

½ cup minced scallions

1 cup fresh cilantro or Thai basil leaves, torn if large

½ cup fresh mint leaves, torn if large

Sriracha sauce, for serving

Fish-Free Sauce (Nuoc Cham, recipe follows), for serving

Cook the rice noodles according to the package directions. Drain well, then transfer to a large bowl, drizzle with the sesame oil, and toss to coat. Set aside.

Heat the grapeseed oil in a large skillet over medium heat. Add the shallots and garlic, and cook for 1 minute. Add the lemongrass and stir-fry for 30 seconds, or until fragrant. Add the seitan and stir-fry to brown nicely. Sprinkle on the sugar, soy sauce, and lime juice and stir-fry for 1 minute to coat well. Remove from the heat and set it aside.

Divide the reserved noodles on four plates or shallow bowls. Arrange the seitan on top of the noodles, dividing evenly. Pour any remaining liquid from the pan over the noodles. Next to the seitan, arrange mounds of carrot, cucumber, lettuce, and bean sprouts. Sprinkle all over with peanuts, scallions, cilantro, and mint. Serve chilled or at room temperature, with sriracha and *nuoc cham* to add at the table.

Serves 4

QUICK AND EASY

Fish-Free Sauce (Nuoc Cham)

Fish sauce, known as *nuoc cham* in Vietnam, is used as an all-purpose seasoning in Vietnamese cuisine to add a rich depth of savory flavor to dishes. This vegan version made with dried seaweed, mushrooms, and soy sauce creates a similarly complex umami flavor without using fish.

In a saucepan, combine the mushrooms, seaweed, garlic, sugar, soy sauce, peppercorns, salt, red pepper flakes, and water and bring to a boil. Lower the heat to a simmer and cook for 30 minutes. Strain the mixture and return the liquid back to the pot. Add the vinegar and bring the liquid back to a boil. Cook until the sauce is reduced by half. Remove from the heat and allow to cool completely. Pour the sauce into a jar with a tight-fitting lid and store in the refrigerator where it will keep for a month.

Makes about 1¼ cups sauce

GLUTEN-FREE
NO OIL
QUICK AND EASY

¼ cup dried shiitake mushrooms

¼ cup chopped dried seaweed (kombu or wakame are good choices)

1 clove garlic, crushed

1 tablespoon sugar

⅓ cup soy sauce

½ teaspoon black peppercorns

½ teaspoon salt

½ teaspoon red pepper flakes

2 cups water

2 tablespoons rice vinegar

Lemongrass Asparagus and Edamame Stir-Fry

This dish is filled with the fresh fragrant flavors of lemongrass and cilantro, and loaded with edamame, asparagus, carrots, cashews, and other goodies. It's seasoned with a luscious sauce made with vegan oyster sauce, rice vinegar, and sambal oelek, a paste of ground hot chiles. Even though it's a long list of ingredients, it goes together quickly—the hardest thing about this stir-fry is not eating the whole thing yourself in one sitting.

In a small bowl, combine the soy sauce, water, oyster sauce, vinegar, sambal oelek, coriander, and sugar. Stir to mix well. Set aside.

Heat the oil in a large wok or large skillet over high heat. Add the onion, garlic, lemongrass, and ginger, and stir-fry for 30 seconds. Add the asparagus, bell pepper, edamame, and carrots. Stir-fry for 3 minutes, then stir in the reserved sauce and bring to a boil. Lower the heat to a simmer and cook for about 3 minutes to reduce the sauce a little. Stir in the cilantro and cashews. Taste and adjust the seasonings if needed. Serve hot with rice.

Note: Vegan oyster sauce is sold at Asian markets—it is labeled as "vegetarian" oyster sauce. If unavailable, look for mushroom soy sauce. If you can't find either, you can omit it and just add a little extra of your regular soy sauce, as needed.

Serves 4

GLUTEN-FREE
LOW OIL
QUICK AND EASY

¼ cup soy sauce

¼ cup water

2 tablespoons vegan oyster sauce (see Note)

2 tablespoons rice vinegar

1 teaspoon sambal oelek (ground fresh chili paste)

1 teaspoon ground coriander

1 teaspoon natural sugar

1 tablespoon grapeseed oil or other neutral oil

1 medium yellow onion, halved lengthwise, then thinly sliced

3 cloves garlic, minced

2 fresh lemongrass stalks, tender inner white bulb only, minced

1 teaspoon grated fresh ginger

12 ounces thin asparagus, trimmed, and cut diagonally into 1½-inch pieces

1 red bell pepper, seeded and cut into julienne strips

1 cup steamed fresh or frozen shelled edamame

2 medium-size carrots, coarsely shredded

½ cup chopped fresh cilantro or basil

¼ cup toasted cashews

3 to 4 cups freshly cooked long-grain rice, for serving

Corn Pudding with Coconut Sauce

It may seem odd to serve a corn pudding for dessert, but one taste will convince you that it's actually a pretty good idea. This flavorful pudding topped with a coconut sauce is called *chè bắp*. If you have coconut sugar on hand, it's a great choice for this recipe.

2 tablespoons small tapioca pearls

1½ cups fresh or frozen corn kernels, thawed

6 tablespoons natural sugar

¼ teaspoon salt

1 (13-ounce) can unsweetened coconut milk

1 teaspoon vanilla extract

2 teaspoons cornstarch blended with ¼ cup water

2 tablespoons sesame seeds

Soak the tapioca in a bowl of warm water for 30 minutes. Set aside.

In a saucepan, combine the corn kernels, 4 tablespoons of the sugar, ⅛ teaspoon of the salt, and all but ½ cup of the coconut milk. Stir to combine. Bring just to a boil, then decrease the heat to low and simmer for 10 minutes. Taste and adjust the seasonings, adding more sugar or salt, if needed.

Drain the soaked tapioca pearls, then stir them into the corn mixture and simmer for 5 to 8 minutes or until the tapioca is soft and translucent and the pudding is thickened. Stir in the vanilla. Remove from the heat to cool to room temperature, then refrigerate for 30 minutes or longer to chill.

While the pudding is chilling, make the coconut sauce. In a small saucepan, combine the remaining ½ cup of coconut milk with the remaining 2 tablespoons sugar and ⅛ teaspoon of salt and bring almost to a boil. Decrease the heat to medium-low and stir in the cornstarch mixture, stirring constantly to thicken. When the sauce thickens, remove the saucepan from the heat.

To serve, top each serving of pudding with a couple of tablespoons of the coconut sauce and garnish with the sesame seeds.

Serves 4

GLUTEN-FREE
SOY-FREE
NO OIL

Southeast Asia Islands

The cuisines of the island nations of Southeast Asia—particularly Malaysia, Indonesia, and Singapore—have always intrigued me, not just for their delicious flavors but also because the food in these nations are true melting pots of cuisines. Malay food, for example, is a delectable amalgam of the culinary traditions of China and India, Indonesia, Thailand, and its own indigenous roots. It is this combined cultural influence that makes Malaysian food so delicious. In Malaysia you'll find noodle and rice dishes reminiscent of China, fragrant Indian-inspired curries and *dosas*, and the sweet and pungent flavors of Southeast Asia, with an abundant use of tropical fruits, herbs, tamarind, and most notably hot chiles and coconut. For all of its cultural influences, the cuisine of Malaysia has managed to produce a number of distinctly Malaysian dishes. Many Malay dishes feature a *rempeh*, a spice and herb paste that is sautéed in oil to deepen the flavors, while the national dish of Malaysia is *nasi lemak*, or "creamy rice," a fragrant rice dish cooked in coconut milk and pandan leaves. Vegan-friendly Malaysian specialty dishes include *rasam*, a lentil soup made with coriander and cumin, *mee rebus*, a noodle dish served with a tangy, spicy and sweet potato–based sauce, fried yam cakes, radish cakes, and spring roll–style crepes stuffed with tofu and vegetables.

Not to be outdone are Indonesia and Singapore, also pastiche cultures out of which come distinctly fascinating cuisines. Once known as the "Spice Islands," it is not surprising that Indonesians favor cooking with the many indigenous aromatics, such as ginger, garlic, coriander, lemongrass, chiles, and coconut. Though the culture and cuisine throughout the islands are diverse, the most popular meals consist of rice served with several savory side dishes and accompanied by a popular, often spicy condiment, called a *sambal*, made with chiles and other ingredients.

While Indonesian cuisine has been influenced by China, the local herbs, spices, and produce, such as lemongrass, coriander, and coconut, lend their distinctive characteristics, as evidenced in Lemongrass Coconut Rice on page 258. Chiles are often paired with these ingredients as well as ginger and garlic to flavor many of the dishes. Tempeh, a plant-based protein made from compressed soybeans, originated in Indonesia, where it is often prepared in coconut milk.

Laksa Noodle Soup

Singapore is home to several kinds of *laksa*, a spicy noodle soup that is also popular throughout Malaysia. The most popular type of *laksa* features curry and a coconut milk base, with thick noodles. Another type, called *asam*, is a sour fish-based soup. There are many variations of both, some using thin noodles, fish, bean sprouts, herbs, and even pineapple. In this version, I include some of my favorite elements, such as cilantro, pineapple, and coconut milk, for a luscious soup that is both refreshing and satisfying.

8 ounces dried rice noodles

1 cup coarsely chopped shallots or yellow onion

2 dried red chiles, softened in hot water

1 stalk lemongrass, white part only, crushed

2 teaspoons grated fresh ginger

2 teaspoons ground coriander

2 teaspoons curry powder

1 teaspoon paprika

½ teaspoon ground turmeric

½ teaspoon cayenne

1 tablespoon grapeseed oil

5 cups vegetable broth

2 teaspoons sugar

1 teaspoon salt

¼ teaspoon freshly ground black pepper

1 (14-ounce) can unsweetened coconut milk

8 ounces extra-firm tofu, cut into ½-inch cubes

1 cup fresh bean sprouts, blanched

3 scallions, sliced

1 cucumber, peeled, seeded, and chopped

1 bunch cilantro, chopped

1 cup chopped pineapple (optional)

Lime wedges, for serving

Asian chili paste (sambal), for serving

Soak the rice noodles in a bowl of hot, not boiling, water and set aside.

In a food processor, combine the shallots, chiles, lemongrass, ginger, coriander, curry powder, paprika, turmeric, and cayenne and process until blended to a paste.

Heat the oil in a large pot over medium heat. Add the shallot mixture and cook, stirring for 3 minutes, adding a small amount of the broth to prevent burning. Add the remaining broth and bring to a boil. Lower the heat to medium and add the sugar, salt, and pepper. Simmer for 20 minutes, then strain through a sieve or colander and return the liquid to the pot. Stir in the coconut milk and heat until hot; do not boil. Add the rice noodles and tofu and simmer for another 10 minutes. To serve, divide the bean sprouts and scallions among four soup bowls and ladle the soup into the bowls. Garnish with the cucumber, cilantro, and pineapple, if using. Serve with lime wedges and *sambal*.

Note: Since most of us don't keep handy a stockpile of fresh *laksa* leaves and candlenuts traditionally found in this spicy soup, the recipe calls for readily available ingredients. This soup is pretty spicy, especially depending on the heat of your chiles, so if you prefer it milder, use less cayenne (or leave it out) and/or cut back on the chiles.

Serves 4 to 6

GLUTEN-FREE

Singepore Mei Fun

Mei fun noodles are thin Chinese rice noodles (also called rice vermicelli) that are extremely popular in Singapore. Basic mei fun is somewhat bland, usually stir-fried with shiitake mushrooms, soy sauce, and a few other ingredients, with additional condiments served on the side. Singapore *mei fun*, on the other hand, is distinctive for its addition of curry powder. It usually features a number of vegetables, and shrimp, meat, or tofu (or a combination). My version calls for tofu, but you can substitute seitan, tempeh, or even jackfruit.

8 ounces rice vermicelli (mei fun)

4 teaspoons grapeseed oil

8 ounces extra-firm tofu, drained, pressed, and cut into ½-inch dice

¼ cup soy sauce

1 to 2 tablespoons good-quality Madras curry powder (mild or hot)

1 medium-size yellow onion, halved lengthwise and thinly sliced

1 red bell pepper, seeded and cut into thin matchstick strips

1 carrot, coarsely shredded

2 ounces snow peas, trimmed and cut into 1-inch pieces

1 teaspoon sugar

½ teaspoon salt

½ teaspoon red pepper flakes

1 cup vegetable broth

2 cups small broccoli florets, steamed

2 tablespoons chopped fresh cilantro

Soak the rice noodles according to the package directions until softened. Drain well and set aside.

Heat 2 teaspoons of the oil in a large skillet or wok over medium-high heat. Add the tofu and stir-fry until nicely browned, adding 2 tablespoons of the soy sauce and a sprinkling of curry powder while cooking. Remove from the skillet and set aside on a plate.

Reheat the skillet with the remaining 2 teaspoons of oil. Add the onion, bell pepper, carrot, and snow peas, and stir-fry for 2 to 3 minutes to soften. Stir in the remaining curry powder and stir-fry for 10 seconds, or until fragrant.

Add the remaining 2 tablespoons of soy sauce, along with the sugar, salt, and red pepper flakes, stirring to mix well. Stir in the broth and bring to a boil over high heat.

Add the drained rice noodles and return to a boil, stirring to coat the noodles in the sauce. Add the steamed broccoli and reserved tofu, and cook, stirring, 1 to 2 minutes, or until the liquid has been absorbed by the noodles. Taste and adjust the seasonings, if needed. Serve hot sprinkled with the cilantro.

Note: If rice vermicelli noodles are unavailable, you can make this with angel hair pasta instead (cooked al dente before adding to the skillet). Feel free to change up the vegetables used (zucchini instead of broccoli, or green peas instead of snow peas, for example). Adjust the seasoning to your taste, by adding more red pepper flakes or more curry powder for more heat.

Serves 4

GLUTEN-FREE
QUICK AND EASY

Eggplant Rempeh

The Malaysian spice and herb paste known as *rempeh* is sautéed in oil to deepen the flavors. Rempeh is a delicious way to prepare tempeh or tofu, as well as vegetables such as eggplant. Use coconut aminos instead of soy sauce to make this soy free.

3 fresh hot red chiles, seeded and coarsely chopped

2 shallots, coarsely chopped

4 cloves garlic, coarsely chopped

2 to 3 teaspoons grated fresh ginger

2 tablespoons tomato ketchup or chili sauce

1 tablespoon soy sauce

1 tablespoon freshly squeezed lime juice

½ teaspoon sugar

1 pound Japanese eggplants, ends trimmed, halved lengthwise

2 tablespoons grapeseed oil

½ cup chopped fresh basil leaves

3 to 4 cups freshly cooked brown rice, for serving

In a food processor, combine the chiles, shallots, garlic, and ginger and process to a paste. Set aside. In a small bowl combine the ketchup, soy sauce, lime juice, and sugar and stir to mix well. Set aside.

Cut the eggplant halves crosswise into thirds. Heat the oil in a large skillet over medium-high heat. Add the eggplant pieces and cook until browned on both sides, about 4 minutes per side. Add the reserved chile paste mixture to the eggplant and cook until fragrant.

Stir in the reserved sauce mixture and continue cooking until the eggplant is tender and the sauce has thickened. If the sauce becomes too dry, add a tablespoon or two of water. When ready to serve, stir in the basil. Serve hot over rice.

Serves 4

GLUTEN-FREE
SOY-FREE OPTION
QUICK AND EASY

Pineapple-Cucumber Salad

Fruit and vegetable salad enjoyed throughout Malaysia, Indonesia, and Singapore are often referred to as *rojak*, the Malaysian word for "mixture." There are numerous variations throughout the region, and this one is similar to those made in Indonesia. I like to serve it with Eggplant Rempeh (page 256). Use coconut aminos instead of soy sauce to make this soy free.

In a bowl, combine the cucumber, pineapple, and scallions. Set aside.

In a small bowl, combine the lime juice, sambal oelek, sugar, soy sauce, and salt. Stir to mix well. When ready to serve, pour the dressing over the salad and mix well to combine.

Serves 4 to 6

GLUTEN-FREE
LOW OIL
SOY-FREE OPTION
QUICK AND EASY

1 English cucumber, peeled and cut into ½-inch dice

½ small pineapple, peeled, cored, and cut into ½-inch dice

3 scallions, minced

Freshly squeezed juice of 2 limes

½ to 1 teaspoon sambal oelek or 1 fresh hot red chile, seeded and pounded to a paste

1 teaspoon sugar

1 teaspoon soy sauce

¼ teaspoon salt

Lemongrass Coconut Rice

Fragrant jasmine rice gets even more fragrant when prepared with lemongrass, lime juice, garlic, scallions, and coconut. This delicious side dish can be served with any Southeast Asian dish, including curries and stir-fries. Use coconut aminos instead of soy sauce to make this soy free.

1 tablespoon grapeseed oil or coconut oil

3 cloves garlic, minced

1 (2-inch) piece lemongrass (tender white end), finely sliced

1¾ cups jasmine rice

2 (13-ounce) cans unsweetened coconut milk

1 cup vegetable broth, plus more as needed

2 tablespoons shredded unsweetened coconut

1 tablespoon soy sauce

½ teaspoon ground turmeric

Salt

1 tablespoon freshly squeezed lime or lemon juice

2 scallions, finely minced

Heat the oil in a large saucepan or Dutch oven over medium-high heat. Add the garlic and lemongrass and cook, stirring, for 30 seconds or until fragrant. Stir in the rice, coconut milk, broth, shredded coconut, soy sauce, tumeric, and salt to taste. Bring just to a boil, stirring occasionally to keep the rice from sticking. Decrease the heat to low, cover the pot tightly with a lid, and cook for about 15 minutes, or until the liquid has been absorbed. Turn off the heat, but leave the covered pot on the burner to steam for another 5 to 10 minutes. Just before serving, add the lime juice and use a fork to fluff the rice. Taste and adjust the seasonings, if needed. Serve hot sprinkled with the scallions.

Serves 4

GLUTEN-FREE
SOY-FREE OPTION
QUICK AND EASY

Coconut Fried Bananas

Popular throughout Southeast Asia where fried bananas are called *goreng pisang*, this version features shredded coconut in the batter. They are especially good served hot out of the pan alongside a scoop of coconut or vanilla vegan ice cream.

In a bowl, combine the flour, sugar, baking soda, and salt. Add the water and mix well. Stir in ½ cup of the shredded coconut. Mix the batter until well combined. It will be thick.

Place the cornstarch in a shallow bowl. Add the remaining ¼ cup of coconut and stir to combine.

Dip the banana pieces into the batter, then gently dredge them in the cornstarch-coconut mixture and set on a plate.

Heat the oil in a deep skillet over medium-high heat. Add the coated bananas to the hot skillet, in batches as needed. Cook until golden brown on the bottom, then flip over and continue cooking until the bananas are completely golden brown.

Remove from the skillet and drain on paper towels. Transfer to shallow dessert bowls. Serve hot sprinkled with peanuts alongside a scoop of ice cream, if desired.

Serves 4

GLUTEN-FREE
SOY-FREE
QUICK AND EASY

¾ cup rice flour or all-purpose flour

¼ cup sugar

½ teaspoon baking soda

Pinch of salt

¾ cup water or unsweetened coconut milk

¾ cup shredded unsweetened coconut

¼ cup cornstarch

2 tablespoons coconut oil or neutral oil

4 large firm, ripe bananas or 8 ripe baby bananas, peeled and halved lengthwise (also halved crosswise, if large)

½ cup crushed dry-roasted peanuts

Vegan ice cream, for serving (optional)

Recipes By Category

Following is a list of the recipes grouped according to category. Several recipes can be found in more than one group. The recipes listed in each group refer to the recipe when made with the primary ingredients for each recipe, without optional ingredients or variations.

GLUTEN FREE

These recipes contain no wheat, rye, or barley. You'll need to make sure certain ingredients you use that may contain gluten (such as soy sauce, oats, mustard, etc.) are gluten free. In addition to the recipes listed here, several other recipes are marked with "gluten-free option," indicating that a simple ingredient sway (such as gluten-free pasta for wheat pasta) will make the recipe gluten free.

24-Hour Kimchi (page 230)

Aji Salsa (page 125)

Ajvar (page 160)

Akara Dipping Sauce (page 138)

Avocado and Tomato Salsa Verrines (page 100)

Baharat Spice Blend (page 156)

Baharat-Spiced Baba Ghanoush (page 153)

Baklava Bites (page 57)

Banh Mi Spring Rolls (page 240)

Basil Pistou (page 30)

Berbere Spice Blend (page 144)

Black Bean Caldillo (page 107)

Black-Eyed Pea Fritters (page 138)

Bolivian Quinoa Pilaf (page 124)

Brigadiero Chocolate Fudge Truffles (page 131)

Caakiri Pudding with Pineapple (page 148)

Cardamom Chickpea Cookies (page 187)

Carrot-Mung Bean Salad (page 179)

Cauliflower Colcannon (page 78)

Chickpea and Kale Wat (page 137)

Chickpea and Potato Patties (page 169)

Chimichurri-Grilled Vegetables (page 130)

Chipotle Corn-Stuffed Peppers (page 108)

Cilantro Jicima Slaw with Lime-Orange Dressing (page 105)

Coconut Sambol (page 186)

Coconut Spinach and Lentil Dal (page 177)

Coconut Fried Bananas (page 259)

Corn Pudding with Coconut Sauce (page 248)

Cottage Pie (page 74)

Cucumber and White Bean Ceviche (page 122)

Easy Boston Baked Beans (page 93)

Easy Chapchae (page 232)

Eggplant Kabayaki (page 219)

Eggplant Piri-piri (page 41)

Eggplant Rempeh (page 256)

Eggplant Satays (page 207)

English Garden Salad (page 72)

Farinata with Sun-Dried Tomatoes and Olives (page 4)

Fennel Gremolata (page 7)

Fish-Free Sauce (page 245)

Garlicky Greens and Beans (page 92)

Greek Rice and Spinach (page 56)

Green Beans Provençal (page 26)

Harissa Sauce (page 135)

Hoisin-Peanut Dipping Sauce (page 241)

Injera (page 141)

Jamaican Jerk Vegetable Skewers (page 114)

Laksa Noodle Soup (page 252)

SOY FREE

These recipes contain no tofu, tempeh, edamame, soy sauce, or miso. In addition to the recipes listed here, many other recipes are noted as "soy-free options," meaning they can be soy free with a simple ingredient swap, such as using a soy-free vegan buttery spread (Earth Balance makes one) or using coconut aminos instead of soy sauce.

LOW OIL/NO OIL

These recipes use 1 tablespoon of oil or less. Many of them can be made oil free simply by substituting a few tablespoons of water for the oil to "water sauté."

QUICK AND EASY

These recipes can be prepared in less than 30 minutes of active time.

Note: This does not include time spent soaking nuts, a final chilling, or other inactive time.

Menus

The recipes in this book are designed to be enjoyed any way you like: alone, with other recipes from the same region, or paired with recipes from other regions. Feel free to develop your own menus, or choose from among these menus for some of my personal favorite combinations. Here you will find a menu for each country or region featured in the book along with a few cross-cuisine menus "without borders."

SIMPLY ITALIAN
Artichoke Crostini with Chickpeas and Arugula (page 6)
Trofie alla Pesto with Green Beans and Potatoes (page 11)
Tiramisu Pie (page 16)

TEMPTING TAPAS
Pan-Seared Mushrooms with Garlic and Sherry (page 35)
Patatas Bravas (page 36)
Eggplant Piri-piri (page 41)
Roasted Romesco Vegetable Stacks (page 37)
Saffron-Almond Rice Pudding (page 42)

FRENCH À LA CARTE
Pâté au Champignon (page 21)
Brandy-Laced Onion Soup (page 20)
Potato Gratin Dauphinois (page 25)
Portobellos with Béarnaise Sauce (page 24)
Mousse au Chocolat (page 31)

GREEK TAVERNA DINNER
Baked Eggplant Fries with Tzatziki Sauce (page 52)
Stifado (page 55)
Greek Rice and Spinach (page 56)
Baklava Bites (page 57)

COMFORT FOOD FEST
Triple Mushroom Soup with Sour Cream and Dill (page 60)
Seitan Jagerschnitzel (page 63)
Roasted Brussels Sprouts and Walnuts (page 66)
Potato Pancakes (page 61)
Easy Apple Strudel (page 69)

PUB FARE
English Garden Salad (page 72)
Soda Bread Scones (page 76)
Cottage Pie (page 74)
Lemon Posset (page 80)

ALL-AMERICAN SUPPER
Butternut Mac and Cheese (page 90)
Garlicky Greens and Beans (page 92)
Blue Ribbon Chocolate Layer Cake (page 95)

MEXICO AL FRESCO
Avocado and Tomato Salsa Verrines (page 100)
Garden Fideos (page 103)
Watermelon Paletas (page 109)

SOUTH AMERICA SAMPLER
Cucumber and White Bean Ceviche (page 122)
Brazilian Feijoada (page 128)
Brigadiero Chocolate Fudge Truffles (page 131)

CARIBBEAN SUNSET SUPPER
Roasted Corn Chowder (page 113)
Jamaican Jerk Vegetable Skewers (page 114)
Piña Colada Squares (page 118)

MIDDLE EAST FEAST
Kale-Stuffed Phyllo "Pens" (page 154)
Za'atar Roasted Cauliflower (page 161)
Sleek-Stuffed Eggplant with Pomegranate Sauce (page 158)
Stuffed Dates, Three Ways (page 162)

OUT OF AFRICA
Spicy Lemon Chickpeas (Fasting Eggs) (page 136)
Chickpea and Kale Wat (page 137)
Injera (page 141)
Caakiri Pudding with Pineapple (page 148)

JEWELS OF INDIA
Papri Chaat (page 170)
Hakka Noodles (page 175)
Manchurian Cauliflower (page 176)
Cardamom Almond Chickpea Cookies (page 187)

Glossary of Ingredients

Many of the ingredients used in this book are explained right in the recipe headnotes. Other ingredients, notably the ones that are used throughout the book, such as tofu, tempeh, and seitan, are explored at length beginning on page xii. Still, there may be some ingredients that you may not be familiar with and, although you can find them explained in the recipes, I thought it might be convenient to provide a separate list of some of these terms so you can become familiar with them. To further familiarize yourself with the various ingredients used in this book, check out the pantry lists beginning on page xx.

Cardamom. Aromatic seeds used for baking, flavoring coffee, and to season Indian dishes.

Chipotle. A dried and smoked jalapeño which can be found dried or reconstituted and sold in adobo sauce. These chiles are very hot.

Chutney. A condiment used in Indian cooking. Fresh chutneys have a bright, clean flavor and are usually thin, smooth sauces. Cilantro, mint, and tamarind are common in fresh chutney. Cooked chutneys have a deeper, broader flavor and often have a chunky texture.

Curry Powder. A mixture of spices used to season Indian food. It can be mild with spices like cumin, fennel, and coriander; hot, when made with chiles and pepper; or fragrant when made with cinnamon and saffron.

Five-Spice Powder. A spice mixture used in Chinese cooking consisting of ground cinnamon, star anise, Szechuan peppercorns, cloves, and fennel.

Galangal. A root spice related to ginger, which has a musky flavor reminiscent of saffron. It is found dried whole or in slices, and also in powder.

Garam Masala. An Indian spice mixture with a complex flavor and aroma. The mixture may include cumin, fennel, coriander, cardamom, cinnamon, saffron, pepper, chiles, and caraway.

Harissa. A spice mixture used as both a condiment and a seasoning. Harissa contains chiles that are ground with cumin, garlic, coriander, and olive oil to make a thick paste.

Hoisin Sauce. A rich, dark, sweet barbecue sauce used in Chinese cooking, it is made from soybeans, garlic, chiles, red beans, and spices, including star anise.

Kochujang. Spicy-sweet Korean chili paste, it is used to make many classic Korean dishes such as bimimbap.

Lemongrass. A subtropical root that provides a fresh lemon flavor to Southeastern Asian dishes.

Liquid Smoke. Concentrated smoky water used to give foods a smoked flavor.

Mirin. Used in Japanese cooking, mirin is a slightly sweet and syrupy nonalcoholic version of sake or rice wine.

Miso. A paste made from fermented soy beans that is used in Japanese cooking to make soups and sauces.

Mole. A type of thick, rich sauce with a complex flavor used in Mexican cooking made with chiles, cumin, coriander, cinnamon, nuts, seeds, and chocolate.

Nori Seaweed. Thin dry sheets of seaweed used in Japanese cooking, primarily to wrap sushi.

Nutritional Yeast. A source of vitamin B_{12}, this yellow, cheesy-tasting powder or flake is used to provide flavor and nutrients to vegan recipes. It is not to be confused with brewer's yeast or active dry yeast.

Oyster Sauce. A dark brown delicate sauce that adds richness to Asian dishes. Look for vegan versions of oyster sauce under the names "Vegetarian Oyster Sauce," "Vegetarian Stir-Fry Sauce," and "Mushroom Soy Sauce."

Paprika. Ground dried red chiles used as a spice and garnish. It ranges in flavor from mild and slightly sweet, to smoky, to hot.

Rice Paper Wrapper. A thin, crispy wrap made from rice flour and water that is softened in water and used to wrap spring rolls.

Saffron. A spice with a pungent aroma and flavor, and bright yellow color. It is expensive and used sparingly. Turmeric may be used to substitute for the yellow color, although there is no substitute for its unique flavor.

Soy Sauce. A salty, tangy, brown seasoning or sauce brewed from fermented soy beans. Darker, stronger sauces are used for cooking while lighter ones are used as sauces and seasonings. Japanese soy sauce is called *shoyu* or tamari.

Spring Roll Wrapper. A thin, crispy wrap made from rice flour and water used to wrap spring rolls. Also called rice paper wrappers.

Tahini. A paste made from sesame seeds, used in hummus and baba ghanoush.

Tamarind. The pulp of a fruit pod, tamarind is very sticky and has a bittersweet flavor with citrus overtones. It is used in both savory and sweet dishes and is sold as concentrate, syrup, and in bricks of pulp that must be soaked, kneaded, and strained before using.

Wasabi. Called Japanese horseradish, it is a root that is dried and ground to a fine powder that is then reconstituted and made into a paste. It is used as a condiment with soy sauce when eating sushi.

Worcestershire Sauce. A condiment or seasoning made of a blend of ingredients including tamarind, molasses, vinegar, and cloves. The vegan version omits the anchovies.

Online Resources

Here are some great online resources for vegan ingredients as well as international specialties, spices, and seasonings.

Bob's Red Mill
www.bobsredmill.com
800-349-2173

Food Fight Grocery
www.foodfightgrocery.com
503-233-3910

Herbivore Clothing Company
www.herbivoreclothing.com
503-281-TOFU (8638)

International Food Shop
www.internationalfoodshop.com
949-582-2645

International Spices
www.internationalspices.com
402-727-4600

Pangea (The Vegan Store)
www.veganstore.com
800-340-1200

Penzeys
www.penzeys.com
800-741-7787

**The Mail-Order Catalog
for Healthy Eating**
www.healthy-eating.com
800-695-2241

Vegan Essentials
www.veganessentials.com
888-88V-EGAN

Vegie World
www.vegieworld.com
212-334-4428

World Market
www.worldmarket.com
877-967-5362

Metric Conversions and Equivalents

METRIC CONVERSION FORMULAS

To Convert	Multiply
Ounces to grams	Ounces by 28.35
Pounds to kilograms	Pounds by 0.454
Teaspoons to milliliters	Teaspoons by 4.93
Tablespoons to milliliters	Tablespoons by 14.79
Fluid ounces to milliliters	Fluid ounces by 29.57
Cups to milliliters	Cups by 236.59
Cups to liters	Cups by 0.236
Pints to liters	Pints by 0.473
Quarts to liters	Quarts by 0.946
Gallons to liters	Gallons by 3.785
Inches to centimeters	Inches by 2.54

APPROXIMATE METRIC EQUIVALENTS

Volume

¼ teaspoon	1 milliliter
½ teaspoon	2.5 milliliters
¾ teaspoon	4 milliliters
1 teaspoon	5 milliliters
1¼ teaspoons	6 milliliters
1½ teaspoons	7.5 milliliters
1¾ teaspoons	8.5 milliliters
2 teaspoons	10 milliliters
1 tablespoon (½ fluid ounce)	15 milliliters
2 tablespoons (1 fluid ounce)	30 milliliters
¼ cup	60 milliliters
⅓ cup	80 milliliters
½ cup (4 fluid ounces)	120 milliliters
⅔ cup	160 milliliters
¾ cup	180 milliliters
1 cup (8 fluid ounces)	240 milliliters
1¼ cups	300 milliliters
1½ cups (12 fluid ounces)	360 milliliters
1⅔ cups	400 milliliters
2 cups (1 pint)	460 milliliters
3 cups	700 milliliters
4 cups (1 quart)	0.95 liter
1 quart plus ¼ cup	1 liter
4 quarts (1 gallon)	3.8 liters

Length

⅛ inch	3 millimeters
¼ inch	6 millimeters
½ inch	1.35 centimeters
1 inch	2.5 centimeters
2 inches	5 centimeters
2½ inches	6 centimeters
4 inches	10 centimeters
5 inches	13 centimeters
6 inches	15.25 centimeters
12 inches (1 foot)	30 centimeters

Weight

¼ ounce	7 grams
½ ounce	14 grams
¾ ounce	21 grams
1 ounce	28 grams
1¼ ounces	35 grams
1½ ounces	42.5 grams
1⅔ ounces	45 grams
2 ounces	57 grams
3 ounces	85 grams
4 ounces (¼ pound)	113 grams
5 ounces	142 grams
6 ounces	170 grams
7 ounces	198 grams
8 ounces (½ pound)	227 grams
16 ounces (1 pound)	454 grams
35.25 ounces (2.2 pounds)	1 kilogram

OVEN TEMPERATURES

To convert Fahrenheit to Celsius, subtract 32 from Fahrenheit, multiply the result by 5, then divide by 9.

Description	Fahrenheit	Celsius	British Gas Mark
Very cool	200°	95°	0
Very cool	225°	110°	¼
Very cool	250°	120°	½
Cool	275°	135°	1
Cool	300°	150°	2
Warm	325°	165°	3
Moderate	350°	175°	4
Moderately hot	375°	190°	5
Fairly hot	400°	200°	6
Hot	425°	220°	7
Very hot	450°	230°	8
Very hot	475°	245°	9

COMMON INGREDIENTS AND THEIR APPROXIMATE EQUIVALENTS

1 cup uncooked white rice = 185 grams

1 cup all-purpose flour = 140 grams

1 stick butter (4 ounces • ½ cup • 8 tablespoons) = 110 grams

1 cup butter (8 ounces • 2 sticks • 16 tablespoons) = 220 grams

1 cup brown sugar, firmly packed = 225 grams

1 cup granulated sugar = 200 grams

Information compiled from a variety of sources, including *Recipes into Type* by Joan Whitman and Dolores Simon (Newton, MA: Biscuit Books, 2000); *The New Food Lover's Companion* by Sharon Tyler Herbst (Hauppauge, NY: Barron's, 1995); and *Rosemary Brown's Big Kitchen Instruction Book* (Kansas City, MO: Andrews McMeel, 1998).

Index

Andrews McMeel Publishing, LLC
an Andrews McMeel Universal company
1130 Walnut Street, Kansas City, Missouri 64106

14 15 16 17 18 TEN 10 9 8 7 6 5 4 3 2 1

ISBN: 978-1-4494-4708-3

Library of Congress Control Number: 2014930776

Photography: Sara Remington
        iStock: xxiv, 2, 18, 44, 70, 82, 98, 110, 120, 129, 150,
        133, 139, 144, 147, 201, 202, 214, 226, 238, 250
Food Stylist: Erin Quon
Prop Stylist: Ethel Brennan
Designer: Julie Barnes
Composition: Diane Marsh

Special thanks to Roni Jaco of the Loaded Trunk
www.loadedtrunk.com

www.andrewsmcmeel.com
www.robinrobertson.com

ATTENTION: SCHOOLS AND BUSINESSES
Andrews McMeel books are available at quantity discounts with bulk purchase or educational, business, or sales promotional use. For information, please e-mail the Andrews McMeel Publishing Special Sales Department: specialsales@amuniversal.com.